Economic Fundamentals of Financial Markets

ECONOMIC FUNDAMENTALS OF FINANCIAL MARKETS

Bart Taub
University of Glasgow

World Scientific
NEW JERSEY • LONDON • SINGAPORE • BEIJING • SHANGHAI • TAIPEI • CHENNAI

Published by

World Scientific Publishing Co. Pte. Ltd.
5 Toh Tuck Link, Singapore 596224
USA office: 27 Warren Street, Suite 401-402, Hackensack, NJ 07601
UK office: 57 Shelton Street, Covent Garden, London WC2H 9HE

Library of Congress Control Number: 2025013902

British Library Cataloguing-in-Publication Data
A catalogue record for this book is available from the British Library.

ECONOMIC FUNDAMENTALS OF FINANCIAL MARKETS

ISBN 978-981-98-1496-1 (hardcover)
ISBN 978-981-98-1497-8 (ebook for institutions)
ISBN 978-981-98-1498-5 (ebook for individuals)

For any available supplementary material, please visit
https://www.worldscientific.com/worldscibooks/10.1142/14360#t=suppl

Desk Editors: Soundararajan Raghuraman/Geysilla Jean

Typeset by Stallion Press
Email: enquiries@stallionpress.com

In memory of my mother

Preface

This book tells a story with a beginning, a middle, and an end.

The beginning is about how interest rates show up in unexpected places: the prices of things in the distant past as well as in the modern day. The middle fleshes out how people interacting in markets motivate exactly those prices. And the end solves a riddle: if we think market behaviour is the correct description of the world, why has it seemingly failed so many statistical tests? The exciting conclusion is that, by applying new ideas in those statistical tests, it works.

To tell the story, this book uses a consistent technical framework (continuous time) to analyse how interest rates are determined in macroeconomic equilibrium, building a modern treatment of the influence of risk on interest rates. The first half of this book builds foundations, including basic calculus, using only examples typically used in economics and finance models. With those foundations in place, we develop the basic consumer optimisation problem but incorporate Lagrange multipliers explicitly and intuitively, as Lagrange multipliers are an essential part of the later parts of this book. These ideas are then extended to develop the theory of optimal control, applying it to develop the basic model of economic growth. The basic growth model is then used for a quantitative and precise theory of the interest rate in a growing economy, and also the basic theory of asset pricing in general equilibrium. We can then hit several other nails with the control-theory hammer: seasonal cycles, how taxes impact economic growth, and the optimal use of renewable and exhaustible resources.

The second half of this book builds basic foundations for stochastic models, including basic stochastic differential equations, Ito's lemma, and stochastic control, with applications using classical examples. The stochastic control model is then used to develop the basic Merton model of portfolio choice. The Merton model is refined to mimic a general equilibrium stochastic growth model, and this model is used to develop the theory of interest rates in risky environments.

The subsequent stage of this book develops the risk-neutral measure, establishes the validity of the capital asset pricing model in stochastic general equilibrium, and also develops the theory of option pricing without resorting to partial differential equations methods.

The final parts of this book examine the empirical implications of the stochastic general equilibrium model, including tests related to the so-called excess volatility problem. The empirical arguments make use of publicly accessible data and use only spreadsheets to compute the relevant statistics.

About the Author

Bart Taub is Professor of Finance at the University of Glasgow. Prior to taking up his position at Glasgow he most recently held positions at the University of Durham and the University of Illinois. He received his PhD from the University of Chicago.

Contents

List of Figures

List of Tables

Introduction: A Hidden World

Our goal is to connect financial theory with macroeconomic theory, using a new approach. We want a theory of the interest rate, both from the financial side and from the macroeconomic side so that the two sides are consistent with each other.

Interest Rates

Interest rates are prices. Everyone makes financial decisions based on the interest rate, so you, as finance students, are probably already aware of and have been exposed to portfolio choice and investment decisions as depending heavily on the characteristics of the interest rate. But in financial theory, we don't think very hard about where the interest rate comes from.

A modern macroeconomic theory generates predictions of the interest rate. As we shall see, it is the intertemporal marginal rate of substitution — we said it is a price, but really it is the ratio of two prices: the ratio of the price of consuming in the future to the price of consuming in the present. This marginal rate of substitution emerges in models of economic growth. To be of use in a financial setting, we have to have a theory that also allows for the fact that the environment in which the growth model is operating is stochastic: it involves risk.

There are three principles that we respect in building this theory.

The first is optimisation under constraints. We want to have people in our model, so we express the idea that they maximise their happiness while respecting the physical limitations they face.

The second is rationality: we are going to assume that the people in the models we construct are aware of the environment that they are in and in particular, the information relevant to their decision-making. When they make decisions, they will use the information correctly; "correctly" means respecting statistical theory in settings where information is explicit as the central focus of the model.

The third principle is equilibrium. We are going to assume that markets operate in the world that we're going to model and that the markets are in equilibrium. So we're going to appropriately define the constituents of markets and then be very careful about finding equilibrium in those markets.

It is actually a tall order to combine macroeconomic growth theory, stochastic environments, and financial elements while respecting these principles. The question becomes as follows: How do you approach this technically? The problem is that a lot of financial theorising of the sort that we're concerned with uses continuous time, whereas in macroeconomic growth theoretic modelling, the standard is discrete-time dynamic-programming approaches. The conclusion I drew was that it would be better to go with continuous time because we can then connect everything. This is especially true for the final chapter, where we examine the excess volatility puzzle through the lens of the Hansen–Jagannathan test: the test is much easier to construct and to understand with a continuous-time approach.

Interest Rates in Medieval Times

Let's start with an empirical examination of interest rates in medieval times in the UK.

Medieval institutions such as churches and courts kept records. Churches kept books with records of births, marriages, and deaths, for example — these were parish registers. There's a great deal of data that can be obtained from these sources: you can figure out how long people lived and you can look at what they were named and follow the people with those names through centuries of history. And there are court records that go back centuries as well.

The court records have interesting information about people such as how much money they had when they died because they gave it to their heirs in their wills and those wills had to go through probate, which is a courtroom process, so it was all recorded and kept for centuries. And now economic historians are looking at that data, and there are other useful data, such as who was executed, and who was jailed, because those records are kept.

McCloskey and Nash (1984) looked at archival data of this sort from institutions, primarily monasteries, and manorial estates, in England in medieval times, specifically the price of wheat that these institutions paid when they bought supplies of wheat and other grains.

Using monastery records, the McCloskey–Nash article took the average of the price paid for wheat in each month over the seasons of the year, over more than a hundred years, 1260–1400. So, for example, they took the price paid for wheat in September. For all of those years and for many different monasteries around England and then averaged the September price paid, and similarly the October price, the November price, and so on for all of the months because the records are there.

After taking the averages of the prices, they then looked at the change of the average price from month to month, over the course of the year. The results of this calculation are displayed in Table 1. The September number of 3.55, for example, is the percentage change of the price paid for wheat from September to October. You can see that the numbers are somewhat big; we think of 3.55% as a fairly big *annual* rate of return, but these are *monthly* returns or changes in price. As we look across the table, what we see is that all of the numbers are big. (McCloskey and Nash averaged the returns, finding the average month-to-month return to be 2.37%, implying an annual rate of change of 32% — certainly large by modern standards.)

Table 1. Averaged month-to-month price changes of wheat, 1260–1400.

September–October	3.55	January–February	1.91	May–June	1.52
October–November	2.25	February–March	2.04	June–July	1.78
November–December	1.85	March–April	2.12	July–August	1.29
December–January	2.03	April–May	1.78		

Source: McCloskey and Nash (1984), Table 3; reproduced by permission.

Since the monasteries were paying for the grain, we know they were not the ones growing the grain and putting it in the storage bins and silos; somebody else was doing that and then charging money for the grain. That raises the following economic question: suppose that you are a farmer expecting to sell your grain to the monastery, but in December, months after the harvest. Your thought process is the following: after the harvest, I'm going to put my grain into the storage bin or the silo on my farm, and I'm going to get a price when I sell it to the monastery that justifies not selling it right after I have harvested it. And in order to justify doing that, I have to be paid a compensation for waiting. And what is the compensation for waiting? It is the interest payment. So alternatively, if we are in medieval times, we could think about taking the harvest of the grain, selling all of it immediately upon the harvest in the grain market, to the extent that a grain market existed back then.

The farmer could take the payment for the grain to the bank. The banker would say, well, I will pay you interest if you leave that money with me. And as you probably understand already, the banker would then take the money and invest it in something to generate the interest and a little profit. But the farmer who had deposited his money would expect an interest payment.

So there are two possible alternative scenarios: the first where he sells his grain and gets the money right away and puts it in the bank, and the second where he puts the harvested grain in a storage bin and then sells it directly to the monastery in December. They have to be equivalent. Otherwise, somebody could make a profit by either increasing the sales of grain at the harvest or putting more grain in storage and waiting until December to sell it.

How can we be confident of that? Well, first of all, we are going to assume that the farmers were rational. Rationality means that just because they lived in medieval times doesn't mean that they were in some sort of fairyland where everybody was happy, or that they were in some sort of primitive natural state where everybody was friendly to each other, always got along, and didn't have to worry about mundane things like markets. It's more appropriate to think, well, we're routinely modelling people in modern days as rational people who solve problems, optimisation problems subject to the constraints that they face. Certainly, there's no reason to think that wasn't the case back in medieval times. So, this arbitrage argument dictates that the price of grain over the season had to rise after the harvest to justify putting it in storage and selling it later. McCloskey and Nash took that as the starting point and reasoned, well, if that's true, then we should be able to look at the prices of grain and in particular, look at the increase in prices over the course of the season, especially in the fall and midwinter, and can back out from that what the interest rate had to be, or at least an upper bound on what the interest rate had to be.

What they concluded was these implied interest rates look pretty high. They themselves mentioned that the increase in the price does not just pay you interest if you have put grain into the grain silo for later sale. It's costly to store grain. So if you put grain into a grain silo, you're going to attract rats, for example, and you have to do something to prevent the rats from getting the grain. And that means that you actually have to hang around the grain storage silo and keep them away somehow. And there also are dishonest people who will try to steal the grain from your grain silo, so you have to hire security guards to keep the grain safe until it's saleable. And the silo itself costs money to create and it can develop leaks and the rain might get in, so you have to constantly patch the roof, and so on. So, those little stories are just to remind you that it's costly to store grain, or anything for that matter, and somebody has to be paid for that cost. And it's the farmer in this case, if he owns the storage. That cost has to be included in the compensation he receives when he sells the grain at a later time, and the rate of increase of the price is going to be exaggerated beyond what the interest rate is because of that cost. So, these very high numbers that we're seeing as the percentage rate of change in the price of grain are partly explained by the fact that there had to have been costs. We can be sure that the costs would have been higher per bushel of grain in medieval times than they would be today.

A key lesson from the McCloskey–Nash article, aside from the fact that the interest rate permeates life in ways that we don't always think about, is that there is a force, arbitrage, operating at all times. The story about the alternative, selling the harvest immediately and taking the proceeds to the bank, is really an arbitrage story. And the consequence of the arbitrage idea is that everybody has to obtain the same interest rate. If you're a banker, you have to pay that interest rate and it's determined in an equilibrium. That equilibrium is being forced on everybody in ways that are not always directly in front of you. The prices of grain going up while in storage is not directly obvious, but it's not only reflecting the interest rate, it's helping to force the interest rate to be what it is in equilibrium. The bankers, as well as the farmers, have to obey the force because they're all in competitive equilibrium with each other.

Storage in the Modern Day

In 2020, world consumption of kerosene (used as heating oil) was 12,250,000 barrels.[1] For perspective, the volume of this production is a cube that is slightly less than 1 km on a side, or 0.7 miles on a side, or about a third of a cubic mile. And that is just the kerosene: total crude production was about 7 times this figure. Although governments are involved in taxing this product, it is almost entirely the outcome of private activity. (It can also be observed that it is not necessary to store the 0.3 cubic mile of heating oil: it is mostly burned as it is produced.)

Suppose you want to make money in the heating oil market. I'm going to propose a way. Let's look at some heating oil futures. A futures contract lets you buy or sell a commodity at a pre-agreed time and price. A typical textbook would gush over how nice it is that retail heating oil companies can hedge against a cold winter by setting up some futures contracts to avoid excessive price rises over the winter, and to ensure their supplies, even if it turns out to be a cold winter. After all, their business depends on reliably supplying oil when the weather is at its worst.

But let's take a more cold-blooded look at the heating oil futures market. Even though you are probably not a person who has a major oil storage tank, you could get involved in futures in the following way. Look at the price of October 15, 2024 heating oil; this is easy to find on Yahoo Finance.

As of September 2024, the spot price of heating oil was $\$X_{\text{Sept12}} = 2.1333$/gallon. The October 15 future price was $\$X_{\text{Oct15}} = 2.14$. You could contract to buy one million gallons of oil at that price and

[1] British Petroleum Statistical Review of World Energy 2021.

hire a storage company to store it until you decide to sell it. (When October 15 rolls around, you will need to pony up \$2.14 million for the oil.)

Now, note that the futures price of oil for delivery in February 2025 is higher: it is $X_{\text{Feb25}} = 2.17$, much higher than the October price. You could sell your stored oil for that price and make a tidy profit of 0.03/gallon. Multiply this by a million gallons — these sorts of large trades are allowed — and you've made \$30,000.

It gets better. You could go to a bank, or a stock broker who lends money for stock purchases — margin. Just point out to him that if he lends at a low rate, he will get paid back with certainty because this is a no-lose situation. There is no speculation here: the prices in the previous paragraph have already been determined in the futures contracts, and they are locked in. So, you can easily borrow the \$2.14 million to pay for the oil contract in September.

Why stop here? You could borrow much much more and buy many more than one million gallons. You could become quite rich this way and in a hurry.

But we need to be careful here. Even though this is a sure thing, the interest rate is going to matter. To pay back the loan on each barrel you contract for, you have to make sure that the interest rate is no bigger than

$$\frac{X_{\text{Feb25}} - X_{\text{Oct24}}}{X_{\text{Oct24}}} = \frac{2.17 - 2.14}{2.17} \times 3 = 0.014018692 = 0.014018692$$

This is the return (in fractional form) for storing the oil for four months, or a third of a year. We can convert it to an annual rate of return via compounding:

$$(1 + 0.014018692)^3 - 1 = 0.042648401$$

or 4.3% equivalent annual rate of return, not counting the storage cost. Let's look at the interest rate that matters for this arbitrage.

Since it is a sure thing, we want an interest rate that reflects the absence of risk. One interest rate that has low risk is the yield on US treasuries because these have little risk of defaulting. As of mid-September 2024, the interest rate for US treasury bills with a six-month maturity was 4.82%.

What we see is that the interest rate is really too high to make this arbitrage work. Why? The market has priced the futures contracts so that this is so. If your arbitrage could work, other people would also try it. In so doing, their desire to buy September oil would bid up the October price, and their desire to set up a sell in February would force down the February futures price.

What if you wanted to be on the other side of the market? You could be the person standing ready to buy oil in February and selling it in October. If the February price were the same as the October price, you could sell October oil, put the proceeds in an interest-bearing account, and then use the principal to buy the oil back in February. You can do this even if you don't have access to oil by selling it short in October and buying it back in February. You keep the interest after paying back the oil in February. What spoils this arbitrage is that the price of oil is not flatter than the interest rate: it goes up by the interest rate.

We can extract that interest rate — the one that initiates in the future — by looking at treasury bonds of different maturities, noting that the long term yield is the product of two gross short term yields, one near term and one long term. By dividing out the short term yield, we obtain the *future* short-term yield.

Carrying out this exercise, we can note the following (annualized) yields on US treasuries in fractional form: $r_{\text{6-month}} = 0.04701$ and $r_{\text{3-month}} = 0.05025$. To find out the three-month future interest rate commencing in three months, we carry out the following calculation:

$$\begin{aligned} & (1 + r_{\text{6-month}})^{\frac{1}{2}} = (1 + r_{\text{future 3-month}})^{\frac{1}{4}}(1 + r_{\text{3-month}})^{\frac{1}{4}} \\ \rightarrow \quad & (1 + 0.04701)^{\frac{1}{2}} = (1 + r_{\text{future 3-month}})^{\frac{1}{4}}(1 + 0.05025)^{\frac{1}{4}} \end{aligned}$$

The exponents $\frac{1}{2}$ and $\frac{1}{4}$ stem from the requirement to convert the annual yields reported for the treasury yields into half-year and quarter-year yields. Solving for $r_{\text{future 3-month}}$ yields 0.04378 — remarkably close to the implied rate of return in the oil futures prices. Although we haven't lined up the dating perfectly with the futures contract dating, this number is much closer to being the relevant number for the borrowing leg of the proposed arbitrage. (Real-world arbitrageurs would work harder to make the dates line up properly.)

To effectively obtain that interest rate for the arbitrage, we could buy a three-month treasury bill and finance it by selling a six-month treasury short; this would leave roughly half of the shorted bond's value to use to pay for the oil when purchasing the oil at the start of the arbitrage. At the end, you would sell the oil and use the proceeds to repurchase the bonds to wind down the short — effectively paying back the loan. And what we see is that the implied future interest rate is a little too big to make the arbitrage work.

Of course, we have left out other details: someone has to pay the storage fees for the physical oil that is underneath the contract, and there are financial transaction fees. This reduces the feasibility of the proposed arbitrage even more.

There are some key conclusions. First, it is apparent that the time pattern of oil futures prices has been forced into conformity with the future interest rate by the pressure of the potential for arbitrage. There is no visible process by which this happens, but it does happen because the thousands of market participants around the world — refineries, traders, heating oil retailers, and oil storage companies — stand ready to exploit small deviations from the pattern. These 21st-century forces are no different from the 13th-century forces that we documented before.

It is also fundamental that the intertemporal pattern of futures prices that we have documented is not driven by weather, nor does it stand as some sort of market prediction of the weather. This is not to say that heating oil prices are not affected by weather: if it develops that there is a forecast of a cold winter come October, *all* prices will rise, but the *intertemporal* pattern will continue to be driven by interest rates.

Joseph

There's one thing missing from the arbitrage discussion, which is inspired by the following story you might be familiar with, the story of Joseph from the Bible. The beginning of the story of Joseph is that he is on the losing end of a family dispute and as a result is sold into slavery in Egypt. And after he gets to Egypt, there are some events that he can't really control very well, and he ends up in prison, and while in prison he talks to the other prisoners. The other prisoners tell him about their dreams, and Joseph makes predictions from those dreams. On hearing one of the dreams, he predicts that one of the prisoners, a baker, will eventually get released; this does happen, and the prisoner goes back to his job as a baker for the Pharaoh, the leader of Egypt.

Pharaoh is very bothered by his own dream. The beginning of the dream is that there are seven cows that come out of the Nile river and the cows are fat, healthy cows. But then another seven cows come out. The second seven cows are skinny, scrawny, and starving, and they eat the first seven cows.

Pharaoh keeps having this dream. He tells his servants, including the baker, about the dream, and he wants to know what it means. The baker says, well, I know this guy who's good at interpreting dreams. Since Joseph had already proven himself in interpreting dreams, he is brought up from the dungeon to interpret Pharaoh's dream. His interpretation is that there are going to be seven fat years and then seven lean years. That's what the cows are symbolising. And to get ready for this event, you should store up your grain during the seven fat years. So, as a result of that, Pharaoh bought into the explanation and he had storage bins created and the grain that was harvested in the good years was then available for the seven lean years that did follow in famine years.

This illustrates that in the story about the arbitrage with the grain prices and the interest rate, we didn't mention risk: there is the possibility that harvests can be bad or good and that the farmers who are operating in this setting are aware of that risk of bad harvests. And so they're going to react to that risk. The story of Joseph in Egypt, of course, clarifies what the reaction is, which is to store up a little excess grain, not just what you need to re-plant your crops after. The grain for bread has been consumed at the monastery, but you have to keep a little extra on hand just in case the crop fails and you have to consume and you still want to have enough to replant, of course. So risk, or the perception of risk, is going to induce that kind of precautionary saving behaviour. And we want to be able to talk about that and the effect on the interest rate of that as well. The interest rate is actually going to end up reflecting the existence of risk, both in the data and explicitly in our model, which is going to take a while to develop because we have to develop tools. But in the model, we are going to see exactly how the risk affects the interest rate.

Part I

Deterministic Models

Chapter 1

Non-Scary Algebra and Calculus

We're now ready to begin on the technical side of things. The first thing to say is that we are going to have people in our models, and we need a way to represent them and how they behave. The way we are going to do this is to suppose that people solve optimisation problems. We want to be able to express that in a technical way, and calculus is necessary for this.

We also want to represent equilibrium, that is, how people interact in markets. Again, this has to be done in a technical way because then we can say very precisely what the implications of optimising behaviour are.

Expressing Optimisation with Calculus

How do we represent optimisation? Suppose that we have a function $f(x)$, and suppose that that function has a concave shape like the one in Figure 1.1. What if I want to find the top of that function?

Calculus provides a method to find the top of the function: look at where the first derivative of the function is zero and whatever x that gives us that point is the x we want; we can call that point x^*:

$$\max_x f(x) \quad \rightarrow \quad f'(x^*) = 0$$

We have expressed this command with the notation "$\max_x$."

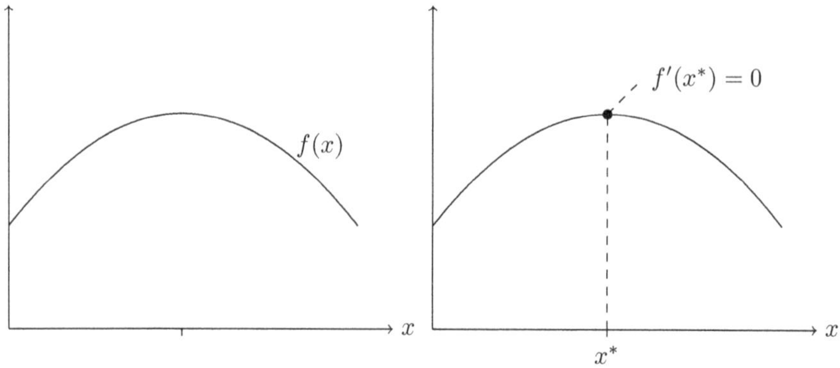

Figure 1.1. Concave function.

Here is an example of a function that we might want to find the top of: $3 - 0.25 * (2.5 - x)^2$. Take the first derivative, set it to zero, and you end up with this value of x^*: 2.5.

Example 1.1. Solve the following optimisation problem:

$$f(x) = x^\alpha - Ax$$

$$f'(x^*) = 0 \rightarrow \alpha x^* x^{\alpha-1} - A = 0$$

$$\rightarrow x^* = \left(\frac{A}{\alpha}\right)^{\frac{1}{\alpha-1}}$$

After setting the derivative to zero, we can do a little more algebra and solve for x^* explicitly. We actually know what x^* is algebraically now.

We can also think of this as equating the slope of x^α with the slope of the straight line Ax — in other words, a tangency. That's where you solve a problem by finding the slope of a line equalling the slope of another line at one point. It comes up in economics quite a bit, of course. If we think of this as let's find a tangency between the straight line described by A times x and the curved line, there's only one point where they're going to have the same slope. So, taking the derivative, setting it to zero, a very common thing in economics models, is solving an optimisation problem.

Basic calculus facts

The first calculus fact concerns notation. These two ways of expressing the derivative are equivalent:

$$f'(x) \quad \frac{d}{dx}f(x)$$

There is an additional special notation: if you take the derivative with respect to time you can use a dot,

$$\dot{f} \quad \frac{d}{dt}f(t)$$

Which notation gets used depends on the context.

There is one additional notation, the partial derivative, that will occasionally arise:

$$f_x \quad \frac{\partial}{\partial x}f(x,y)$$

just means, "take the derivative with respect to x, treating y as if it were a constant." There is shorthand here too: the subscript form f_x denotes the partial derivative.

There is one more additional subtlety about notation: because we are very concerned about dynamics, our functions will often be functions of time, and to represent them as time dependent, we write X_t instead of $f(t)$; in this special context, the subscript t does *not* denote the partial derivative. And there will be a number of contexts where we have partial derivatives as well as time dependence: f_X denotes the partial derivative of the function $f(X_t, Y_t)$, where X_t and Y_t are functions of time.

Let's review some basic calculus rules. The first one is that if you have the derivative of the sum of two functions, the function $f(x)$ and the function $g(x)$, and you take the derivative of that sum, then you get the sum of the derivatives of each function, so the derivative of the sum is the sum of the derivatives:

$$\frac{d}{dx}(f(x)+g(x)) = \frac{d}{dx}f(x) + \frac{d}{dx}g(x)$$

Next is the chain rule, which applies if you have a function that's a function of another function. So, for a function $f(g(x))$, to take the derivative of that whole thing with respect to x, we first take the derivative of the f part and keep the inside g part, then multiply by the derivative of the inside part of f, namely $g'(x)$:

$$\frac{d}{dx}f(g(x)) = f'(g(x))g'(x)$$

If we have the product of two functions, then if you take the derivative of the product, you get this rule, which is slightly complicated but straightforward, because it is symmetric. You take the derivative of the first function, so you have $f'(x)$ multiplied by the original function $g(x)$ without the derivative. And then you trade places so that you have the original function $f(x)$ times the derivative of the g function. This is called the product rule:

$$\frac{d}{dx}f(x)g(x) = f'(x)g(x) + f(x)g'(x)$$

If you have a constant times any function, the derivative is the constant times the derivative of the function. And the derivative of a constant is zero:

$$\frac{d}{dx}af(x) = af'(x) \quad \frac{d}{dx}a = 0$$

Special functions and their derivatives

There are special functions that frequently arise in economic modelling: the exponential function, the logarithm, the geometric function, and the quadratic function.

The exponential function. The derivative of the exponential function, $e^{f(x)}$, is that same thing, $e^{f(x)}$, you just keep it, but in addition, using the chain rule, you then multiply by that first derivative of $f(x)$.

Many situations will come up where we want the derivative of e^{bx}, where b is some constant. Applying the rule, we get be^{bx}; the original function stays unchanged, but you bring this constant out by taking the derivative of the exponent.

There are some additional useful rules for the algebra of exponents:

$$
\begin{aligned}
\text{Derivative: } & \frac{d}{dx}e^{f(x)} = e^{f(x)}f'(x) \\
\text{Example: } & \frac{d}{dx}e^{bx} = be^{bx} \\
\text{Sums in the exponent: } & e^{x+y} = e^{x}e^{y} \\
\text{Product of exponentials: } & = e^{x}e^{y} = e^{x+y} \\
\text{Exponential of exponential: } & (e^{x})^{y} = e^{xy} \\
\text{Exponential of log: } & e^{\ln(x)} = x \\
\text{Sums of exponentials: } & e^{x} + e^{y} = ?
\end{aligned}
\tag{1.1}
$$

The key property in this list is as follows: If you have the product of two exponentials, that is the same as the exponential of the sum of the two exponents.

If you have an exponential taken to a power, that is, you have e^x and that is then taken to another power y, then you can just multiply the powers: $(e^x)^y$ becomes e^{xy}.

The logarithm is the opposite of exponentiation, if we're talking about the natural logarithm, so $e^{\ln(x)}$ is just x and $\ln(e^x)$ is just x going the other way.

The final entry highlights that if you have the sum of two exponentials, it's not so easy; there's no general rule for the sum of exponentials.

The logarithm function. The logarithm function also has some rules. For

$$\ln(f(x))$$

where $f(x)$ is some other function, the rules are as follows:

$$\text{Derivative: } \frac{d}{dx}\ln(f(x)) = \frac{1}{f(x)}f'(x) \quad \text{(by the chain rule)}$$

$$\text{Example: } \frac{d}{dx}\ln(bx) = \frac{1}{x}$$

First of all, the derivative of the logarithm function is one over the original function times the derivative of the function. And if you have the log of a constant b multiplying the variable x, then you get the derivative of this, which is $\frac{1}{bx}\frac{d}{dx}bx$ by the chain rule, so the bs cancel.

The algebra rules for the logarithm are as follows:

$$\begin{aligned}
\text{Log of product: } & \ln(xy) = \ln(x) + \ln(y) \\
\text{Log of geometric: } & \ln(x^\alpha) = \alpha \ln(x) \\
\text{Log of exponential: } & \ln(e^x) = x \\
\text{Sums in the argument: } & \ln(x + y) =?
\end{aligned}$$

The logarithm of a geometric expression x^α is α times the logarithm of x; the logarithm of a sum is not the sum of the logarithms. So again, you have to be careful about some of the rules.

The geometric function. The geometric function more generally looks like the following:

$$x^{f(x)}$$

where $f(x)$ is some other function.

Derivative

$$\frac{d}{dx}x^{f(x)} = \frac{d}{dx}e^{\ln(x)f(x)} = x^{f(x)}\left(\frac{f(x)}{x} + \ln(x)f'(x)\right) \tag{1.2}$$

Here is an example:

$$\frac{d}{dx}x^\alpha = \alpha x^{\alpha-1}$$

We can apply the chain rule. And let's go to this example, the derivative of x^α. Multiply the exponent out front. Subtract one from the exponent. You have $\alpha x^{\alpha-1}$. That will come up a lot.

There's just a little bit more to say about exponents. We had this special exponential function. But if we have a geometric exponential function like this, then the sums in the exponent become the product of the exponentials:

$$
\begin{aligned}
\text{Sums in the exponent: } & x^{a+b} = x^a x^b \\
\text{Log of geometric: } & \ln(x^\alpha) = \alpha \ln(x) \qquad (1.3) \\
\text{Powers of geometric functions: } & (x^a)^b = x^{ab}
\end{aligned}
$$

as with the exponential operation that we saw before and except the x is in the base instead of in the exponent. For the derivative of the logarithm of the geometric function, we take the α and we multiply it out front and then the logarithm. And if we have powers of a geometric function, that is equivalent to a geometric function with the product of the exponents.

Integrals

Now, we're going to leave our comfort zone a little bit. The integral symbol is

$$\int$$

The integral symbol started out as an elongated version of S, which just means sum, so an integral is actually a sum of some other sort.[1] You may have seen a discussion of integration in a calculus class where you add up little boxes under a curve. To get the integral and to make the boxes, the width of the box is smaller and smaller — this is the expression of the idea that we're adding something up. Just as with the previous calculus rules, because this is not a mathematics text, we're not going to justify the integral by drawing those pictures and talking about taking limits and so on. We just want to know what are the rules and have a little bit of intuition for what integration is about. And then we're going to apply the rules.

For an arbitrary function of the sort we encounter, $f(x)$, the integral is

$$\int_{\ell_1}^{\ell_2} f(x)dx$$

[1]In Isaac Newton's days, the symbol was used as an "s" in regular text — it had a natural meaning.

The integral is simply a sum, so it is common to think of the integral from ℓ_1 to ℓ_2 as the area under the curve between those two points.

We need to develop the notation a bit. When you write down an integral, there are immediately some complications because it's not just that simple elongated S in the integral sign. If you follow the rules, you have to have other things in the expression of the integral. So first of all, of course, we're going to have the expression of the function that we're interested in integrating. So, we're calling that arbitrary function $f(x)$, and soon enough we will talk about specific versions of $f(x)$. But we have these other things ℓ_1, ℓ_2, and the dx. The dx is the width of the little boxes that you may have seen in the development of the integral. But their width is infinitesimal, so dx is the mathematical notation for that infinitesimally small width as you go along, adding up the little boxes. There is a branch of mathematics that formalises the dx as an algebraic object and develops an entire theory that is actually somewhat non-standard in its approach to calculus, which treats that and it treats that dx as an algebraic object in the conventional sense and also in physics, for example, you would just do that anyway and not worry too much about breaking mathematical rules. That's the approach we take when it comes up: the dx is to be treated like just an algebraic object with conventional rules like multiplication and division.

For now all it means is you have to put it there just to be notationally correct, and then you can stop worrying about it because really the main action is about this function: what does the integration operation do to the function?

The next issue is the ℓ_1 and ℓ_2. When we take the derivative of something, we don't have these extra elements hanging around that we have to worry about when we take the derivative. But when we integrate, we do. These are called the limits of integration, hence the letter ℓ. These specify the starting and stopping points for your adding up of the little boxes.

One of the confusing things about integration is that when you integrate, there is typically going to be something you do to $f(x)$ before you worry about the ℓ_1 and ℓ_2; in your calculus class, they might have called it the anti-derivative. So, there are some quasi-algebraic rules that apply to the operation of integration that are separate from the limits of integration: the ℓ_1 and ℓ_2. Once you realise that there those two aspects of integration can be contemplated somewhat separately, it becomes a little less scary.

Let's think about the primary application of integration in economics: where you think about optimising an individual's utility over his or her lifetime. There would be a summation sign in front of the utility to signify that you're adding up not just today's utility but future utilities as well. And you might have an expectation sign out front, which we put in later:

$$\int_{t=0}^{t=\infty} e^{-rt} u(C_t) dt$$

So what you see is exactly the same thing, except we're integrating instead of adding that is to say we are allowing for the reality that people live their lives from moment to moment, not just one year at a time, which is what the summation approach does. It's not different economics or different mathematics, ultimately.

There are several things going on in that integral. First of all, let's look at the utility function, $u(\cdot)$. Figure 1.2 is a very crude graph of it; on the horizontal axis, we have consumption, c. Consumption is our abstract economist's way of thinking about what you eat, what you use as you go through life to improve your happiness, all rolled into one. And u is the payoff that you get from that consumption and this function, $u(\cdot)$ has two basic features. One is that it is an increasing function: if your consumption goes up, your utility goes up — that's what the u stands for. Utility is just a fancy word for happiness. But it's the *flow* of happiness that we're interested in, not some ultimate happiness that you achieve, and then that's it.

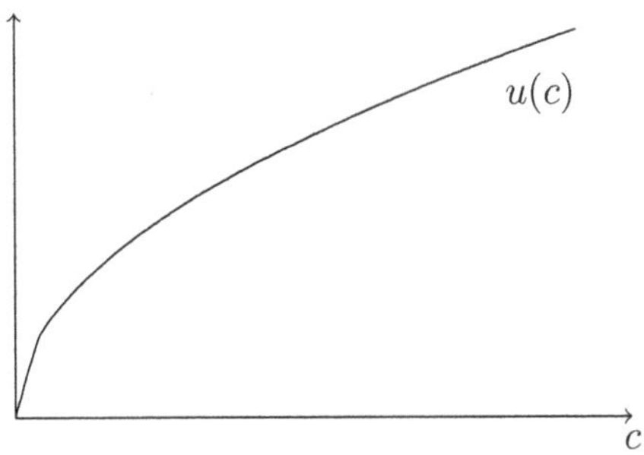

Figure 1.2. Utility function.

The other feature is that it is not a straight line. The slope gets shallower and shallower as you increase your consumption. Geometrically, it is concave. And this expresses the idea that the more you consume, the less *incremental* pleasure you get from consuming. If you're starving and you get a little bit of food, your utility shoots up in a very sensitive way. But if you've had a very full meal and then you look at the dessert menu, you might say, well, it looks good, but you'll only get a little bit of additional pleasure from having that dessert.

Note that there is a time subscript on consumption that is being added up in the integral. An abstract individual who we are trying to model would care about that flow of utility over time. If that flow of consumption, which we're representing as C_t, can go up and down, then the utility of that consumption, $u(C_t)$, can also go up and down: there's no law that says that consumption is some constant. We're going to model individuals as looking ahead and caring about their utility flow that they're getting, not just now, but in the future. So, you have a meal now and you get a flow of utility, but you also care about the meals that you're going to have in the future in the coming weeks. And you're going to take account of that in your assessment of your own happiness if you are this individual. You're going to add it up, and so this integration that is here is adding that up.

There's an additional term in the integral, e^{-rt}, which is a somewhat complicated looking expression. There are two things in the exponent: r and t. So are is the interest rate you can think of it intuitively as the number 0.02 or the number 0.05, if we're thinking about things on an annual basis. So, we are integrating but multiplying by this exponential.

What is the function of the e^{-rt} term? It is discounting the future. It's useful to take a minute to ponder this. So let us suppose that r is in fact 0.05. Let's try $t = 0$, $t = 1$, $t = 2$. You can use your calculator to fill in the numbers. (Answers: 1, 0.95, 0.91)

This is a very crude way of illustrating that as time progresses into the future, the weight that is put on $u(C_t)$ gets reduced. And this is the technical meaning of discounting. By the way, what would happen if we said $t = \infty$? Zero. So, as you go infinitely into the future, you don't care about what happens in the infinite future.

What we are capturing is the decreasing weight that people put on future events relative to early events. One can do little thought experiments such as, what if you had the opportunity to have your favourite flavour of ice cream in one minute vs. your favourite flavour of ice cream in one year from now. Would you pay the same price for those two things? And the answer is, intuitively, you know you would pay more for the current one, you would care more about the current one because it's immediate. We're capturing that desire for immediacy via discounting.

Now, this is going to be an aside, but one might ask the following: do we all have little utility functions in our heads? When they dissect cadavers, is there a place, next to the pineal gland or something, where they see the utility function? And the answer is no, there isn't a utility function. Nature didn't evolve a utility function. So, how is it that we take the reality of the utility function seriously and make it the centrepiece of our models? There is an answer for this: one can go at this from a different point of view, and that point of view is survival. It is acceptable to think of organisms in general and people in particular as attempting to maximise the probability of their survival. If we model that mathematically, we end up with behaviour that effectively duplicates what we see with this utility function; this was demonstrated by Majumdar and Radner (1991), and we revisit this assertion later in the book.

The beginning of the analysis of survival optimisation posits that one can build up a kind of abstract capital that generates a return and that one can also use up that capital to stave off death. As an example, we can store up grain after the harvest and deplete the store of it over the winter, but the more we use it up, the less is available to plant in the spring. By consciously storing excess grain, we stave off the possibility of having no grain at all after a bad harvest in the following spring. The survival model expresses this fundamental physical reality: that there is a trade-off between return and risk. One cannot ensure survival by never taking risk because the physical realities do not encompass zero-risk strategies. The next step in the survival model is to model the dynamics of the survival probability directly: it is a function of the state of capital.

An individual trying to maximise his survival optimally trades off risk and return and, specifically takes on some risk. But this is exactly the same way an individual attempting to maximise his long run utility behaves, as we see in the second half of the book.

The limits of integration in the integration — the ℓ_1 and ℓ_2 — are zero and infinity. It is easy to understand that the lower limit of integration, zero, denotes the current instant of time; but time infinity? People don't live forever, so how is it that we can so calmly put in infinity as the conventional upper limit of integration? That is, we're adding up the utility of consumption over an infinite life and there is no person with an infinite life. The justification is that we have children, we have descendants that we care about. And we're very abstractly capturing that, caring about our descendants and them caring about their descendants and so on into the future by putting infinity there.

Practical examples for integration

Let's now develop some of the practical rules for integration for our primary function examples, completely skipping all of the mathematical justifications. The simplest case is the integral of a constant:

$$\begin{aligned}\int_{\ell_1}^{\ell_2} adx &= a\int_{\ell_1}^{\ell_2} dx \\ &= a\left(x\Big|_{x=\ell_2} - x\Big|_{x=\ell_1}\right) = a(\ell_2 - \ell_1)\end{aligned}$$

As a practical matter, there are two things we have to keep track of: One is what we referred to as the anti-derivative. Since integration is the opposite of taking the derivative, it's sometimes called the anti-derivative aspect of it. The anti-derivative is just the constant times x, but there are two terms here because we are being careful about the fact that there are limits of integration. The rule that we follow is to first find this anti-derivative, then evaluate it at the first limit of integration, which is to say, the upper limit of integration, and, finally, subtract the evaluation of it at the lower limit of integration.

The integral of the exponential function e^{ax} also comes up a lot. We integrate this function with some limits of integration. If you take this the integral of this exponential, then you get the exponential back, but you divide by this coefficient a:

$$\int_{\ell_1}^{\ell_2} e^{ax}dx = \frac{e^{ax}}{a}\Big|_{x=\ell_2} - \frac{e^{ax}}{a}\Big|_{x=\ell_1}$$

So, as a matter of just checking, without worrying about the limits of integration yet, what if we take the derivative of this object with respect to x? Then we can invoke our rules that we developed of derivatives in the previous slides, so let's actually do that. Going back to the rules for derivatives of exponentials, we see that $\frac{d}{dx}\frac{e^{ax}}{a} = e^{ax}$: we get the original function e^{ax} back.

Another function that's going to come up a lot is the geometric function, x^a, with a constant. When we integrate it, well, first of all, we have this anti-derivative $\frac{x^{a+1}}{a+1}$. For the definite integral, we calculate the difference of the two terms evaluated at the limits of integration:

$$\int_{\ell_1}^{\ell_2} x^a dx = \left.\frac{x^{a+1}}{a+1}\right|_{x=\ell_2} - \left.\frac{x^{a+1}}{a+1}\right|_{x=\ell_1}$$

As a matter of notation, the big bar means, evaluate this function next to the bar at ℓ_2 and similarly for ℓ_1. In the geometric function integral, we have an anti-derivative and we can verify that this anti-derivative is correct by taking its derivative and seeing if we get x^a.

Exercises

(1) Derive the rule for the derivatives involving constants, $\frac{d}{dx}ax = a$ and $\frac{d}{dx}a = 0$ using the product rule or the chain rule.

(2) Solve the following integral:

$$\int_0^2 \frac{1}{2}x^\alpha dx$$

Chapter 2

Optimisation

In the introduction, we noted that we were going to represent individuals as optimising. In this chapter, we express this in a technical way.

Picturing optimising as getting to the top of a hill, you have seen how this translates into a calculus problem. But this way of thinking about the problem needs to be augmented in a slightly non-intuitive way: Lagrange multipliers. We develop the idea in three steps: first, with an elementary single-good consumption problem, second with two goods, and third with consumption of goods over time.

Lagrange Multipliers

It is useful to start with a trivial example:

$$\max_{c} u(c)$$

subject to the constraint

$$c \leq y$$

For now, forget about integration and forget about time and just think about an abstract individual who wants to maximise his utility of consumption, just in the here and now, without regard for the future. We've already seen c, consumption, and $u(\cdot)$, the utility of consumption. We use this notation, $u(\cdot)$, to remind ourselves that it is a function, not just a number.

When we talked about the utility of consumption before, we didn't worry about where that consumption came from. But now we're going to start worrying about it. We're going to represent what individuals are as people who maximise their utility, so they actually take an action — the maximisation — to become happy.

The problem that pervades economics is that there isn't enough consumption to go around. We're going to have to maximise the utility within the constraints that we face. A constraint just expresses the fact that resources in general are scarce. As an individual, your income is what it is and no bigger; you can't suddenly decide that going to double your income. You have to do what you can to maximise your utility within the income that you have.

We are representing things in an extremely abstract way: we are supposing that there is only one kind of consumption; for the purposes of visualisation let's think of it as ice cream.

There's an income, which we denote by y, and you have to stay within the bounds of that income, and that income is also expressed in, well, scoops of ice cream. We are expressing the fact that you can't eat more than your income with the expression

$$c \leq y$$

We want to express the fact that there is maximisation, but in addition that there is maximisation subject to the constraint of income, mathematically. There is a way to do it, but before we do it, we can note that this problem has a trivial solution. Remember that the utility function was increasing, so if you want to make your utility as big as possible, you want to make your consumption as big as possible. How big can you make it? Well, you can make it as big as y. And so this is the answer to the problem of maximising utility: it's the utility of your income, y. The "brute force" approach is to substitute the constraint $c = y$ into the objective, yielding the solution $u(y)$.

To maximise utility in a mathematically methodical way, the discussion in the previous chapter suggests that we should take the derivative and set it to zero; that should yield the same result as brute force:

$$u'(c) = 0$$

But that doesn't really work: to set the derivative of a standard utility function to zero, you have to have infinite consumption — recall

Figure 1.2 — there is no top of the utility hill. That isn't allowed by the constraint: consumption cannot exceed income. There is another way to think about the problem, and it's actually more complicated at first, but it will help us think about the problem in other ways.

First, restate the problem as follows:

$$\max_{c} \{u(c) + \lambda(y - c)\}$$

This reformulation of the problem has a generic name: it is called a Lagrangian.[1]

In the Lagrangian formulation, we are still maximising by choosing consumption, and we still have the utility function that we are interested in maximising. But now there's this additional term.

The additional term, which we add to the utility function, has two pieces: λ and $y - c$. The difference $y - c$ expresses the constraint that consumption has to be less than or equal to income; λ is the Greek letter for L and L stands for Lagrange multiplier. We're going to treat λ as if it's a variable like consumption.

Let's just naively pretend that this is our optimisation problem. What happens if we solve it by taking the derivative with respect to c? Well, first of all, we need to use our rules of derivatives. We take the derivative with respect to c of this whole thing. The first-order condition is

$$u'(c) - \lambda = 0 \quad \rightarrow \quad c = u'^{-1}(\lambda)$$

The derivative of a sum is the sum of the derivatives and therefore we can break this into two parts. The derivative of $u(c)$ is $u'(c)$. And λ doesn't involve c. Now, we have the derivative with respect to c of λc. We treat λ as a constant so the derivative is λ.

Let's go back to an abstract function, $f(\cdot)$, which has this concave shape. The utility function was concave, but it was upward sloping everywhere. This one actually has a place where it starts to slope down. We found that there is a mathematical operation that determines where the top of this function is: the derivative is the slope of the function, and the slope at the top is zero.

[1]The name honors the 18th–19th century French-Italian mathematician J. L. Lagrange, and the Lagrangian approach was originally formulated to express physics problems in which the constraints expressed the conservation of energy and momentum rather than income.

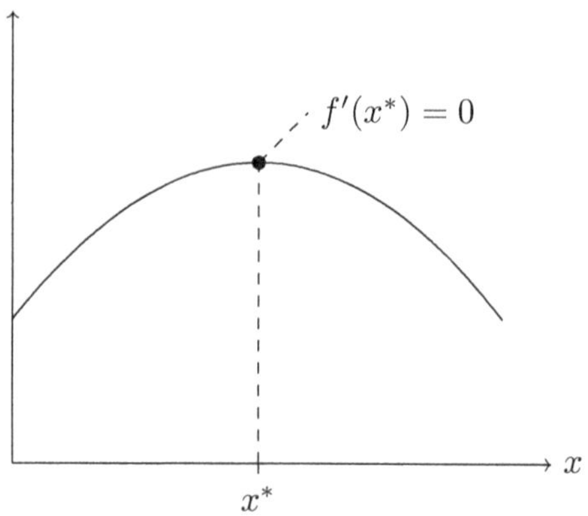

We're not done. We wanted to figure out what consumption is when you solve the optimisation problem. If we pretend that we're optimising over a concave function and we've got c instead of x as the thing we're choosing, there's going to be a c that sets the derivative to zero. If we could call it c^* and we want to figure out what it is now, we already know the answer. This is a trivial problem. But we can go through the steps that we would go through if it wasn't so trivial, and in a minute we see how it might not be so trivial in a more complicated setting. So, we take this first-order condition and we take the inverse of that $u'(c)$. And that's our answer, apply that inverse function to λ.

But the full solution requires knowledge of λ; up until now we have been treating it as an abstract quantity. We can solve for λ by going back to the budget constraint. Substitute the solution for consumption into the budget constraint and then invert the inverse of the marginal utility function:

$$u'^{-1}(\lambda) = y \quad \rightarrow \quad \lambda = u'(y)$$

We can take the solution for λ and go back to the solution for consumption c, and now we have the full solution — that consumption equals income:

$$c = u'^{-1}(u'(y)) = y$$

Of course, we already knew that, but now it is in formal terms.

Economists have their own terminology for the derivative of utility: marginal utility. Maybe you've heard of this and that reminds us that it's a slope of the utility function. So, λ is the marginal utility of income. And that's actually a general statement as we see in a minute. So, when we have a Lagrange multiplier it is going to have the interpretation of the marginal utility of income or something analogous to income.

There is something else to note: when you take the derivative of the Lagrangian with respect to λ, you just get the budget constraint back. You can think of this as the first-order condition with respect to λ. Combining it with the first-order condition for consumption, you get two equations in two unknowns, c and λ, and we can solve them simultaneously:

$$\begin{aligned} u'(c) - \lambda &= 0 \\ y - c &= 0 \end{aligned}$$

In the bonus material, there is a detail: you don't maximise with respect to λ, you minimise. It is therefore more correct to write the Lagrangian problem as

$$\min_{\lambda} \max_{c} u(c) + \lambda(y - c)$$

But operationally it works the same way — you take the derivative and set it to zero.

Example 2.1. Let's pause here and do an example of with a geometric utility function:

$$u(c) = \frac{c^{1-\gamma}}{1-\gamma}$$

It has this special form, which we've already explored a little bit with the derivatives and also the integrals. The $1-\gamma$ term is in the denominator because it cancels out when you take the derivative. This is just for convenience, as we spend more time with the derivative of utility than with the utility function itself. (The parameter γ has a special meaning: it expresses the risk aversion; we talk more about this later.)

We can immediately state the marginal utility:

$$u'(c) = c^{-\gamma}$$

To be concrete, we can suppose that γ is equal to one half, so $u(c)$ is equal to the square root of c. It is an upward sloping function and it is concave. You then have $u'(c)$: it is $c^{-1/2}$, or one over the square root.

We want to figure out the inverse function. We have $u'(c) = \lambda$ in the first-order condition. To obtain to the solution for c, we use the exponent rules. Recall that if we have $(x^a)^b$ and that's x^{ab}, we have $a = -\gamma$ and we set $b = -\frac{1}{\gamma}$, and they cancel. This gives us $c = \lambda^{\frac{1}{-\gamma}}$: this is our function for c. It is a function of λ, except we don't know what λ is yet. So, we have to go back to that problem.

The individual solving this problem faces the constraint. Let's suppose that that constraint holds with equality: $c = y$. And so we go from $c = y$ to $u'^{-1}(\lambda)$, which is c. Apply the constraint so that c is equal to y. And now we have our solution for λ:

$$\lambda = y^{-\gamma} \tag{2.1}$$

In our numerical example. γ can be $\frac{1}{2}$, the square root. This yields $c = \lambda^{-2}$. Now, we can solve for λ: because $c = y$ in this fundamental setting, λ is $y^{-\frac{1}{2}}$.

Two goods

What if there are two goods? An individual wants to maximise his utility. He has an income but there are two things to buy: let's revert to a classic pair of goods: wine and cheese. You would like to bring some wine and some cheese to your picnic, but you want to consume them in the optimal proportion to each other. Eating cheese but not drinking any wine isn't as much fun as having some wine with your cheese; drinking only wine, but eating no cheese, also leaves you in a different place that's not as good as having both the cheese and the wine.

But what combination of the cheese and the wine do you pick? If wine costs £1,000/L and cheese is £1/kg, you'll eat more cheese and just have a little tiny sip of wine. And on the other hand, if wine is £1/L and cheese is a £100/kg, you'll consume wine but just a crumb of cheese, other things equal.

The main point is as follows: the prices of the two things that you're going to choose matter. And they're going to influence the ratio of the consumption of the things that you choose. We want to capture that idea but in a more technical way. There is a way to solve the optimisation problem of not just how much total wine and cheese you consume, like the previous problem we just examined, but also the ratio of the two things. And now the prices are going to matter.

First of all, we have to write down the problem that we want to solve:

$$\max_{c} u(c_1, c_2) \quad \text{subject to } p_1 c_1 + p_2 c_2 \leq y$$

We now have a utility function that is a utility function of two things, not just one. And there is a budget constraint, which says that what you consume of the first good, the wine, and of the second good, the cheese. When multiplied by their prices, p_1 and p_2, that has to add up to no more than the income that you have. So, in the previous slides, we didn't think about prices, but now we have to. This is our constraint — the budget constraint. We are still expressing the idea that an individual is solving a maximisation problem, making decisions, and taking actions that we want to characterise. And that's what this max operation does.

We can again express this idea in a compact mathematical form with a Lagrangian:

$$\min_{\lambda} \max_{\{c_1, c_2\}} \{u(c_1, c_2) + \lambda(y - (p_1 c_1 + p_2 c_2))\}$$

The Lagrangian says maximise, by choosing both c_1 and c_2, the two types of consumption, wine and cheese, to maximise this utility function. Additionally, we also know we have to optimise with respect to the multiplier, λ (and as set out in the bonus material it is proper to minimise with respect to λ, not maximise). We express the constraint as y minus the stuff on the left-hand side of this inequality. Note that if c_1 and c_2 are such that y was actually strictly greater than what was spent on the consumption, then y minus the left-hand side would be positive. So, the budget constraint is always going to be either positive or zero. And intuitively, we know it's going to be zero at the end of the day, but mathematically we allow for the possibility that it could be positive.

How do we solve this problem? The same approach that we used before is going to work again. We take the derivatives with respect to c_1 and with respect to c_2 and with respect to λ — the first-order conditions:

$$u_1 = \lambda p_1$$

$$u_2 = \lambda p_2$$

$$y = p_1 c_1 + p_2 c_2$$

(*A reminder*: the derivative u_1 informally means to take derivative with respect to c_1, treating c_2 as a constant, and vice versa; if we were being more formal, we would write the partial derivative as $\frac{\partial u}{\partial c_1}$.)

In order to find the top of the utility function, it's that the utility function is now a little more complicated. It isn't just a function of one thing, it's a function of two things. So instead of this object that has a top that we just look at where the first derivative is zero, it's like a hill. It has multiple dimensions, directions in which we are taking the derivative, but it is still true, however, that when all of the derivatives are zero, we're at the top of the hill.

Here is a visual analogy: you are on a hike, ascending a hill, but there is a fence that runs in a straight line up the side of the hill and then down the other side — it doesn't reach the top of the hill. If you are on the downhill side of the fence, climbing upward along it, the highest point you can reach is the optimum. At that point you are at the top of the fence, not the top of the hill.

So we have three equations and three things we want to figure out: c_1, c_2, and λ.

Dividing the two first-order conditions yields the ratio of prices on the right-hand side because the λs cancel:

$$\frac{u_{c_1}}{u_{c_2}} = \frac{p_1}{p_2}$$

This solves the problem of what ratio of wine and cheese we choose. Do we choose a little wine and a lot of cheese or a lot of wine and a little cheese? And this expression tells us the answer. The relative proportions of the wine and cheese are going to be driven by the relative prices, the ratio of the prices.

Example. We can solve explicitly for specific examples:

$$u(c_1, c_2) = \frac{c_1^{1-\gamma}}{1-\gamma} + \frac{c_2^{1-\gamma}}{1-\gamma}$$

$$\frac{u_{c_1}}{u_{c_2}} = \frac{c_1^{-\gamma}}{c_2^{-\gamma}} = \frac{p_1}{p_2} \to \frac{c_1}{c_2} = \left(\frac{p_1}{p_2}\right)^{-\frac{1}{\gamma}}$$

This is an extension of the geometric utility example we did for the one-good case.

It is useful to substitute a specific value for γ in this example — $\frac{1}{2}$. It is clear that increasing the price of good 1 reduces the relative consumption of good 1.

Units of the Lagrange multiplier

If we were in physics or chemistry, we would want to check the units to make sure that everything lines up properly. What is the Lagrange multiplier measuring? As we already established, it is the marginal utility of income. We want to determine the units of marginal utility.

In the Lagrangian, we have this extra term, $\lambda(y-c)$. And because in this Lagrangian we have utility, this extra term also has to be measured in terms of utility units for consistency. However, income and consumption are measured in, well, you can think of it as pounds or dollars — units of money. And so λ has to convert money into utility. Therefore, the Lagrange multiplier has to be in units of utility per dollar or utility per pound.

At the optimum, that is where the problem is solved. The Lagrange multiplier tells us the price of an extra unit of utility in terms of income, that is, the marginal increase in income needed to get an extra unit of utility. So, we can think of that Lagrange multiplier as a sort of a price.

The fence-on-the-side-of-a-hill analogy also helps with the marginal utility of income idea. You can imagine moving the entire fence up the hill, parallel to its original track, by one foot — the analogy of increasing income. The maximum point along the fence will also move uphill by one foot — this is the analogue of the marginal utility gain from an increase in income.

Summarising, we have the following:

- In the Lagrangian, we are maximising utility, so the extra term, $\lambda(y-c)$, must be in utility units to be consistent.
- The budget constraint term $(y-c)$ is in money income units (£).
- Thus, the Lagrange multiplier must be in units of $\frac{\text{utility}}{£}$ — it converts money income units to utility units.
- So, at the optimum, it tells us the price of an extra unit of utility in terms of income — the increase in income needed to get an extra unit of utility — the marginal utility of income

The same good at two different times

Let's next think of c_1 and c_2 not as two different goods like wine and cheese but as basic consumption — back to ice cream — abstractly defined at two different times. Can we use the same reasoning to get at what the consumer should do? The answer is yes. Exactly the same reasoning applies. However, the definitions of the prices are a bit different: prices are going to have something to do with the interest rate. Then, if we arbitrarily define the price of the good at time 1 as 1, so $p_1 \equiv 1$, then we can write the budget constraint down as

$$y \geq c_1 + \frac{1}{1+r}c_2$$

where y is *wealth*: the discounted value of income over several periods. We know that for the budget constraint to be obeyed properly, you can't consume more than you have in wealth, appropriately defined.

Therefore, the sum of current consumption and also discounted future consumption cannot be bigger than the wealth that you start out with. We take $\frac{1}{1+r}$ as the discount factor times whatever we consume in the second period.

What is meant by "discounted?" Ignoring the formula for a minute, we can ask the following question: Suppose that, separate from c_1, just thinking about c_2, suppose that you plan to consume c_2 in the next period of your existence. We can ask the following: how much money would we need to put into the bank so that in that second period, period 2, we would be able to take the money out of the bank, along with the interest, and buy c_2 and consume it? The answer is quite simple.

Let's call that initial amount of money that we put into the bank x. And we want to be able to buy c_2 when we take the money out of the bank in a year: how much money will we have? We will have the initial deposit x plus the interest on x when we take it out in a year. Well, we want this to equal c_2 because we're planning to consume c_2 by doing that. Therefore, $(1+r)x = c_2$, and x is equal to $\frac{1}{1+r}$ times c_2. This is called the discounted value.

Therefore, $\frac{1}{1+r}c_2$ is the amount you need to put into the bank to get c_2. And of course, if you consume something immediately, then you don't need to discount it by putting some something in the bank to pay for it. So when we add these two things up, we get the total resources available for consuming now and consuming later.

It is key that we can interpret the discount coefficient $\frac{1}{1+r}$ as a price. And also, we didn't make it explicit, but we've got a one multiplying c_1. So the price of consuming c_1 is 1 — that was an assumption — and the price of consuming a good later is $\frac{1}{1+r}$. There's no mathematical distinction between those two prices and the prices p_1 and p_2 that we had in the wine and cheese two-good problem.

And that means that we can solve it the same way. Solving the problem exactly as in the two-good model:

$$\frac{u_{c_1}}{u_{c_2}} = \frac{1}{\frac{1}{1+r}} = 1+r$$

Thus, when we go through the steps that from the two-good case, we got that the marginal utility of consuming good 1 divided by the marginal utility of consuming good 2 has to be the ratio of those prices: $1+r$. And if we reduce the price of good 2, that is the equivalent of raising the interest rate, so we consume more of good 2 in response.

The Lagrange multiplier has an interpretation: it's the marginal utility of y, but now y is wealth, so we're interpreting that as the marginal utility of wealth.

Example 2.2. Let's do our geometric utility example in this context. We define a utility function that is the sum of two pieces, each of which looks familiar — consumption to the power $1-\gamma$ divided by

$1-\gamma$ — geometric utility:

$$u(c_1, c_2) = \frac{c_1^{1-\gamma}}{1-\gamma} + \frac{1}{1+\rho}\frac{c_2^{1-\gamma}}{1-\gamma}$$

We add together the utilities of the consuming now and consuming later, but we have this extra term, the coefficient $\frac{1}{1+\rho}$; ρ is the Greek letter for r, suggesting that it's behaving somehow like an interest rate. And indeed, if you look at the structure of this piece of the utility function, it does kind of look like an interest rate that's discounting the future, and that's exactly the right interpretation. Indeed, when we talked about the integral of utility in the previous chapter, we had that discount factor, e^{-rt}, and we talked about how it operates. So, this $\frac{1}{1+\rho}$ behaves similarly to e^{-rt}: it puts a lower weight on future utility of consumption than on current utility of consumption. If we think of ρ as a thousand, then $\frac{1}{1+\rho}$ is almost zero — 0.0001. So, the bigger ρ is, the smaller the weight. The relative weight that we put on future utility and the smaller ρ is the more weight we put on future utilities. So, if we think of ρ as zero, then we put equal weigh — 1.0 — on current utility of consumption and future utility of consumption.

It is useful to think of ρ as measuring impatience, so a low value of ρ means you're very patient and a high value of ρ means you're very impatient. And if ρ is equal to a thousand, as we noted earlier, you would be very impatient and you would care very little about the future and put most of the weight on current utility.

ρ isn't the same as r, the interest rate, but ρ is something that is internal to the person solving the problem. So, it's commonly referred to as the subjective rate of time discount: there is discounting in the sense that we described earlier, but it is subjective in the sense that it represents the personal preferences or tastes of the individual solving the problem. Intuitively, we should expect that ρ and r will have some sort of relationship. That is the case, and we'll be getting to that.

Solving this problem using the previous methods, the left-hand side of the equation resulting from taking the derivative, setting them to zero and so on is going to be the marginal utility of consumption at time 1. (Note that $\rho = r$ is not required.) Carrying through with the algebra, we obtain the ratio

$$\frac{c_1^{-\gamma}}{c_2^{-\gamma}} = \frac{1+r}{1+\rho} \quad \rightarrow \quad \frac{c_1}{c_2} = \left(\frac{1+r}{1+\rho}\right)^{-\frac{1}{\gamma}}$$

We can conduct a couple of thought experiments. For the first experiment, set $\rho = 0$. Suppose that α is 0.07 and r is 0.03, which would correspond to an interest rate of 3%. Then what is this object on the right-hand side? 0.9062. This is a number less than 1, and this means that $\frac{c_1}{c_2}$ is less than 1. This means that consumption at time 1 is less than the consumption at time 2.

If ρ is equal to zero, the economic interpretation is that the person solving this problem is perfectly patient. A person who is perfectly patient, that is, who equally waits current and future consumption, notes that if he puts money in the bank, he gets interest. And if he does a little bit of sacrificing today, then tomorrow he'll get that interest in addition to whatever is whatever he put in the bank. And so that sounds like a benefit. So, he'll consume a little more in the future because of that payment.

For our second numerical example, let $\rho = r$, and continue with $r = 0.03$. The ratio on the right-hand side is 1, 1 to any power is just 1, and so the right-hand side becomes 1. And so this means that consumption now and consumption later are the same.

So, if the subjective rate of time discount is the same as the interest rate, then consumption is even over current and future consumption. But if r is bigger than ρ, then the individual we're thinking about whose problem we're solving will consume more in the future because they get this benefit from saving. Big r means the expression $\frac{1}{1+r}$ becomes small, and that's like lowering the price, given the interpretation we're putting on it as a price. So, you're consuming more of the cheaper good, that is to say, more of the future good.

There's a side comment to make, which is we know what r is because we can observe it in markets, but we don't necessarily know what ρ is. And we don't actually necessarily know what γ is. These are theoretical constructs at this moment, and a question lurking in the background is how are we going to measure these numbers γ and ρ. That is for later.

Chopping the constraint period by period

We now see that the Lagrange multiplier is a price, and the algebraic expression $\frac{1}{1+r}$ is a price; how are they related? And in any case, we are really interested in the *relative* price — that determines relative consumption. So, it makes sense to chop up the Lagrangian so that the consumption in each period has a Lagrange multiplier attached to it. Then, we can look at the relative price between periods, as we already have done.

To get this to work however, we need an additional feature: there has to be a way for an individual to trade current and future consumption. This will be achieved via savings.

Instead of the budget constraint

$$y \geq c_1 + \frac{1}{1+r} c_2$$

we can chop the intertemporal budget constraint into pieces so that there is one constraint per period. Each of the constraints has its own Lagrange multiplier:

$$y = c_1 + s$$

$$(1+r)s = c_2$$

where s is the savings. The Lagrangian then consists of of the utility function plus the constraints multiplied by their Lagrange multipliers:

$$\min_{\{\lambda_1,\lambda_2\}} \max_{\{c_1,c_2,s\}} \{u(c_1,c_2) + \lambda_1(y - s - c_1) + \lambda_2((1+r)s - c_2)\} \quad (2.2)$$

So, there are now two Lagrange multipliers and an additional choice variable, savings s:

$$\max_{\{c_1,c_2,s,\lambda_1,\lambda_2\}} \{u(c_1,c_2) + \lambda_1(y - s - c_1) + \lambda_2((1+r)s - c_2)\} \quad (2.3)$$

There are now five first-order conditions:

$$u_{c_1} - \lambda_1 = 0$$

$$u_{c_2} - \lambda_2 = 0$$

$$-\lambda_1 + (1+r)\lambda_2 = 0$$

$$y - s - c_1 = 0$$
$$(1 + r)s - c_2 = 0$$

These are five equations in the unknowns c_1, c_2, s, λ_1, λ_2. We get the same answer as when we had just one intertemporal equation.

Note that we can calculate the ratio of the marginal utilities as we did in the earlier wine and cheese consumption problem, and that ratio is equal to the ratio of prices, that is, the relative price, but that relative price is expressed strictly as the ratio of the Lagrange multipliers from each period:

$$\frac{u_{c_2}}{u_{c_1}} = \frac{\lambda_2}{\lambda_1}$$

What the λs express is the *relative* price of good 1, namely $p_1 = 1$, and λ_2, namely $p_2 = \frac{1}{1+r}$; we capture this by normalizing λ_2 by dividing by λ_1:

$$\frac{\lambda_2}{\lambda_1} = \frac{1}{1 + r}$$

What is that relative price? We already know the answer from our earlier analysis of the two-period problem using the single wealth constraint: it is $1 + r$. We therefore need to establish that the same relative price emerges here:

$$\boxed{\lambda_2 = \frac{1}{1 + r}\lambda_1}$$

that is, the Lagrange multipliers have a time pattern that looks like the discounting of future asset values — the relative price of future consumption relative to current consumption, as embodied in the Lagrange multipliers, is the discount factor, $\frac{1}{1+r}$. This pattern is going to show up in the richer models we are going to develop.

We can add up the two constraints; the constraints add to original constraint:

$$\lambda_1(y - s - c_1) + \frac{1}{1 + r}\lambda_1((1 + r)s - c_2)$$
$$= \lambda_1 \left(y - c_1 - \frac{1}{1 + r}c_2\right)$$

which was our earlier budget constraint, so the two approaches to the intertemporal problem are equivalent.

Extending the intertemporal model: Growth

There is a very similar problem, Robinson Crusoe's investment problem,

$$\min_{\{\lambda_1,\lambda_2\}} \max_{\{c_1,c_2,s\}} \{u(c_1, c_2) + \lambda_1(k_1 - s - c_1) + \lambda_2(f(s) - c_2)\}$$

where $f(s)$ is the output from investment s ($f(s)$ takes the place of $(1+r)$).

When we take the derivative, the marginal product acts like the interest rate:

$$\begin{aligned} \lambda_1 &= c_1^{-\gamma} \quad \text{use previous solution for } c_1 \\ \lambda_2 &= \frac{1}{1+\rho} c_2^{-\gamma} \\ \lambda_2 &= \frac{1}{1+r} \lambda_1 \\ y - s - c_1 &= 0 \\ f'(s)s - c_2 &= 0 \end{aligned}$$

$f'(s)$ is going to behave like $(1+r)$. Using the geometric utility example, the first-order conditions can be broken out period by period. We extend this idea further in the coming chapters.

Exercises

Exercise 2.1. Basic consumer optimisation. Substitute numbers in the 1-good Lagrangian model and work out relative consumption and also the Lagrange multiplier λ:

$$u(c) = \frac{c^{1-\gamma}}{1-\gamma}$$

(i) $\gamma = 1/2$
(ii) $\gamma = 2/3$

Exercise 2.2. Substitute numbers in the 1-good Lagrangian model and work out relative consumption and also the Lagrange multiplier λ but for exponential utility:

$$-(1/\gamma)e^{-\gamma c}$$

(i) $\gamma = 1/2$
(ii) $\alpha = 1/3$

Exercise 2.3. Two-good consumer optimisation. Repeat the derivation but for additive utility:

$$u(c_1, c_2) = \frac{c_1^{1-\gamma}}{1-\gamma} + \frac{1}{1+\rho}\frac{c_2^{1-\gamma}}{1-\gamma}$$

(i) $\gamma = 1/2$
(ii) $\gamma = 2/3$

Exercise 2.4. Establish that the Lagrange multiplier is still the marginal value of income in the two-good consumer optimization problem.

Exercise 2.5. Solve the consumption ratio for the two-period consumer optimization problem example with geometric utility, using the following parameterizations:

(i) $\gamma = 0.3$, $r = 0.03$, $[\rho = 0; \rho = r]$
(ii) $\gamma = 0.3$, $r = 0.09$
(iii) $\gamma = 3$, $r = 0.03$

Exercise 2.6. One-good model. Consider the utility function

$$u(c) = \frac{1 - e^{-\gamma c_1}}{\gamma}$$

A consumer solves

$$\max_c u(c)$$

subject to the constraint

$$y = cp$$

Use the following values:

$$y = 35{,}000 \quad \gamma = 2.7 \quad p = 12$$

(i) As a preliminary step, write down the formula for $u'(c)$.
(ii) Write down the Lagrangian.
(iii) Solve for optimal consumption c as a function of the Lagrange multiplier.

Hint: Start by writing down the first-order condition for c. Then take the logarithm.

(iv) Solve for the Lagrange multiplier.

Hint: Substitute the answer from the previous question into the budget constraint.

Exercise 2.7. One-good model. Consider the utility function

$$u(c) = \gamma \ln(c)$$

A consumer solves

$$\max_{c} u(c)$$

subject to the constraint

$$y = cp$$

Use the following values:

$$y = 35{,}000 \quad \gamma = 2.7 \quad p = 12$$

Carry out the same steps as in Exercise 2.6.

Exercise 2.8. Two-good model. Consider the utility function

$$u(c_1, c_2) = -\frac{1}{2}(\bar{c} - c_1)^2 - \frac{1}{1+\rho}\frac{1}{2}(\bar{c} - c_2)^2$$

where $\bar{c}$ is a fixed constant.

A consumer solves

$$\max_{c_1, c_2}$$

subject to the constraint

$$y = c_1 + \frac{1}{1+r}c_2$$

(i) As a preliminary step, write down the formulas for $u'(c_1)$, $u'(c_2)$.
(ii) Write down the Lagrangian.
(iii) Solve for the optimal consumption *difference* $c_1 - c_2$.
Hint: Start by writing down the first-order conditions for c_1 and c_2. Take the ratio of these two conditions, which involve the marginal utilities that you calculated above.
(iv) Solve for c_1 and c_2 as functions of λ.
(v) Solve for the Lagrange multiplier.

Bonus Material

Second-order conditions and the saddle point

How do we know we are at the top of the Lagrangian "hill?" We can look at the second-order conditions. The second-order condition for optimal consumption in the basic Lagrangian is negative:

$$u''(c) < 0$$

But we devolved onto the realisation that we also need to optimise with respect to the Lagrange multiplier, λ. The second-order condition for λ is zero!

$$\frac{d}{d\lambda}(y - c) = 0$$

We can take further derivatives: the cross derivative of the first-order condition with respect to c is -1, and the cross-derivative with respect to the first-order condition with respect to λ is also -1.

Gathering all of the derivatives in a matrix, we can check whether the matrix is negative definite, that is, whether the determinant is negative; the matrix is

$$\begin{pmatrix} u''(c) & -1 \\ -1 & 0 \end{pmatrix}$$

which does in fact have a negative determinant; this is the multi-dimensional generalisation of the negative second-order condition that goes with ordinary maximisation. But this means that the objective in terms of the two-dimensional problem is in fact a saddle point. This is a general property of Lagrangian formulations.

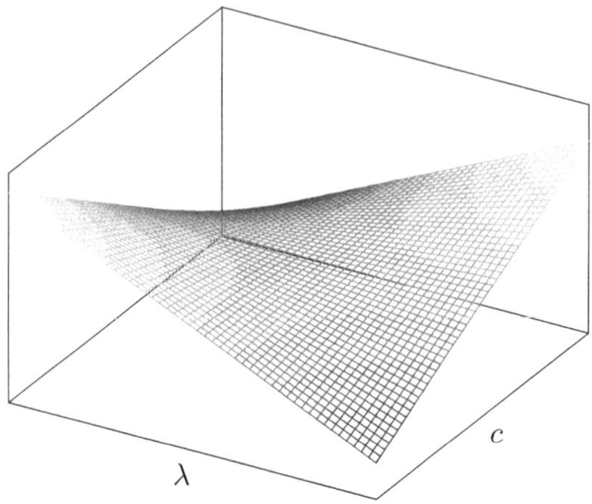

Figure 2.1. Lagrangian is a saddle.

We express the fact that we are looking for a saddle point, not the top a hill, when we have a Lagrangian, by noting that we *minimise* with respect to λ:

$$\min_{\lambda} \max_{c} \{u(c) + \lambda(y - c)\}$$

that is, maximise over c and minimise over λ (see Figure 2.1).

As a practical matter, in well-posed economic models, our focus is on the first-order conditions, and the first-order conditions will be unchanged.

Prices are probabilities

We can convert prices to probabilities. Suppose we multiply and divide by the sum of the prices:

•

$$\max_{\{c_1, c_2\}} \left\{ u(c_1, c_2) \right.$$
$$\left. + \lambda(p_1 + p_2)\left(\frac{y}{p_1 + p_2} - \left(\frac{p_1}{p_1 + p_2}c_1 + \frac{p_2}{p_1 + p_2}c_2\right)\right)\right\} \tag{2.4}$$

- Define new notation:

$$\max_{\{c_1,c_2\}} \{u(c_1, c_2) + \tilde{\lambda}(\tilde{y} - (\tilde{p}_1 c_1 + \tilde{p}_2 c_2))\}$$

- Now, the prices are also *probabilities*: $\tilde{p}_1 + \tilde{p}_2 = 1$.

The optimal consumptions don't change; we've just changed units. These prices are known as Arrow–Debreu prices.

Chapter 3

Economic Growth: Preliminaries

We're nearly ready to apply the tools we have developed to take on the next method: deterministic optimal control. And we're going to be aggressively going towards modelling economic growth, which as a side product will produce the theory of the interest rate as our main application. So the first thing to say is, again, this is a very big subject, and we are just looking at the surface, focusing only on examples. Before proceeding, we need an additional technical tool, differential equations, which we use to generalise the idea of the budget constraint to the continuous time model. Once we do that we'll have some bookkeeping to go through so that we can write down the Lagrangian for the continuous time problem. We do that in the following chapter.

Differential Equations

To begin, we observe that we can often describe physical phenomena and many economic phenomena using differential equations, that is, in equations where a derivative appears. We start with an easy example, in which the derivative is a constant.

Suppose we have something happening physically that we want to describe; a very familiar physical phenomenon is driving in a car, and that car is moving across the ground at a certain speed. If we're on the the motorway (the equivalent of the US interstate), we could be going at 70 miles an hour and just stay at 70 miles an hour. Can we describe that situation physically? Mathematically, the answer is yes. If we denote the location of the car on the ground as $y(t)$, we would say that the time derivative of the location of the car is a constant. The location is changing over time at a constant rate, and we could give that rate a name, a, and we would interpret a as 70 miles an hour. Note that we don't actually have to solve for $y(t)$ to describe what's going on with this equation. So, the key thing about differential equations is although we're interested in solving them in the sense that we'll get to soon, you don't always have to solve them explicitly. You can just use them as a way to describe a phenomenon.

Expressing this in mathematical notation:

- Location of the car at any time t:

$$y(t)$$

- Speed of your car is the change in location y per unity of time — time derivative

$$\frac{d}{dt}y(t)$$

- Then if your speed is a constant ($a = 70$ MPH), this can be described by an ODE (ordinary differential equation)

$$\frac{d}{dt}y(t) = a$$

Note that we don't necessarily have to solve for $y(t)$ — the ODE itself gives a lot of information.

There is a little notational thing to bring up, which is we've been using $\frac{d}{dx}f(x)$ as a way to say the derivative of $f(x)$, and you also have seen the notation $f'(x)$ as a way to notationally express the derivative. But, as we noted in the chapter on calculus, there's a third notation that's very commonly used, which is to put a little dot over a variable: $\frac{d}{dt}y(t) = y'(t) = \dot{y}$; that denotes the time derivative, that is, if the variables are a function of time or if the function is a function of time, the dot means take the derivative with respect to time. So, if we're thinking about velocity or speed, that is, and we're looking at the position of a car over the ground describing it with $y(t)$, then the time derivative in shorthand notation is $\dot{y}$

The simplest example of a differential equation where something actually happens that's interesting is exponential growth. Let's start from the solution that we're going to get to, which is that there might be some initial state of the world, such as happened in the early 1800s when a few rabbits were brought over to Australia. They start breeding and so the number of rabbits grew exponentially.[1] They're having a similar problem with mice and cane toads because there are no natural predators — just kangaroos.

Just as we can describe the location of the car on the motorway, we can describe the size of the rabbit population at a particular time t with a variable: p_t. (A reminder that in this context, the notation p_t means that p is a function of time — it is not the partial derivative.) There's some initial value p_0. The exponential growth can be represented with this exponential function. In notational terms, we have

$$p_t = p_0 e^{\gamma t}$$

starting from p_0. If we put in a number for a γ, which is some constant, then after a certain time soon after time zero, this is the number of rabbits that we will have. So, γ is referred to as the growth rate.

We can then take the time derivative of the population of the rabbits. So what is $\frac{dp}{dt}$? Take the derivative of both sides:

$$\frac{dp_t}{dt} = p_0 \gamma e^{\gamma t} = \gamma p_t$$

with initial value p_0. In words, the time change of the population of rabbits is a function of the number of rabbits at that moment.

We can equivalently write ODEs where the underlying function is a function of time using shorthand

$$\dot{p}_t = \gamma p_t$$

How do we take this derivative? Going back to our rules for derivatives, the derivative of $e^{\gamma t}$ is $\gamma e^{\gamma t}$, that is, we preserve the exponential, so we can write the derivative as γp_t. The result is a (an ordinary) differential equation; when you include the initial value p_0, you can fully solve it.

[1]This led to several rabbit plagues, the worst of which was in late 1940s and early 1950s. The plagues were finally stopped by the introduction of a rabbit virus, myxomatosis.

The real agenda is to go in the reverse direction: there are many situations where it is relatively straightforward to quantitatively describe it in terms of derivatives: the speed of a car or the rate of change of a rabbit population. But our ultimate interest is to predict the final location of the car in terms of elapsed hours, or the total population of rabbits after a year. This means we have to solve the equation. If you can write down a differential equation (in our setting, motivated by economic theorising), then you can solve for the underlying variable (in our case population p_t). Thus, the key thing about differential equations is that we go the other way: start with a differential equation and solve it.

Intuitively, you should expect that integration would come in because integration is the anti-derivative, as we discussed, and that's the beginning of how you would approach solving this equation. However, we're not interested in that deep solution method because this book is about the models that are applications of these ideas. So, we're just going to say that sometimes you can solve and there will be a couple of instances where you can explicitly solve. This is one of them, but in most situations, we won't be explicitly solving differential equations. We use them in their descriptive sense and then use them in models.

If you know what p_0 is, then you can completely solve the differential equation. The solution of

$$\dot{p}_t = \gamma p_t$$

starting from p_0 is

$$p_t = p_0 e^{\gamma t}$$

This is the solution of the differential equation. We established by taking a derivative that you end up with the differential equation. And so logically, we can just reverse that process.

Let's put numbers in an example for intuition.

Example 3.1. Let $\gamma = 0.07$, $p_0 = 100$ (this could be rabbits or a model of the rate of return on an index of stocks in some initial year):

- Then at time 10, we have

$$p_{10} = 100e^{0.07\times 10} = 100 \times 2.014 = 201.4$$

- But if you have a different starting point, you get a different answer:

$$p_{10} = 200e^{0.07\times 10} = 200 \times 2.014 = 402.14$$

that is, *initial conditions matter.*

So, after 10 years of rabbit reproduction in Australia, you will get the initial value of 100 times this exponential of the coefficient γ times the number of years that we let this go on. And if you do the calculation with your calculator, then you get that it roughly doubled in 10 years. If instead we start with the point 200, we then do the same exponential of our ten years of growth. We end up with a different number, but note that it is really the same in the sense that it has doubled the initial value.

Thus, the initial value determines where we end up. If we start with the bigger initial value, we end up with the bigger final value. That initial value expresses the initial condition, and it matters. So, when we're thinking about differential equations, when we actually solve them, we need to think about the starting point — the initial condition — as well as the behaviour of the equation itself. The initial value is a specific case of the general thing that we have to be concerned about with differential equations, namely initial conditions, or more generally, boundary conditions. So where does the equation begin? Where does it end? This matters a lot.

Discounted Utility and Investment: Robinson Crusoe

The basic problem. We want to solve in order to maximise this object, the discounted utility of consumption

$$\max_{c} \int_{0}^{\infty} e^{-\rho t} u(c_t) dt$$

subject to a constraint. This is the bigger version of the two periods of consumption that we talked about in the previous chapter and which relates to that earlier object. We briefly encountered the infinite-horizon discounted utility of consumption when we were talking about integrals.

The integral runs over a certain period of time time: zero, which we can think of as the time of now, and infinity. And we argued that infinity is actually a reasonable thing to put as the upper limit of integration because that represents the fact that we care about our descendants and they care about their descendants and they care about their descendants off into the indefinite future. So, it's appropriate to think of the person solving the consumption problem as solving an intergenerational consumption problem that goes off to infinity.

And as we also discussed, there's this discount factor, ρ, the same ρ that we saw in the discussion of the two periods of consumption, the subjective rate of time discount.

The bigger the ρ, the less the weight put on future utility and the smaller the ρ, the more the weight put on future utility. And so again, ρ has the economic interpretation as impatience. The more impatient you are, the bigger the ρ and the less you care about the future and the more you care about the present in relation to the future.

The constraint. The following part is new. We express the constraint facing the person solving the optimisation with a differential equation:

$$\dot{k}_t = f(k_t) - c_t \qquad k_0 = k^* \tag{3.1}$$

that is, capital k_t grows according to a production function f that uses existing capital as an input, less the flow of consumption.

Note that we have not stated the solution of the differential equation, and we're not going to state the solution explicitly at all. We're going to use this differential equation as a way to describe what's going on.

What can we say about that differential equation? First of all, we've used the letter k. If we were sticking with the intuitive approach from the two goods to two periods of consumption now and later, the constraint would have something to do with wealth. But we're using the letter k: k is the letter that economists typically use to denote capital. We say more about what capital means, but why is it k? Well, in German, capital is K as in "Das Kapital," which you may have heard of, so that k has stuck as the notation for capital. Also, in English, "capital" begins with the letter c, but we like to denote consumption with the letter c.

What is capital in intuitive terms? Well, intuitively, of course, capital is something like the machine tools that are in a factory, or the factory itself, but it actually encompasses a wider set of possibilities for capital. We think of capital as something that can be used in production and something that requires some sort of sacrifice to create. So, of course, it takes sacrifice to create a factory. We would call that investment; it's the same thing as sacrifice. It requires sacrifice to create a machine tool. It requires sacrifice to create a building in which the factory is operating; it requires sacrifice and investment to create the trucks that bring supplies to the factory to turn them into final products and, of course, to take them to customers after they're made.

There are other kinds of capital. Knowledge is a kind of capital. It requires a sacrifice to acquire it. And once you have it, you can use it to create things. This is called human capital. It's something that you're actually creating right now.

We can also think of farm animals as capital. It requires sacrifice and investment to create a new farm animal because if it's, let's say, cows, you have to feed the cows so that they can produce calves. And also, they're productive, right? Once you create that investment, then if you create a calf that grows up and becomes a milk cow, you can milk the cow. And that's the kind of production as a result of your investment.

It is helpful to think of a little story to compress this way of thinking into something familiar. You may have heard of Robinson Crusoe. Robinson Crusoe is the title of a book that was written in the early 18th century (1719) concerning a man who was on a ship that was on a commercial voyage in the Caribbean; the ship was shipwrecked, but Crusoe survived the wreck and ended up living on an island all by himself for years. He had to figure out how to survive and the way he survived ultimately was that he discovered that the island had a herd of goats, and he captured some of them and created a pen and kept them in the pen, and he bred them and used them for milk and meat.

Let's just think about the milk part. He bred the goats, and he would then take the female goats and milk them. Now, this fits exactly with the way we've been describing capital. If he wants to create a new goat, then the mother goat has to be able to nurse the kid. Robinson Crusoe would have to refrain from milking that goat and drinking — consuming — the milk. He would therefore have to sacrifice some of his consumption of milk in order to foster the growth of a kid into a mature goat.

Thinking of Robinson Crusoe drinking milk as his consumption c_t, then his herd of goats, which we can think of as k_t, produces milk according to a function. And we know that the more goats you have, the more milk you have. We can think of that function as being an increasing function of k. And also, we can also note that it's possible to increase the size of the herd. But as you increase the size of the herd, it gets harder and harder to make use of the productivity of the herd. If you have too many goats in a pasture, they'll over-graze the pasture. And by adding one goat to your herd, you don't get the incremental benefit that you would get if you had a much smaller herd and you increased the size of the herd. Therefore, this function $f(\cdot)$ has a shape and that shape is a shape you've seen: it's increasing in k, but it's increasing at a diminishing rate — that's the expression of the overgrazing idea. So, it's got this concave shape and one descriptive term or phrase to describe that shape is that it has diminishing marginal returns.

Now, we have the basic description of what's going on on the right-hand side. $f(k)$ is the milk production from the goats, and some of that milk production goes into producing new goats, kids, and the mother goats nursing those kids. But some of it goes to Robinson Crusoe, so whatever goes to Robinson Crusoe is subtracted from the possibilities of creating new goats. And so the increase in the number of goats is then characterised by the left-hand side. $\dot{k}$ on the left-hand side is the time derivative of k, and it is the increase in the number of goats per unit of time. We can think of this as the increase in the number of goats per year.

Note that Robinson Crusoe is making a decision: he is choosing consumption. And so this equation describing the change in the number of goats over time depends on Robinson Crusoe: his choice of c at each time. Let's just note in passing that it's intuitively possible for c to equal $f(k)$. That is, Robinson Crusoe consumes the entire output of milk of the herd. And so $\dot{k}$ would become zero. That is, the herd would not change in size at all if that were the case.

However, if c is less than $f(k)$, that is, if Robinson Crusoe refrains from consuming all of the output of milk from his herd, then the some of the mother goats can foster their kids, and the number of goats will grow. Then $\dot{k}$ is positive — the herd is growing in size.

The next question is obvious: What is the optimal c? That's not so simple because c has to be chosen not only at the beginning, but at all points into the future. We need to note here that there's no risk in this model. So Robinson Crusoe, we're assuming, can actually see into the future and know everything that's coming just as our consumer who is consuming our consumption of wine and cheese at time 1 and at time 2, and just as Joseph with his understanding of Pharaoh's dream.

This assumption has a name: perfect foresight. It's still pretty complicated. But that assumption of perfect foresight allows us to make progress on our ultimate goal of adding uncertainty about the future into the model.

Back to the point we were addressing, you don't just choose c now. You have to choose c now and for every point in the future. Instead of just period 1 and period 2, now we've got every single t in the future over the continuum of time into the future, possibly quite complicated.

The first step in figuring that out is to integrate the original constraint in equation (3.1):

$$k_t = k_0 + \int_0^t (f(k_s) - c_s)ds \tag{3.2}$$

On the left-hand side, we've got capital at time t, and that can be capital at any time in the future.

Starting at time zero, there's some initial stock of capital, k_0, and we can think of that as the herd of wild goats that Robinson Crusoe discovered when he was exploring the island. And then subsequent to that initial discovery of the herd of goats, he solved this problem: you subtract what the consumption is for every time up until time t and you add up all of those differences via integration. So the constraint is that the capital that you end up with at time t has to be obtained by this right-hand side, which expresses the sacrifice of consumption designed to build up the herd. And an important detail is that this constraint holds at every time t, so there is a *continuum of constraints*.

The Lagrangian. We can now write the optimisation problem as a Lagrangian

$$\max_{c} \int_0^{\infty} e^{-\rho t} u(c_t) dt + \int_0^{\infty} \lambda_t \left(k_t - k_0 - \int_0^t (f(k_s) - c_s) ds \right) dt$$

Looking inside these brackets, we take equation (3.2) and subtract the right-hand side; you then get the term inside the brackets. Intuitively, it's the same idea as $y - c$, the constraint that we had in the first simple Lagrangian that we talked about. Each k_t appears in a continuum of constraints.

And what's the other big part of this object? We already have seen that it is the ultimate objective for Robinson Crusoe to maximise his utility, but discounted over his entire future, which, as we talked about, goes into infinity. The expression is inside the round brackets, the analogue of that constraint $(y - c)$, but extended to this more interesting situation.

And there's λ, our Lagrange multiplier, except λ now has a time subscript on it. Note again that there is a continuum of constraints, one for each time t; we add them up by integrating, with a Lagrange multiplier for each constraint (just as in the two-period model).

So, there isn't just one λ; there's one λ for each t. So, this constraint defining $\dot{k}$ is a constraint that has to be true for every t. And so there has to be a λ that goes with it. The Lagrangian, which in our previous discussion had only one constraint, now has more than one constraint. So what do we do? We just add up the constraints and we have a λ for each constraint. That's what we did in the two-period model. This results in the double integral; also, note that the constraints are not discounted; this comes up in the bookkeeping we have to undertake when we are solving the model.

Intuitively, from our previous work, we know that to solve this model, we are going to take the derivative with respect to c for each time t because each time t gives us a separate good associated with that time, a separate consumption, goods associated with that time just as in the two good model.

But when we take that derivative, we're going to also be taking the derivative with respect to the constraint, the appropriate constraint. And that's going to engage the λ. So, we're going to end up with some sort of first-order condition that says $u'(c_t) = \lambda$ times something else.

So, all of the ideas that we've generated are going to extend to this situation.

Some bookkeeping

We need to do a little bit of work to make that logical flow that we just talked about where you take the derivative with respect to each consumption c_t and so equal to a price times the Lagrange multiplier. As a first step, wc want to restructure the notation.

As our first bookkeeping manoeuvre, we we're going to take the λ that we originally had and multiply it by $e^{\rho t}$; it' is related to the $e^{\rho t}$ that we had in the integral of discounted utility, except there's no minus sign:

$$\tilde{\lambda}_t \equiv e^{\rho t}\lambda_t$$

If we multiply our original λ up by $e^{\rho t}$ and then to call that product $\tilde{\lambda}$, we can rewrite the Lagrangian in the following way:

$$\max_{c} \int_0^\infty \boxed{e^{-\rho t}} u(c_t)dt + \int_0^\infty \boxed{e^{-\rho t}} \tilde{\lambda}_t \left(k_t - k_0 - \int_0^t (f(k_s) - c_s)ds \right) dt \quad (3.3)$$

with the boxed terms highlighting the effect of the redefinition of λ_t. However, instead of λ, we have $\tilde{\lambda}$ and if we multiply $\tilde{\lambda}$ by $e^{-\rho t}$, then we get our original λ.

With this bookkeeping manoeuvre, we end up with $e^{-\rho t}$ multiplying all of the λs, except it's now called $\tilde{\lambda}$. Now, is that going to make a difference? Well, remember from the two-good case that λ appears in the first-order condition $u'(c) = \lambda p$. But then when we divide the marginal utilities for c_1 and c_2, the λ cancels out. And so actually, this isn't going to harm our our analysis because that $\tilde{\lambda}$ ultimately is going to cancel out as well in some way. That's step one in this somewhat complicated argument that we're going to go through now.

We still have to handle the continuum of constraints. Our notational bookkeeping strategy leaves the double integral in place — we're adding up all of these constraints, each with its own $\tilde{\lambda}_t$. We still have the problem that c_t is not the same as c_s so we can't just take the derivative with respect to c_t. Why is it s? This is because we're integrating from zero at a time to adding up all of the assets of $k_s - c_s$ all the way from the initial period up to time t. And so the case that we are all handling here because we're integrating over, does that mean c_s isn't the same as c_t? The c_t is this c at the particular time t, but the c_s are the times, all of the times between zero and two. And so it's not the same thing. So, we cannot just take the derivative. We have to do more work.

Exercises

Exercise 3.1. Let the production function be $f(k) = k^{\alpha}$.

(i) State and plot $f(k)$ and also $f'(k)$

Exercise 3.2. Let the utility function be $u(c) = 1 - e^{-\gamma c}$.

(i) State and plot $u(c)$, $u'(c)$, and also $u'^{-1}(\xi)$
(ii) Calculate the growth rate of marginal utility $\dot{\ln}(u'(c_t))$ and also the growth rate of consumption $\dot{\ln}(c_t)$

- (It might be more useful to calculate $u'(\dot{c_t})$ and also the growth rate of consumption $\dot{c}_t$, that is, the growth "speed" rather than the growth *rate*)

Chapter 4

Optimal Control

In this chapter, we carry out the additional tasks needed to determine the optimal control for the growth problem we set out in the previous chapter. We then flesh out the model of economic growth, demonstrating the effect of growth on interest rates. Finally, we apply the ideas to the problem of optimal grain storage and consumption over the annual cycle that we touched on in the introduction.

Optimal Control Derivation

We want to solve the problem of optimising the integral of discounted utility going off into the future,

$$\max_{c} \int_0^{\infty} e^{-\rho t} u(c_t) dt$$

subject to a constraint, the constraint being that capital, k_t, grows at a certain rate,

$$\dot{k}_t = f(k_t) - c_t$$

which is the result of output from production using existing capital minus the consumption that takes place along the way. The consumption enters utility, and we discount this utility using the subjective discount rate ρ. There is a starting value of capital, k_0. There is a standard way to approach this problem but we're going to go at it in a different way, in order to emphasise the Lagrange multiplier side of optimal control.

If we integrate the constraint equation for capital over time, we convert it to an expression in k_t at each instant of time, including the accumulation that has taken place before that instant. The integrated equation is still a constraint, but there's a constraint for each period t like this, and so we have a continuum of constraints. We have to handle the Lagrange multipliers for those constraints so it's a bit complicated, and the first part of this chapter is devoted to developing the tools to deal with that.

In a two-period model, where there is consumption at time 1 and consumption at time 2, we saw that you could divide the constraint into two constraints, with two Lagrange multipliers attached to them. Those multipliers ended up having a relationship with each other indexed by the interest rate. The same thing is going to happen here: we have a continuum of constraints, instead of just two constraints, with a Lagrange multiplier indexed by time for each of those constraints. At the end of the day, we're going to see that these Lagrange multipliers also behave in a way over time that is characterised by the interest rate.

Transforming the Lagrangian Using Integration by Parts

Our starting point is where we got stuck in the last chapter: we have a continuum of constraints, with a multiplier for each constraint, but when we write down the Lagrangian,

$$\max_c \int_0^\infty e^{-\rho t} u(c_t)dt + \int_0^\infty e^{-\rho t}\tilde{\lambda}_t \left(k_t - k_0 - \int_0^t (f(k_s) - c_s)ds\right)dt \tag{4.1}$$

the timing doesn't work. Although we have redefined the multiplier so that the constraints are discounted the same way as utility, if we attempt to find the optimum by taking the derivative with respect to c_t, this does not correctly capture the c_s terms. The way forward is to undertake a bookkeeping manoeuvre, integration by parts, so as to align the c_t and c_s terms.[1] Integration by parts is reviewed in Appendix A.

[1] A similar development can be found in Kamien and Schwartz (2012, pp. 114–115).

The integration by parts formula has this fundamental form:

$$\int_a^b F(x)G'(x)dx = F(x)G(x)\Big|_a^b - \int_a^b G(x)F'(x)dx$$

The first step in our bookkeeping process is to identify elements of the constraint term in our original Lagrangian with the functions F and G in the formula. Write the double integral part of the constraint as follows:

$$\int_0^\infty e^{-\rho t}\tilde{\lambda}_t \int_0^t (f(k_s) - c_s)ds\, dt$$

- Identify F with the integral:

$$F \sim \int_0^t (f(k_s) - c_s)ds \qquad \rightarrow \qquad F' \sim (f(k_t) - c_t)$$

- Identify G' with the other part:

$$G' \sim e^{-\rho t}\tilde{\lambda}_t \qquad \rightarrow \qquad G = \boxed{\int_t^\infty e^{-\rho s}\tilde{\lambda}_s ds \equiv \mu_t}$$

Starting from the double integral, identifying the functions F and G with the pieces of that integral and passing through that process, we end up with a new object which we called μ_t, which is the summation of weighted Lagrange multipliers through the future. There is a single μ for each t and μ_t doesn't have an integral on it; that's what we wanted. Note that the order of integration changed in the last step when we define μ; that is because the integration over the constraints moves forward through time.

We can then go back to our Lagrangian and plug in all these manipulations and we get this object, the modified Lagrangian:

$$\max_c \int_0^\infty e^{-\rho t}u(c_t)dt + \int_0^\infty e^{-\rho t}\tilde{\lambda}_t(k_t - k_0) - \int_0^\infty \mu_t(f(k_t) - c_t)dt$$

The key observation is that now everything inside the integral has the same timing, and the double integral is gone, so we can just take the derivative with respect to c_t!

There's still a $\tilde{\lambda}$ there, so we have a little bit more work to do, but the key thing is that we have an integral over time in the utility objective part and an integral over time in the constraint part, and so, if we took the derivative with respect to c_t, in this Lagrangian, we will be taking the derivative at each time t, at the same time. In the original Lagrangian, we saw that that was not possible. What we've done is essentially some bookkeeping to make that derivative possible.

We can take the time derivative of μ and we get something that is related to what we already saw; it's the negative of λ, the original Lagrange multiplier, and if we take the derivative of $\tilde{\lambda}$ that we have defined, we get this expression:

$$\frac{d}{dt}\mu = -e^{-\rho t}\tilde{\lambda}$$

We then can re-write the Lagrangian purely in terms of μ, noting that we lost the discounting in the $\dot{\mu}$ term, yielding this structure:

$$\boxed{\max_c \int_0^\infty e^{-\rho t}u(c_t)dt - \int_0^\infty \dot{\mu}_t(k_t - k_0)dt - \int_0^\infty \mu_t(f(k_t) - c_t)dt}$$

Now, take the derivative with respect to c_t at each time t, keeping in mind that k_t might be influenced by c_t:

$$e^{-\rho t}u'(c_t) - \dot{\mu}_t\frac{\partial k_t}{\partial c} - \mu_t\left(f'(k_t)\frac{\partial k_t}{\partial c} - 1\right) = 0$$

We then group terms and what we end up with is something that needs to be zero so we can achieve the optimum:

$$\left(e^{-\rho t}u'(c_t) + \mu_t\right) + \left(-\dot{\mu}_t - \mu_t f'(k_t)\right)\frac{\partial k_t}{\partial c} = 0 \tag{4.2}$$

It has two pieces, so we can see that if each piece is zero, then we will be at the optimum. We can write these two requirements separately, as a pair of equations:

$$\begin{aligned} u'(c_t) + e^{\rho t}\mu_t &= 0 \\ -\dot{\mu}_t - \mu_t f'(k_t) &= 0 \end{aligned} \tag{4.3}$$

Thus, we satisfy the first-order condition if we satisfy these equations.

We have one final bookkeeping step. Let's define yet another object that is related to the λ and the μ, namely the Greek letter ξ: this is the discounted version of μ:

$$\boxed{\xi_t \equiv -e^{\rho t}\mu_t} \quad \rightarrow \quad \mu_t = -e^{-\rho t}\xi_t,$$
$$\dot{\mu}_t = \rho e^{-\rho t}\xi_t - e^{-\rho t}\dot{\xi}_t$$

We can take the time derivative of ξ and we can then substitute for the $\dot{\mu}$ term. The pair of equations (4.3) becomes the pair:

$$\dot{\xi}_t = (\rho - f'(k_t))\xi_t$$
$$u'(c_t) = \xi_t$$

In the second equation, the marginal value of consumption is the (adjusted) multiplier.

To reiterate, we've gone from λ to $\tilde{\lambda}$ to μ to ξ,

λ_t	$\tilde{\lambda}_t$	μ_t	ξ_t
	$e^{\rho t}\lambda_t$	$\int_t^\infty e^{-\rho s}\tilde{\lambda}_s ds$	$-e^{\rho t}\mu_t$

but, at the end, we want to stick with ξ.

The 18th and 19th century mathematics literature took these ideas and they said let's express this problem as a sort of formalised static optimisation problem with no integrals in it, so we define this thing called H, which is for Hamiltonian; Hamilton was a 19th-century Irish mathematician and physicist:

$$H \equiv u(c_t) + \xi_t(f(k_t) - c_t)$$

If we take the derivative of the Hamiltonian with respect to c_t, it ends up being the same as taking the derivative with our somewhat messier expression earlier on, and this equation has a name: the optimality condition. Following the intuition we developed in the one-good and two-good model cases, we can also take the derivative of ξ with respect to time; this equation has a name as well: it is called the costate equation.

Finally, we had an original equation that expressed how capital moves over time, that is, the $\dot{k}$ equation, so if we take the derivative of the Hamiltonian with respect to ξ, we get $\dot{k}_t = f(k_t) - c_t$ — that was our original constraint and that also has a name: the law of motion. It is entirely in the spirit of taking the derivative of the Lagrangian with respect to the Lagrange multiplier for the one-good model or the two good model that we described in Chapter 2 and when you do that, you just get the original constraint back.

$0 = \frac{\partial}{\partial c} H$	$u'(c_t) = \xi_t$	optimality condition
$\dot{k} = \frac{\partial}{\partial \xi} H$	$\dot{k}_t = f(k_t) - c_t$	state equation
$\dot{\xi} = \rho\xi - \frac{\partial}{\partial k} H$	$\dot{\xi}_t = \rho\xi_t - \xi_t f'(k_t)$	costate equation

We have therefore reduced the model to these three equations: the optimality condition, the state equation, and the costate equation. We can now use these three equations to analyse the growth model.

You might expect that the analysis can consist of solving the differential equations, just as we did in our highway travel and rabbit population growth examples, through some sort of integration step. But these equations are highly complex and don't lend themselves to explicit solutions except in very special situations. We are left with indirect approaches to the solution: phase diagrams. This approach, although not providing explicit solutions, will generate a significant amount of economic intuition.

Phase diagrams

As is the case with many dynamic models, it's not always possible to fully solve the model in algebraic form or so-called closed form, so we have to go to indirect ways of characterising the solution, and in this particular model, we do it with a diagram which is called a phase diagram. The diagram has two axes: k and ξ. Both k and ξ are moving simultaneously as determined by the differential equation for each; they interact with each other, and the phase diagram expresses these interactions.

At the point where the costate variable ξ_t satisfies $\dot{\xi} = 0$, we can divide out ξ from the costate equation, leaving the equation

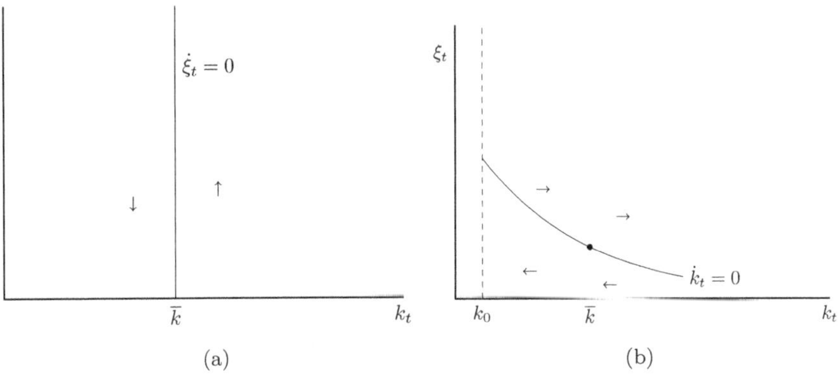

Figure 4.1. Phase diagram fundamentals. (a) Direction of movement for ξ_t. (b) Direction of movement for k_t.

$f'(k) = \rho$. We denote the value of k for which this equation is true as $\overline{k}$, and this is depicted in Figure 4.1(a).

We can similarly characterise the equation that holds when $\dot{k} = 0$; in that case, $f(k) = c$. We know the solution for c from the optimality condition: $u'^{-1}(\xi)$. Substituting the solution for c yields the equation relating k and ξ, $f(k) = u'^{-1}(\xi)$. Because u and u' have shapes driven by the characteristics of utility functions, we can work out the relationship between k and ξ when $\dot{k} = 0$: you get a line that looks like the curved line in Figure 4.1(b).

Now, we can start filling in with arrows, based on the behaviour of the equations we've been talking about around these lines or manifolds that we've set out in the phase diagram. So in particular, to the right of the $\dot{\xi}$ manifold, if k is above $\overline{k}$, ξ will increase over time, and ξ will decrease over time to the left of that manifold. Then, for a small value of k, $f'(k)$ becomes large and that swamps ρ, it becomes bigger than ρ, and so this whole expression becomes negative and $\dot{\xi}$ becomes negative. This gives us the direction of the arrows in Figure 4.1(a).

We can do the same thing for the $\dot{k}$ equation. To the right of this curved manifold where $\dot{k} = 0$, k will tend to increase, and to its left k will decrease, as shown in Figure 4.1(b).

Now that we have filled in these arrows, we see that there are four quadrants of the diagram and in each quadrant the combined direction of k and ξ is different in each case. In the lower right quadrant, the direction of movement is to the northwest; in the lower

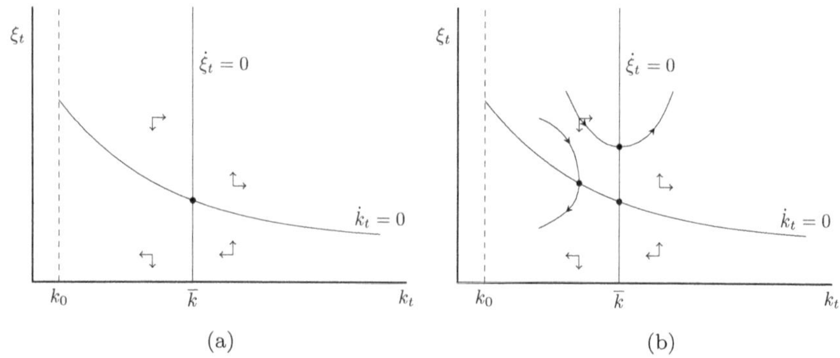

Figure 4.2. Phase diagram combined flow and paths. (a) Combined flow directions. (b) Flow paths.

left quadrant, the direction of movement is to the southwest; in the upper left quadrant, the direction of movement is to the southeast, and the movement in the upper right quadrant is to the northeast; this is illustrated in Figure 4.2(a).

It is now evident that there are going to be paths along which k and ξ will evolve over time, as they obey the equations that we have derived; Figure 4.2(b) shows examples. A key feature of the two example paths in the figure is that they cross the manifolds we discussed above: the upper example crosses the $\dot{\xi}_t = 0$ manifold and is exactly horizontal at that point; the lower left example path crosses the $\dot{k}_t = 0$ manifold and is exactly vertical at the point where it crosses. If you choose the right path, however, the path will cross both manifolds where the manifolds themselves cross. It is clear from the figures that there is exactly one such path. The point where the $\dot{\xi}_t = 0$ and $\dot{k}_t = 0$ intersect is the long run steady state where you reach $\overline{k}$; k doesn't change and neither does ξ; this is shown in Figure 4.3.

It is possible to end up at on a different path, such as those illustrated in Figure 4.2(b), and if you end up at a different path, you will diverge — you will never reach the steady state. To achieve the convergent path, your starting point has to include both the initial k, which is predetermined as k_0, and also some correct initial value of ξ_0; if you don't choose it correctly, then you end up deviating from the path that ends up at $\overline{k}$. There is only one ξ_0 that gets on the long run path to $\overline{k}$.

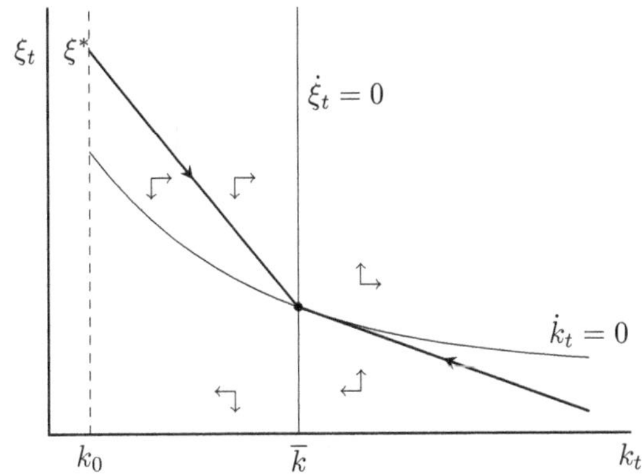

Figure 4.3. Paths and unique path from initial k.

Why Is the Convergent Growth Path Optimal?

Why is the path that converges to the steady state optimal? As we have seen, many paths that satisfy the Hamiltonian equations are possible. The proof that the convergent path is optimal is mathematically intense, so we eschew it here. However, we can get a great deal of intuition simply by examining the alternative paths in the phase diagram.

There are two types of non-convergent paths. In the first case, capital grows beyond the steady state, without bound. This happens if you set the initial value of ξ too high, that is, above ξ^*. In the second case, capital eventually shrinks to zero. This happens if you set the initial value of ξ too low, that is, below ξ^*.

In the first case, where capital grows without bound, we see that the costate variable ξ_t also increases without bound. We know from the optimality condition that $u'(c_t) = \xi_t$ at all times, and because ξ_t is growing, consumption c_t is therefore shrinking. Thus, along these paths, there is over-saving: Robinson Crusoe is starving himself even as his goats overrun the island.

It is intuitive that this case is suboptimal because Robinson Crusoe can simply take the milk from just a few of his excess goats, increasing his consumption and therefore his utility, before again moving along an excess saving curve, and this will increase his discounted utility unambiguously. We can represent this as a one-time downward vertical move from his current path to a new similar path.

This means that the original path he was on wasn't optimal since we can improve on it with this thought experiment. But, of course, this reasoning works no matter how far above the convergent path we are.

In the second case, where capital shrinks towards zero, we can reason symmetrically. We see that the costate variable ξ_t also decreases towards zero, along with capital. We know from the optimality condition that $u'(c_t) = \xi_t$ at all times, and because ξ_t is shrinking, consumption c_t is therefore increasing. Thus, along these paths, there is under-saving: Robinson Crusoe is eating his goats. Eventually, the goats will hit zero; to be concrete, let's label this date as T. Once Robinson Crusoe hits T, consumption becomes zero, and therefore utility becomes zero. The marginal utility of consumption becomes as high as possible (possibly infinite); recalling the two-period model, we want the ratios of the marginal utilities of current and future consumption to be related to the interest rate, but this condition will obviously fail here. However, Robinson Crusoe can move the ratio in the right direction by refraining from consuming a little bit just before T; by saving a goat, he can get a little bit of positive consumption goat's milk after T and therefore reduce the marginal utility of consumption at T. That is, by making a small sacrifice in consumption before T, he gets a huge payoff at T.

This thought experiment is equivalent to jumping from the original path in the phase diagram to a higher path and then following the higher path. Because this clearly results in improved discounted utility, we can see that the original path was also suboptimal.

Thus, in both cases, a jump towards the convergent path improves utility, so this path must be optimal.

Firms

In the previous discussion, we saw that we can think of this as a sort of a Robinson Crusoe problem. Robinson Crusoe ends up on this island alone, nobody else there, except for some goats. He discovers the wild goats, he pens them up, starts breeding them, drinks the milk that they produce, and is able to survive using that strategy. Our abstract model expresses the fact that he has to make decisions about how much to consume versus how much to allow the goats to breed, viewing the goats as his capital.

We can expand on this idea to a more realistic setting: what if this economy is representative of many islands — an archipelago — each with its own Robinson Crusoe, who is, in effect, the owner of his island. With many goat farms interacting with each other via inter-island travel, but identical in every other way, they would comprise a kind of market economy in which they could potentially buy and sell milk and also goats from each other, borrow and save with each other, and so on.

We could think of each goat farm as a kind of firm. Due to the easy movement between islands, that firm would have shareholders and it's quite possible that, even though each individual Robinson Crusoe would have his own goat farm, he might sell shares in that farm to the other farmers, and vice versa. Out of an obligation to the shareholders, as the manager of the goat farm, Robinson Crusoe would maximise the profits of the goat farm.

How do you maximise profit? First, you have to express profit: it is the output of the firm less the expenses of the firm. The expenses in this economy are straightforward: the cost of the goats.

In this economy, the owners of the goats and the owners of the firms aren't necessarily the same people. The owners of the goats are going to charge a goat-rental fee to the manager of the goat farm. What fee should the goat owners charge? What is the price of a goat? It is the price that you pay if you borrowed money in order to acquire the goats and then you would pay back the loan to acquire the goats, with the interest on the loan; you'd roll over the loan every year, so you would end up paying only the interest on the loan. Therefore, that is a cost if you're running this firm: the cost of renting the goats is the interest rate times the number of goats you rent.

The firm maximises profit by creating and selling output using capital optimally with this in mind. Therefore, your profit is the total milk production less this cost[2]:

$$\pi_t = \max_{k_t}(f(k_t) - r_t k_t)$$

[2]Of course, in the real world, there will be other costs, labour being the most obvious. We could want to include this in a more realistic model. However, the fundamental characteristics and behaviour of the model would not change. For the cognoscenti, this is because labour is fundamentally intratemporal in nature.

where r_t is the interest rate the firm pays for borrowing capital for production.

This is a situation where you can optimise by taking the derivative and setting it to zero, and when you do that, you get the following equation:

$$f'(k_t) = r_t$$

The derivative of the production function with respect to k is equal to the interest rate r, and this is the same as saying the marginal product of capital is equal to the interest rate.

The profit is, therefore, equal to the output from the goats that you rent minus this cost. So, in equilibrium, that is, when $f'(k_t) = r_t$, profit is

$$\pi_t = f(k_t) - f'(k_t)k_t$$

The individuals in the economy, the Robinson Crusoes who are the managers, can also own shares in other goat farms as shareholders, and they're also goat owners. These are two separate things: as shareholders, they receive dividend payments. What are dividend payments? They are the profits that we just analysed and derived. But as the owners of the goats, they receive interest payments because they own the goats and they rent them out, and so they have two sources of income: profits and interest.

So, because individuals in the economy own the capital and get paid interest for lending it out, and they own the firms so they get the profits, then when we add these two sources of income together in equilibrium, because the interest rate has to equal the marginal product of capital, we get the total income as the output:

$$\pi_t + r_t k_t = \big(f(k_t) - f'(k_t)k_t\big) + f'(k_t)k_t = f(k_t)$$

That would be what you would get if we had the single Robinson Crusoe on his original island, as we already saw. So, the competitive economy with lots of atomistic Robinson Crusoes, each with his own farm, goats that he rents out, and shares in firms, is entirely equivalent to the stand-alone one-man Robinson Crusoe island economy.

What is the value of a firm in this economy? It is the discounted profits, the discount of dividends, so when we do corporate finance, this is exactly the formula that we would use: we're adding up future profits, anticipating future profits, and discounting them by the interest rate:

$$p_t = \int_t^{\infty} e^{-r_s(s-t)} \pi_s ds \tag{4.4}$$

This is the share price of the firm — if there is only one share. Of course, you can divide up the equity into many smaller shares, as is the practice in the real world.

Firms in the steady state

We have to be a little bit careful because the marginal product of capital is changing as this economy grows, and therefore the interest rate itself, which is that marginal product of capital, will also change, so it needs a time subscript. The equity value of the firm in (4.4) is therefore not trivial to calculate. But at the steady state, the marginal product of capital will be a constant because capital is constant. Substitute that constant in the valuation formula and profits will also be a constant and so you can actually figure out the value of the firm in the steady state.

At the steady state $\bar{k}$, $\dot{\xi}_t = 0$ and therefore from the costate equation, $f'(\bar{k}) = \rho$. Since we have demonstrated that $f'(k_t) = r_t$ at all times due to firm profit maximisation, we have indirectly shown that $r = \rho$, the subjective rate of time discount, at the steady state. It is then straightforward to solve the integral of firm value: it is simply the classic present value formula:

$$\frac{f(\bar{k}) - \rho\bar{k}}{\rho}$$

Example 4.1. We already established that in the basic deterministic growth model, the steady state value of the representative agent's firm is the present value of the profit, which is found simply by dividing the profit by the steady-state interest rate, which is the subjective rate of time preference, ρ. We would like the closed form solution for profit in the geometric utility $\frac{c^{1-\gamma}}{1-\gamma}$ and production function k^{α} example.

At the steady state, the marginal product of capital is equal to the steady state interest rate, ρ, enabling us to determine the steady-state capital:

$$f'(\overline{k}) = \rho \quad \rightarrow \quad \alpha\overline{k}^{\alpha-1} = \rho \quad \rightarrow \quad \overline{k} = \left(\frac{\alpha}{\rho}\right)^{\frac{1}{1-\alpha}}$$

We can then calculate profit:

$$\begin{aligned}
\pi(\overline{k}) &= f(\overline{k}) - \rho\overline{k} = f(\overline{k}) - f'(\overline{k})\overline{k} \\
&= \left(\frac{\alpha}{\rho}\right)^{\frac{\alpha}{1-\alpha}} - \alpha\left(\frac{\alpha}{\rho}\right)^{\frac{\alpha-1}{1-\alpha}}\left(\frac{\alpha}{\rho}\right)^{\frac{1}{1-\alpha}} \\
&= (1-\alpha)\left(\frac{\alpha}{\rho}\right)^{\frac{\alpha}{1-\alpha}}
\end{aligned}$$

The value of the firm is then the present value:

$$\frac{1-\alpha}{\rho}\left(\frac{\alpha}{\rho}\right)^{\frac{\alpha}{1-\alpha}}$$

It will be helpful for comparison later on to write this as

$$\frac{1-\alpha}{\alpha}\left(\frac{\alpha}{\rho}\right)^{\frac{1}{1-\alpha}}$$

Consumption and the costate in the steady state: Example

In the steady state, investment is zero and all output is consumed: $c_t = f(\overline{k})$. Therefore, $\overline{c} = \left(\frac{\alpha}{\rho}\right)^{\frac{\alpha}{1-\alpha}}$.

We also have the $u'(c_t) = \xi_t$ at all times, so for geometric utility, $u'(c_t) = c_t^{-\gamma}$, so $c_t = \xi_t^{-\frac{1}{\gamma}}$. This means we can solve for the steady state value of the costate ξ_t using the fact that consumption equals output in the steady state:

$$\xi_t = \left(\frac{\alpha}{\rho}\right)^{-\frac{\alpha\gamma}{1-\alpha}}$$

This fits entirely with the intuition we developed earlier for Lagrange multipliers. Expressing the right-hand side in terms of output,

$$\left(\frac{\alpha}{\rho}\right)^{-\frac{\alpha\gamma}{1-\alpha}} = \left(\overline{k}^{\alpha}\right)^{-\gamma}$$

we exactly duplicate the formula for the Lagrange multiplier in equation (2.1).

Deterministic Optimal Control Model of Grain Storage

In the story of Joseph, grain is stored in the fat years for later consumption. Something similar happens over the course of the season wherever grain is grown. When the grain is stored, the farmers who store it are starkly aware of a trade-off: they could consume the grain soon after harvest or they can hold it in reserve for consumption in the winter; additionally, they have to hold some of the grain back for spring planting.

In this section, we discuss a technical model of grain storage over the seasonal cycle, Taub (1987) which was intended to further elucidate the McCloskey and Nash model of medieval interest rates. In this model, we see how boundary conditions express some of the economic dimensions of the setting and how they affect the behaviour of the solution.

The model begins by noting that there are two key times in the season: planting and harvest. Time passes continually between planting and harvest, and between harvest and planting. Between the harvest time and the planting time, grain is consumed; at the planting time, there is a discrete fall in the quantity of grain in the storage silos as the grain needed for sowing is withdrawn all at once. The quantity does not fall to zero, however, because the farmers need to eat grain while the crop grows prior to the harvest. Because there is no risk in this model, all of the remaining grain is used up by the harvest and the quantity in storage falls to zero. The harvest then replenishes the stock of grain stored in the silo and the process begins again.

Objective and constraints

The farmers maximise discounted utility of consumption as in the growth model but only up to the next time threshold in the season. In this agrarian economy, they consume only grain (not goat's milk!), and the grain is consumed out of their storage bins. We can therefore define the state of this economy as the total grain remaining in the storage bin at any one time over the course of the year-long seasonal cycle. We denote this as s_t, storage at time t.

The constraint for this problem — that is, the law of motion for the state — is straightforward: over the season, the stored grain gets depleted as it is consumed and as it depreciates from losses due to rodents, mold, and so on,

$$\dot{s}_t = -(c_t + \delta s_t)$$

using the standard notation for depreciation, δ.

During the winter, between harvest and planting, farmers solve

$$V(s_{T_H}) = \max_{c_t, s_t} \int_0^{T_P} e^{-\rho t} u(c_t) dt + e^{-\rho T_P} V(s_{T_P}) \tag{4.5}$$

where S_{T_P} is the stored grain at planting time T_P, ready to be planted. The notation $V(S_{T_P})$ denotes the value at the time of planting, as anticipated by the farmer, and similarly $V(S_{T_H})$ denotes the value at the harvest time T_H.

Between T_H and T_P, the farmers consume grain out of storage for sustenance, all the way up to planting at time T_P. At planting time, the quantity of grain is reduced by a discrete amount, the amount planted that leaves just enough to sustain the farmer through the summer growing season. At planting, determining consumption during the summer between planting and harvest, farmers solve

$$V(s_{T_P}) = \max_{c_t, s_t} \int_0^{T_H} e^{-\rho t} u(c_t) dt + e^{-\rho T_H} V(s_{T_H}) \tag{4.6}$$

Over the summer, during the growth of the crop, the farmer continues to consume until the harvest at T_H, consuming all the remaining grain so that at the moment of harvest, $s_{T_H} = 0$. The harvest brings in a discrete amount of grain, and the process starts again.

It is evident that the summer problem is the same as the winter problem; they are distinguished only by the terminal value function $V(\cdot)$ and the initial state s_t, in each case. The value $V(s_{T_P})$ enters at the end of the period for the problem defining the harvest value $V(s_{T_H})$ in (4.5), and, conversely, the value $V(s_{T_H})$ enters at the end of the period for the problem defining the harvest value $V(s_{T_P})$ in (4.6).

Hamiltonian and basic equations

We can recall the arguments we went through in the development of deterministic optimal control to write down the elements of the model. The Hamiltonian expresses the utility of the farmer as he consumes over the season and also expresses the constraint — the state equation:

$$H(s,q) = u(c) + q(-c - \delta s)$$

The Lagrange multiplier is q_t rather than ξ_t.

There are three optimal control equations: the optimality, state, and costate equations.

Optimality:	$q_t = u'(c_t)$
State:	$\dot{s}_t = -(c_t + \delta s_t)$
Costate:	$\dot{q} = (\rho + \delta)q_t$

There is an additional condition in the paper:

$$q_{T_P} = V'(s_{T_P})$$

This is a terminal condition that states that the multiplier is the marginal (expressed as a derivative) value of the stored grain at planting — similar to our earlier interpretations of the Lagrange multiplier.

Phase diagram

We can use the same strategy we used in the growth model to construct the phase diagram for the grain storage problem. Figure 4.4(a) displays the phase diagram, with the state variable s_t (analogous to k_t in the growth model) on the horizontal axis and the costate q_t (analogous to ξ_t in the growth model) on the vertical axis.

The first step is to draw the manifolds where $\dot{s}_t$ and $\dot{q}_t$ are zero. Examining the Hamiltonian equations, we see that $\dot{s}_t$ will in fact always be negative: you are always consuming, reducing s_t, and the depreciation and storage cost effects work in the same direction: they always reduce the amount of grain in storage. Therefore, there is no manifold where $\dot{s}_t$ is zero; all of the arrows in the phase diagram must point to the left. Examining the costate equation, we have the same thing: the only way to get $\dot{q}_t$ to equal zero is to set the costate to

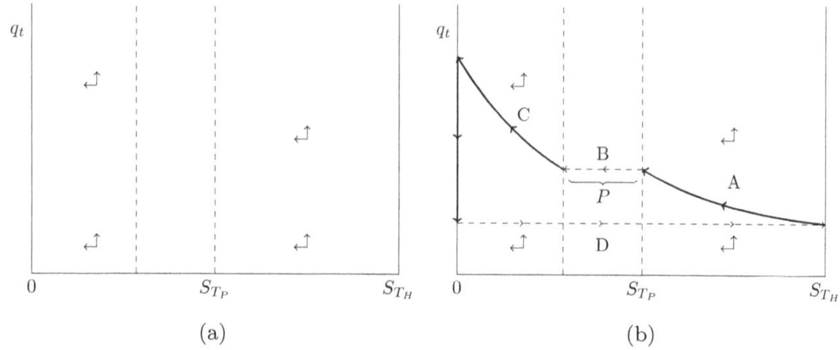

Figure 4.4. Grain storage phase diagram. (a) Direction of movement for S_t and q_t. (b) Optimal path.

zero. For positive q_t, the direction of movement of the costate must be positive: all the arrows therefore point up.

Having established the directions of the arrows, we can proceed to analyse the paths. In the growth model, we identified a special path, namely the only path that led to the steady state point. Is there a similar path here? We can generate some ideas about this using intuition.

The first intuitive idea is that all of the grain will be used up at a particular moment: the harvest. If you have any grain left in the grain silo at the moment of harvest, you have failed to consume enough grain. On the other hand, you don't want to consume so much grain that you run out of grain from the silos before the harvest: your utility will become zero.[3] Thus, our first intuitive conclusion is that the correct path in the phase diagram must hit zero grain at the moment of the harvest. In Figure 4.4(b), the segment labelled C ends with the grain s_t equalling zero. However, this is not enough intuition because all paths end this way, as the arrows always point to the left.

A second element of the diagram is that at the harvest time, the grain silo is replenished by the harvest, going from zero to the maximum storage. In Figure 4.4, the new starting point is therefore

[3]For the geometric utility that we would typically use for examples, this would yield infinite marginal utility; for special cases of such utility functions, such as the logarithm function, utility would become infinitely negative — definitely suboptimal.

at the beginning of path A. The grain is the consumed over the winter, traversing path A.

Path B is the moment of planting in the spring: a discrete amount of grain, P — the length of path B — is planted. To keep the analysis simple, we assume that the amount of grain needed for planting is fixed, due to the fixed amount of land available for crops. (We could embellish the model to allow for planting different amounts of grain, resulting in a greater or lesser harvest later on.)

A key characteristic of path B is that the costate variable q_t does not change; such a change would result in the implicit price to jump: remember that we established that the Lagrange multiplier is the marginal value of income in the consumer problem, and we then developed that the marginal value is therefore a kind of price. Viewing the costate as the price, if the costate variable jumped at the moment of planting, then there would be an arbitrage available: an entrepreneur could buy a few bushels of grain just before planting, store it for a few days, and then sell it at a higher price.

The costate cannot go down at planting either. The arbitrageur could sell a few bushels of grain before planting, put the proceeds in a bank account, and then after the harvest use the proceeds of the savings to buy back the grain at a lower price, leaving a net profit. The conclusion is that path B, which happens in the single instant when the planting is carried out, is horizontal.

Path C traces the grain and costate after planting, up to the moment of the harvest. All of the grain remaining after planting is consumed, leaving zero grain at the moment of the harvest.

The final piece of intuition is to understand that when the harvest takes place, the amount of grain jumps up, and so the costate — the marginal value of the state s_t — must jump down, but in such a way that you start at the beginning of path, A, so that all three paths properly connect — this is path D.

The key feature of the figure is that q_t increases over the season. This reflects the basic intuition in the McCloskey and Nash article: the shadow value of the grain must increase at the rate of interest (with an adjustment for depreciation). This is directly evident from the costate equation:

$$\frac{\dot{q}_t}{q_t} = \rho + \delta$$

We would expect the visible interest rate to incorporate not only the subjective rate of time discount but also the depreciation rate δ, as this must be compensated during storage.

We can also immediately draw a conclusion about consumption. One might conjecture that, once the grain is stored in the silo immediately after the harvest, consumption could then be a constant flow over the season, until the next harvest. However, this is not the case. Consumption is

$$c_t = u'^{-1}(q_t)$$

Because q_t is constantly increasing over the season, the inverse marginal utility function is therefore decreasing, and so consumption decreases over the season. Therefore, there will be a stark contrast between consumption before and after the harvest: it will jump up after the harvest.

We see this reflected in real life: autumn harvest festivals are ubiquitous in all agricultural societies.

Interest Rates and the Black Death

In about 1342, the Black Death (now understood to be the bubonic plague, *Yersinia pestis*, a bacterial disease) killed half the population of Europe, leaving the accumulated capital at the time, houses, buildings, roads, and domestic animal herds, unaffected; these were inherited by the survivors.

From our perspective, on a per capita basis, this would be the equivalent of doubling the capital available to Robinson Crusoe, viewing his goat herd as capital. We can analyse the effect on interest rates and check the empirical validity of the prediction by looking at historical data. Clark (1988) examined the rate of return to capital by examining the ratio of land rents to land purchase prices before and after the Black Death; his Table 3 (reproduced here as Figure 4.5) shows a precipitous decline in the implicit interest rate, as would be predicted by the model. (As a side comment, if we embellish our model to include labour as well as capital, the model also predicts that wages would have risen dramatically, and this is also what we observe.)

TABLE 3
The Rate of Return on Capital in England, 1151–1900 (Percentage)

	Perpetual rent charges (nominal)	Government consols (nominal)	Rent/price ratio on land (real)	Inflation rate (per year)
1151–1200	9.5 (17)			
1201–1250	10.3 (107)		7.3 (2)	+0.5
1251–1300	10.2 (43)		10.3 (4)	+0.5
1301–1350	11.2 (3)		10.2 (5)	+0.3
1351–1400	4.5 (2)		9.4 (2)	0.0
1401–1450			5.6 (17)	0.0
1451–1500	4.0 (1)		5.0 (3)	+0.2
1501–1550	4.6 (5)		5.5 (5)	+1.2
1551–1600	6.0 (21)		5.8 (6)	+1.8
1601–1650	6.0 (42)		5.4 (25)	+0.7
1651–1700	5.3 (65)		5.4 (64)	−0.2
1701–1750	4.3 (49)		4.3 (126)	−0.3
1751–1800	4.0 (29)	4.0	3.6 (91)	+1.4
1801–1850		3.9	3.6 (24)	−0.8
1851–1900		3.0		−0.5

Notes. The numbers in brackets are the number of observations which each interest rate is based upon, where this is applicable. The interest rate is calculated as an average of reported rates for each 50-year period. Before 1650 the rate of inflation is calculated using only the price of wheat.

Sources. Rent charges: Table 1; Table 2; Charity Commissioners (1821, pp. 378–381); Habakkuk (1952, pp. 35–36); Thrupp (1948, p. 123); Harvey, (1977, pp. 396); Salter (1960, pp. 88, 132, 150); Watkin (1952, p. cxci). Consols. Homer (1977, pp. 161–162, 195–197). Land rents. Table 2; Albertson (1932, p. 47); Clay (1974, p. 174); Coss (1974, p. 21); Coss, (1975, pp. 6, 9); Coss (1980, pp. 5–17); Denton (1888, p. 234); Duncan (1986, pp. 560–561); Habakkuk (1952, p. 31); Harvey, (1977, pp. 425–426); Kershaw (1973, pp. 115–117); McFarlane (1981, pp. 185–190); Platt (1973, p. 170); Powicke (1947, p. 536); Salter (1960, pp. 23, 77, 110, 134); Salter (1969, p. 9). Inflation rate: Mitchell and Deane (1962, pp. 468–475, 484–486); Postan (1972, p. 240); Rogers (1866a, pp. 228–232).

Figure 4.5. Medieval rate of return to capital.
Source: Reprinted with permission from Clark (1988, pp. 265–294).

Exercises

Exercise 4.1. Let $f(k) = k^\alpha$; what are π_t and p_t in the steady state?

Exercise 4.2. Deterministic optimal growth model. Let

$$u(c) = \frac{1 - e^{-\gamma c}}{\gamma} \qquad f(k) = \frac{1 - e^{-\alpha k}}{\alpha}$$

A representative individual solves

$$\max_{c} \int_0^\infty e^{-\rho t} u(c_t) dt$$

subject to

$$\dot{k}_t = f(k_t) - c_t \qquad k_0 = k^*$$

(i) Write the appropriate Hamiltonian.
(ii) State the solution for consumption as a function of the costate variable.
Hint: You might need to take a logarithm.
(iii) State the equation for the costate variable.
(iv) State the steady-state capital.
(v) State the steady-state interest rate.
(vi) State the flow of profit in the steady state.
(vii) State the price of an equity share in the representative firm in the steady state.
(viii) State the equation for the interest rate along the growth path (not just at the steady state), assuming that the initial capital is k_0.
Hint: This will require you to take a derivative.

Exercise 4.3. Deterministic optimal growth model. Let

$$u(c) = \gamma \ln(c) \qquad f(k) = \alpha \ln(k - 1)$$

where we assume $k > 1$. A representative individual solves

$$\max_{c} \int_0^\infty e^{-\rho t} u(c_t) dt$$

subject to

$$\dot{k}_t = f(k_t) - c_t \qquad k_0 = k^*$$

Carry out steps (i)–(vii) in Exercise 4.2.

Exercise 4.4. Consider the grain storage model with the following structure:

- Utility is geometric:

$$u(c) = \frac{c^{1-\gamma}}{1-\gamma}$$

- Depreciation is zero ($\delta = 0$).
- A fixed and predetermined amount of grain, P, is needed for planting at the time of planting T_P.
- The time elapsed between the harvest and the planting, followed by the next harvest, is exactly one year, that is,

$$T_P + T_H = 1$$

Solve the following subproblems:

(i) Solve for the time path of the costate q_t, assuming some initial value q_H starting at the harvest.
(ii) Solve for consumption as a function of the costate between the harvest and planting.
(iii) Solve for the time path of grain in the silo between the harvest and the time of planting T_P.
This can be integrated directly, with initial condition $S_0 = S_H$.
(iv) Solve for the time path of grain in the silo between the planting time T_H and the time of harvest T_H.
(v) Solve for the integral of discounted utility between the harvest and the planting.
(vi) Similarly, solve for the integral of utility between the planting and the harvest.
(vii) Find the values $V(S_{T_P})$ and $V(S_{T_H})$.
(viii) The solution for the values in the previous step depends on the initial costate value q_H. What value solves the model?

Bonus Material

Remember that in the two-period model, we had this result that when we added saving to the model, there were two Lagrange multipliers because there were two constraints, and the two constraints were related by the interest rate as follows:

$$\lambda_2 = \frac{1}{1+r}\lambda_1$$

Example

Let's go back to our example in the two-period model, with

$$u(c_1, c_2) = \frac{c_1^{1-\gamma}}{1-\gamma} + \frac{1}{1+\rho}\frac{c_2^{1-\gamma}}{1-\gamma}$$

From the solution of the Lagrangian, we have the ratio

$$\frac{c_1^{\gamma}}{c_2^{\gamma}} = \frac{1+r}{1+\rho}$$

We can take logs and rearrange, yielding

$$\ln\left(c_2^{\gamma}\right) - \ln\left(c_1^{\gamma}\right) \sim \rho - r$$

On the right-hand side, we have used the basic fact that for small x, the approximation $\ln(1+x) \sim x$ holds. Recalling that $f'(k) = r$, the left-hand side is the growth rate of the marginal utility of consumption.

Similarly, in the costate equation of the optimal growth model,

$$\dot{\ln(\xi)}_t = \rho - f'(k_t)$$

is the growth rate of the marginal utility of consumption. We can use this to calculate the growth rate of consumption:

$$c_t = \xi_t^{-\frac{1}{\gamma}} \to \ln(c_t) = -\frac{1}{\gamma}\ln(\xi_t)$$

$$\to \dot{\ln(c_t)} = -\frac{1}{\gamma}\dot{\ln(\xi_t)} = -\frac{1}{\gamma}(\rho - f'(k_t)) = -\frac{1}{\gamma}(\rho - r_t)$$

The interest rate r is going to be bigger than ρ before you reach the steady state, so the whole expression is positive: consumption is growing.

We can see the influence of γ, the coefficient of relative risk aversion, which is an expression of the preferences of the individual that we're talking about in this example. A high value of γ *slows down* growth; people who are risk-averse lack the patience to give up consumption now in order to get consumption later by investing in their goats, as it were.

Boundary Conditions in the Grain Storage Model

Recall that at planting, any grain in the silo is taken out and planted, reducing the amount of stored grain to zero. The quantity of that seed grain is determined in advance by the farmer through his consumption patterns over the winter and therefore constitutes part of his decision process. How does he determine it? Too much consumption over the winter leaves too little to plant, reducing the subsequent harvest. This in turn necessarily reduces consumption over the following winter. Thus, the consumption pattern and the amount of grain planted need to properly mesh.

There is an additional condition required besides the three basic Hamiltonian equations, which fleshes out the solution:

$$q_{T_P} = V'(s_{T_P})$$

This is a terminal condition that states that at the moment of planting the multiplier is equal to the marginal (expressed as a derivative) value of the stored grain at planting — similar to our earlier interpretations of the Lagrange multiplier. The paths on the phase diagram will stitch together to ensure that this condition holds so that the quantity of grain that is planted, when matched with the consumption over the winter, equals the total harvest.

Too much consumption over the winter leaves too little to plant, reducing the subsequent harvest. This in turn necessarily reduces consumption over the following winter, raising the marginal value — the multiplier q. The farmer can carry out arbitrage by reducing his consumption now, raising his marginal value q now, but with the benefit of lowering the future q.

Chapter 5

Additional Growth Model Applications

In this chapter, we examine several variants of the growth model. The growth model posited a single representative agent, but it makes sense to expand the model to encompass foreign countries whose growth status might differ, to understand how their interactions might affect their growth. Additionally, real economies have governments and taxation, and how taxes affect growth is fundamentally important. We also explore how control theory can be used to determine optimal resource use: in one case, when to harvest resources that grow over time, such as trees, and how to optimally use up resources that shrink when used, such as petroleum.

Should a Country Grow on Its Own or Borrow From Foreign Investors to Speed Up Growth?

Suppose you as a developing country have the following choice:

(1) Grow autarkically but fully maintain sovereignty over your own capital.
(2) Borrow from foreign investors but at the cost of becoming a permanent debtor nation.

We can get a little bit of insight into the correct answer by remembering that it is a fundamental and highly general result in economics that trade is beneficial for both parties to a trade. Borrowing capital is a form of trade. One can interpret the trade as the domestic economy receiving investment now in return for — that is, trading — future payments, and the foreign investors are simply on the other side of this exchange.

We can begin by asking whether a country that has initial capital k_0 can benefit from borrowing from foreign investors. The first detail is to determine the foreign interest rate. Since by construction the economy in question starts out with less than the steady-state level of capital, to highlight the results, we an assume that the world at large is near the steady state, so for practical purposes, the world interest rate is the steady state value, ρ.

The borrowing country can decide to test the waters by borrowing a small amount of capital, Δ. The capital will be added to its own capital stock, raising the total to $k_0 + \Delta$, and this total capital enters into the production function, producing output $f(k_0 + \Delta)$. The country owns the output but must pay interest on the borrowed capital, $\rho\Delta$.

We can get at the incremental benefit of the borrowed capital by calculating the difference between the additional output from the borrowed capital and the interest cost. We can use calculus for this calculation. The net financial benefit from borrowed capital, per unit of borrowed foreign capital, is

$$\frac{d}{d\Delta}\left(f(k_0 + \Delta) - \rho\Delta\right) = f'(k_0 + \Delta) - \rho$$

We know that the marginal product of capital, $f'(k_0)$, exceeds ρ because the country is developing, so $k_0 < \overline{k}$, and therefore the marginal product, $f'(k_0 + \Delta)$, is *greater than* ρ. Thus, the borrowing country can pay off the loan, principal and interest, and have additional funds left over. Therefore, the financial benefit of the borrowing is positive. We can label this benefit and the surplus, $(f'(k_0 + \Delta) - \rho)\,\Delta$; this surplus can be used for consumption that would not be available under autarkic growth.

Note that this benefit is positive no matter how large Δ is, as long as $k_0 + \Delta$ is less than the steady state capital $\overline{k}$. (At the steady-state capital $\overline{k}$, the marginal product is ρ, and there would be no surplus.) It makes sense to borrow a small Δ, but it also makes sense to borrow a large value. In fact, as long as the total capital, domestic plus borrowed, $k_0+\Delta$ is less than the steady state capital, the incremental financial benefit for the borrowing country is positive. Thus, it makes sense to borrow so that the total capital is equal to the steady state value, all at once. By doing this, the country achieves full economic growth in an instant!

However, there is a cost. The borrowing country becomes a permanent debtor. Does this make sense? It could repay the principal of the borrowed capital over time and then own the borrowed capital.

To understand the repayment scheme, begin by noting that the surplus can be used for investment as well as consumption. Thus, we can do a thought experiment in which the borrowing country carries on with the autarkic growth path of consumption and investment and plows all of the surplus from borrowing into paying down the principal of the foreign capital. Thus, the discounted utility from this experiment is the same as that for autarkic growth.

It is clear that this is suboptimal: you can take some of the surplus from the long run steady state and increase consumption today; due to discounting at rate ρ, the lost future utility of consumption is outweighed by the current gain of equal consumption. Thus, it makes sense to use all of the surplus for consumption. But again, this means becoming a permanent debtor.

We can be concrete about the nature of imported foreign capital. Subsistence farmers in India irrigate their fields by running bullocks around a water-wheel pump, lifting water into ditches at agonisingly slow rates. The bullocks need to be fed, sheltered, and goaded to tread around the well by a full time attendant. By borrowing money, a farmer can replace the well and the bullock with a gasoline-powered mechanical pump imported from Japan or Korea, drawing water from a much deeper well. Once set in motion, the pump does not need an attendant nor does it need feed grain that could otherwise go the farmer. This story has been played out in India millions of times over the past few decades, and as a result, India has been transformed: GDP per capita went from \$323 in 1965 to \$2,090 in 2022. This is nothing short of miraculous.

The gains from imported capital are not evenly distributed

We've maintained the stance that there is a representative individual in our models, but we can put this assumption aside temporarily to ask the following question: will the owners of capital (the owners of the goats in our Robinson Crusoe story) and firms (the owners of the goat's milk farms) be equally happy to import capital? The answer is no, the owners of the goats will be opposed. The decline in income of domestic capital owners due to influx of foreign capital is

$$(f'(k_t) - \rho)k_t$$

Before the foreign capital comes in, their income is $f'(k_t)k_t$, and after the foreign capital comes in, their income falls because the interest rate falls to its steady state value.

The owners of the firms, on the other hand, gain: their profits increase because capital costs fall. The increase in profits of shareholders due to influx of foreign capital is

$$f(\bar{k}) - \rho k_t - (f(k_t) - f'(k_t)k_t)$$

If the goat owners have political power, they might be able to block the import of foreign capital; this happens in the real world all the time. But we have established that this is to the detriment of the country as a whole. (In India, the government of India argued that domestic "infant industries" needed protection from foreign competition and with that in mind imposed strict restrictions on the import of foreign capital and also banned foreign firms from having ownership stakes in domestic Indian firms. As a result, India's growth was stunted for several decades after independence in 1947.)

What Are the Effects of Taxes on Output, Profits, and Consumption on Economic Growth?

To analyse the effects of taxes, we first need to determine the disposition of the taxes. One idea is to assume that tax revenue is discarded or spent on projects that generate no use for the representative agent. This would be similar to losing income or wealth; the consequence is that overall consumption would go down; with multiple goods the consumption of each good would decrease, but that would be it. We can think of this in intuitive terms as pyramid building: the representative agent gets no benefit from it.

Another idea would be to model the disposition as increasing the provision of some public good, such as national defense. This would be entirely valid, but we would be led on a significant detour to incorporate the utility function for these public goods. Moreover, the process of choosing the public goods, because they are not provided by markets, can be a book in itself.

What we really want to get at is the "distortionary" effect of taxes, that is, the effect of taxes on the relative prices of things. We know that if we change the relative prices (i.e. the ratio of prices that we discussed in the context of the Lagrangian models), then the relative consumptions will also change. Therefore, we model the disposition of taxes simply as lump sum transfers, that is, as simply refunding the tax revenue to the citizens of the country, on a per capita basis. The key aspect of these refunds is that they are given to the representative agent regardless of his consumption or his investment; he cannot affect the refund.

He can, however, respond to the tax. If the tax is on investment, he can adjust his investment to minimise the impact of the tax. If the tax is on consumption, he can alter his consumption in response.

We can reformulate the growth model with taxes as follows. First, consumption includes both consumption in our previous sense, and also the revenue from taxes, g_t ("g" for "government"), that is simply transferred to the representative individual.

The transfers of tax revenue enter the utility function:

$$\max_c \int_0^\infty e^{-\rho t} u(c_t + g_t) dt$$

The law of motion for capital is also affected by taxes: if the tax at rate τ is on output, then the law of motion is altered as shown:

$$\dot{k}_t = (1-\tau) f(k_t) - c_t + g_t \qquad k_0 = k^*$$

The key insight here is that consumption is something that the individual controls, whereas the transfer is taken as given by the individual — he cannot influence it.

The Hamiltonian is adjusted to account for taxes:

$$H \equiv u(c_t + g_t) + \xi_t((1-\tau) f(k_t) - c_t + g_t)$$

The solution method is the same as before, but we have an extra step. In the initial step, the individual solves for consumption as usual, yielding the usual optimality condition:

$$u'(c_t + g_t) = \xi_t$$

However, the costate equation is affected because the tax effectively alters the production function:

$$\dot{\xi} = (\rho - (1-\tau)f'(k_t))\,\xi_t$$

It is key that the optimisation by the representative individual does not take account of his influence on the size of the refund — he takes this as fixed.

$0 = \frac{\partial}{\partial c}H$	$u'(c_t + g_t) = \xi_t$	optimality condition
$\dot{k} = \frac{\partial}{\partial \xi}H$	$\dot{k}_t = (1-\tau)f(k_t) - c_t + g_t$	state equation
$\dot{\xi} = \rho\xi - \frac{\partial}{\partial k}H$	$\dot{\xi}_t = (\rho - (1-\tau)f'(k_t))\,\xi_t$	costate equation

The second and new step is to substitute for the tax revenue g_t in the optimality, state, and costate equations and then carry out the dynamic analysis or phase diagram analysis, with the requirement that the government transfers g_t equal the revenue from taxes — the government's budget constraint:

$$g_t = \tau f(k_t)$$

Once we include the equality between the tax revenue and the government transfer of the per capita tax proceeds, the Hamiltonian equations reflect the equilibrium:

$0 = \frac{\partial}{\partial c}H$	$u'(c_t + \tau f(k_t)) = \xi_t$	optimality condition
$\dot{k} = \frac{\partial}{\partial \xi}H$	$\dot{k}_t = f(k_t) - c_t$	state equation
$\dot{\xi} = \rho\xi - \frac{\partial}{\partial k}H$	$\dot{\xi}_t = (\rho - (1-\tau)f'(k_t))\,\xi_t$	costate equation

Specifically, the state equation is not directly affected by the tax, but the costate equation is affected. As a result, capital accumulation is damped.

We can see that the steady state is affected by the tax on output:

$$f'(\bar{k}) = \frac{\rho}{1-\tau}$$

Since the marginal product of capital at the steady state is increased, the steady state capital is decreased, and therefore, long run consumption, and with it discounted utility, is reduced, despite the fact that government revenue is transferred to consumers.

Tax on profits

We could also have a tax on firm profits; maybe this can mitigate the negative impact of a tax on output. In the analysis of a tax on profits, we have to be careful to distinguish between the profits determined by the firm's choice of capital in the face of the interest rate r_t and the equivalence of the marginal product of that capital with the interest rate:

$$\dot{k}_t = (1-\tau)\left(f(k_t) - f'(k_t)k_t\right) + f'(k_t)k_t - c_t + g_t \qquad k_0 = k^*$$

with

$$g_t = \tau\left(f(k_t) - r_t k_t\right)$$

Therefore, we use r_t when solving the optimisation from the firm's perspective and impose the requirement that the marginal product of capital equal the interest rate *ex post.*

With the tax on profits, we separate the terms $f(k_t) - r_t k_t$, capturing the firm's expenditure on capital $r_t k_t$, and the term $r_t k_t$, capturing the income the owner of the goats receives from renting out the goats, which is not taxed:

$$H \equiv u(c_t + g_t) + \xi_t\left((1-\tau)\left(f(k_t) - r_t k_t\right) + r_t k_t - c_t + g_t\right)$$

which simplifies to

$$H \equiv u(c_t + g_t) + \xi_t\left(f(k_t) - \tau\left(f(k_t) - r_t k_t\right) - c_t + g_t\right)$$

We have to be careful when solving the Hamiltonian equations. From the perspective of the representative agent, he chooses consumption, taking the transfer of per capita tax revenue as a fixed amount that he cannot affect; moreover, as in our previous analysis, he takes the interest rate as fixed — he does not account for the equality between the interest rate and the marginal product of capital in his optimisation. The Hamiltonian equations are therefore as follows:

$0 = \frac{\partial}{\partial c} H$	$u'(c_t + g_t) = \xi_t$	optimality condition
$\dot{k} = \frac{\partial}{\partial \xi} H$	$\dot{k}_t = f(k_t) - \tau(f(k_t) - r_t k_t) - c_t + g_t$	state equation
$\dot{\xi} = \rho\xi - \frac{\partial}{\partial k} H$	$\dot{\xi}_t = (\rho - r_t + \tau f'(k_t))\xi_t$	costate equation

In equilibrium however, we account for these equalities:

$$r_t = f'(k_t) \quad \text{and} \quad g_t = \tau\left(f(k_t) - r_t k_t\right)$$

Substituting these equalities into the Hamiltonian equations yields

$0 = \frac{\partial}{\partial c} H$	$u'(c_t + \tau(f(k_t) - f'(k_t)k_t)) = \xi_t$	optimality condition
$\dot{k} = \frac{\partial}{\partial \xi} H$	$\dot{k}_t = f(k_t) - c_t$	state equation
$\dot{\xi} = \rho\xi - \frac{\partial}{\partial k} H$	$\dot{\xi}_t = (\rho - f'(k_t) + \tau f'(k_t))\xi_t$	costate equation

Due to the refund of the tax revenue, the state equation is unaffected by the tax. However, the incentive to invest is impaired, and this is reflected in the costate equation. With a tax on profits, the optimality condition is again unaffected except for the transfer:

$$u'(c_t + g_t) = \xi_t$$

However, the costate equation is affected because the tax effectively alters the production function:

$$\dot{\xi} = \left(\rho - f'(k_t) + \tau\left(f'(k_t) - f'(k_t) - r_t\right)\right)\xi_t$$
$$\dot{\xi} = \left(\rho - f'(k_t) + \tau f'(k_t)\right)\xi_t$$

(In the second line, we imposed the equality $f'(k_t) = r_t$, obtaining a cancellation.)

The steady state capital is again affected. The steady state capital with a tax on profit is

$$f'(\bar{k}) = \frac{\rho}{1-\tau}$$

Again, the marginal product of capital $f'(\bar{k})$ must be larger than ρ at the steady state, so capital is reduced. This reduces total output, and therefore, the overall long run consumption is reduced — this happens even though the tax revenue is redistributed to the representative agent. There is no difference between the effect of a tax on output and a tax on profit.

When Should You Cut Down a Tree?

Saplings grow fast, large trees grow slowly. This is partly due to scale factors: trees grow by adding layers to their circumference; to support their weight as they grow tall, they must add cross-sectional mass — area — which adds to the circumference. The number of cells in the cambium — the living layer of bark — increases with the circumference, but the mass increases with the square of the circumference; the cambium's role is to create new support mass and to lift moisture to the leaves and this therefore gets harder and harder to do as the tree grows.

We can view the mass of a tree at time t as the tree's state, x_t. The speed of growth of the tree depends on the size of the tree:

$$\dot{x} = f(x_t) \tag{5.1}$$

for some initial tree size x_0. This is the state equation. The growth rate is positive — $f'(\cdot) > 0$ — but the the speed of growth of the tree slows down as the tree gets bigger: $f''(\cdot) < 0$.

The trees we have in mind do not produce any fruit, so there is no flow of utility or profit while the tree is growing. The only payoff from the tree arrives when the tree is cut down. The owner decides the optimal time, T, to cut the tree, and so from the perspective of any time t before T the value of the tree is simply the discounted value of the tree when it is cut:

$$V(x_t) = \max_T e^{-r(T-t)} x_T$$

where x_T is the solution of the differential equation for tree growth from the differential equation in (5.1). Thus, the problem is to determine the optimal T; generically, this is called *optimal stopping*.

To reduce the notational clutter, let's assume we are at time zero, so the problem is

$$V(x_t) = \max_T e^{-rT} x_T$$

Since there is no flow payoff, we can immediately write the Hamiltonian as

$$H \equiv \xi f(x)$$

There is no control *per se*; the only decision is when to cut the tree down.

We can proceed to derive the Hamiltonian equations. We have already stated the state equation. The costate equation is straightforward:

$$\dot{\xi} = r\xi_t - \frac{\partial}{\partial x} H \quad \rightarrow \quad \dot{\xi} = \xi_t \left(r - f'(x_t))\right)$$

It is immediately clear that the optimum is achieved when the marginal speed of growth, $f'(x)$, is equal to the interest rate; the costate stops growing at that point. The remaining issue is to determine the initial value of the costate.

The phase diagram. We can use the state and costate equations to construct the phase diagram (see Figure 5.1). As with the growth

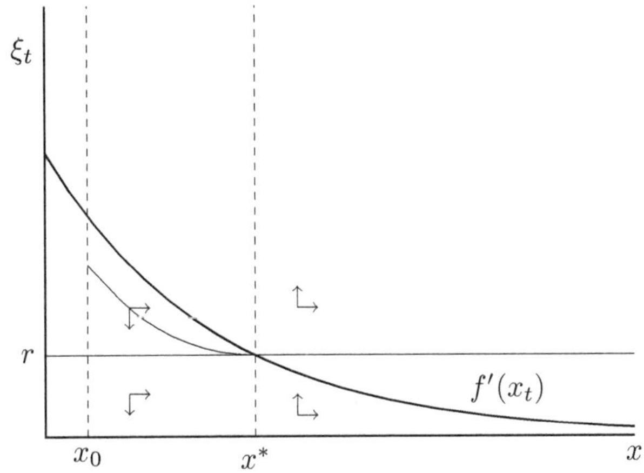

Figure 5.1. Optimal tree harvest phase diagram.

model, we put the state x_t on the horizontal axis and the costate ξ_t on the vertical axis. Next, plot $f'(k)$ as a function of capital. In addition, draw a horizontal line with value r, the interest rate.

Next, draw the arrows. First, it is immediately clear that $\dot{k}$ is always positive — the tree always grows, whether large or small. Thus, every arrow will be rightward pointing. For the vertical arrows, the growth of the costate is negative if the marginal product of capital $f'(k)$ is below r, and vice versa. Completing these directional arrows, we see that there is a just one path that points to the corner where the costate ceases to grow and the path therefore terminates. This therefore uniquely determines the initial value of the costate, ξ_0.

The solution of the optimal cutting time problem is therefore to cut the tree when the growth rate of the tree, $f'(x_t)$, is equal to the interest rate. We can easily see why this is the case with a second diagram (see Figure 5.2[1]), which expresses this same idea, originally put forward by Wicksell (1936) in the early 20th century: cut the tree when it marginal rate of growth equals the interest rate. The logic is simple: if you harvest earlier than that, you are sacrificing an asset that is generating a return that exceeds the return you could

[1]Johnson (1975) has a similar diagram.

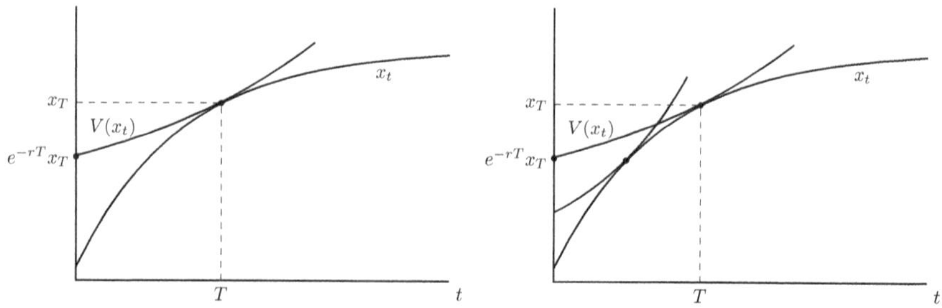

Figure 5.2. Wicksell diagram.

get from investing in a standard financial asset such as bonds or an interest-bearing bank account. If you wait beyond that point, the tree is growing more slowly than would that same financial asset and is therefore suboptimal.

The effect of interest rates

We can analyse the effect of changes in the interest rate on the time of harvest of the tree. The intuition is straightforward: if the interest rate rises, you will harvest the tree when the tree is growing at that higher rate, which means the tree will be younger, when it is growing fast. Thus, increases in the interest rate result in a kind of impatience, and smaller trees, harvested at a faster rate. The idea is illustrated in Figure 5.2.

How Fast Should You Sell Oil Out of Your Oil Well?

Suppose you own an oil well with a finite pool of oil which we can call Q_t. You extract the oil at rate q_t barrels per day, which you control, and which you sell at price p_t; the cost of extraction is c per barrel. Thus, your flow of net income per day is $p_t(q_t - c)$. You want to pump out the oil and sell it at the optimal rate until it is exhausted. How fast should you pump the oil? The problem was analysed by Hotelling (1931) in the 1930; see also the work of Kamien and Schwartz (2012), p. 59.

This problem is different from the tree-cutting problem in that there is a flow of profit, namely the product of the flow of oil, q_t, and the price of oil, p_t, which can change over time.

Here is the basic model. Your objective is to maximise discounted profit:

$$\max_q \int_0^T e^{-rt} p_t(q_t - c)dt$$

where we take account of the unit cost c of pumping the oil.

The state variable is the oil remaining in your well, Q_t, with law of motion:

$$\dot{Q}_t = -q_t$$

You also have to obey the following constraint:

$$\int_t^T q_s ds \leq Q_t$$

at each date t, that is, you can't use more than the available pool of oil available as you go forward from each date t.[2]

It is important to keep in mind that the time path of price is fixed and endogenous for this basic problem, that is, the well owner is a price taker. We look at the requirements that an equilibrium price path must satisfy later on.

The Hamiltonian is

$$H \equiv (p_t - c)q_t + \xi_t(-q_t)$$

with Hamiltonian equations as follows:

$0 = \frac{\partial}{\partial q} H$	$p_t - c = \xi_t$	optimality condition
$\dot{Q} = \frac{\partial}{\partial \xi} H$	$\dot{Q}_t = -q_t$	state equation
$\dot{\xi} = r\xi - \frac{\partial}{\partial Q} H$	$\dot{\xi}_t = r\xi_t$	costate equation

[2]This is an example of an isoperimetric constraint.

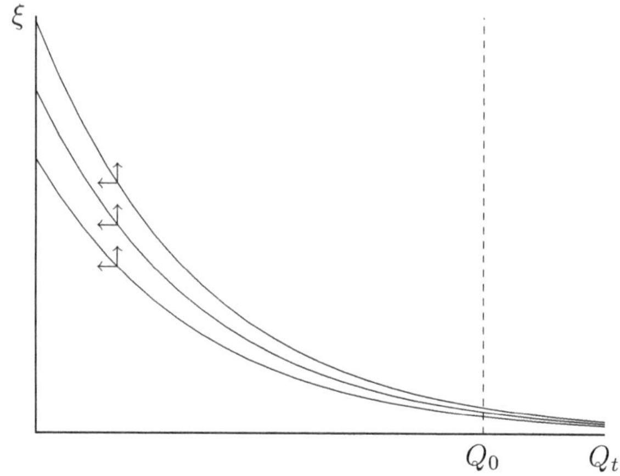

Figure 5.3. Optimal oil extraction phase diagram.

The key observation here is that the costate stands alone: it must rise at the rate of interest (see Figure 5.3). But it must also equal the net price $(p_t - c)$ of oil. So if the net price of oil is rising more slowly than the rate of interest, you don't pump any oil at all. And if the price is rising faster that the rate of interest, you would pump everything you can as fast as possible, using the proceeds from the sale to invest in interest-paying assets.

If we maintain the assumption that the cost of pumping is a function of the speed of pumping, $c(q_t)$, then you'll extract the oil until the *marginal* cost of pumping the oil is such that the net price is increasing at the interest rate.

How do we include the extra dimension of the depletion of the oil? We can have an extended Lagrangian (and hence Hamiltonian) via integration by parts.

The first step in the solution is to solve for the costate variable, which is straightforward:

$$\xi_t = \xi_0 e^{rt}$$

anticipating that the initial value ξ_0 will be such that the oil is depleted optimally.

Next, substitute the solution into the optimality condition:

$$p_t - c = \xi_0 e^{rt}$$

In the simplest case, we can suppose that cost is constant per unit of oil pumped, in which case our combined equation becomes

$$p_t - c = \xi_0 e^{rt} \quad \rightarrow \quad p_t = \xi_0 e^{rt} + c$$

In order for the price to comport with this equation, the price must rise at a rate that is equal to the rate of interest in the long run:

$$\frac{\dot{p}_t}{p_t} = \frac{r}{1 + \frac{e^{-rt}}{\xi_0} c}$$

Since we started out assuming that the oil well owner is competitive with other owners, we actually can't pin down the rate of depletion of the oil and solve for how fast the owner pumps the oil. Since the owner can't affect the price, he will be indifferent between pumping all of his oil at once, or pumping it slowly, or waiting and pumping it later after the price has risen; if he pumps it all now, he can buy a bond that pays the interest rate r and if he waits he will get the equivalent of the bond when he does pump the oil, and if he pumps continuously, then he can put the proceeds in a bank account as the money comes in and build up his wealth that way.

To figure out how fast the oil will be depleted, we need to look at the whole market. In the whole market for oil, the price is in fact dependent on how fast the aggregate of the oil producers deplete their oil. We can express that by positing a demand curve for oil. We can represent this with a function: the per-capita quantity demanded globally is a function of the price: $q_t = D(p_t)$; because it is a demand curve, it is downward sloping, $D'(p_t) < 0$. As with our Robinson Crusoe goat husbandry story, we can propose that there are many oil well owners, and that they also are oil users, all identical, and as such have a demand for the oil they pump — they use it to run their cars.

We can re-examine optimality condition in light of the demand curve. Our requirement is that the flow of oil from the representative well accumulate over time to the initial size of the oil pool:

$$\int_0^T D(p_t)dt = Q_0$$

Substituting from the combined optimality condition and solving the integral will tell us what the initial price has to be.

An example of a demand function is a geometric demand function:

$$D(p_t) = p_t^{-\alpha}$$

If we posit that the cost c of extracting oil is zero, we can fully solve the model. Substituting for the pricing rule into the integral constraint yields

$$\int_0^T p_t^{-\alpha} dt = \int_0^T \left(\xi_0 e^{rt}\right)^{-\alpha} dt = Q_0$$

We can solve the integral:

$$\xi_0^{-\alpha} \frac{e^{-\alpha r T} - 1}{-\alpha r} = Q_0$$

Now, we can solve for ξ_0:

$$\xi_0 = \left(\frac{\alpha r Q_0}{1 - e^{-\alpha r T}}\right)^{-\frac{1}{\alpha}}$$

Once ξ_0 is determined, we have also fully determined the path that the price of oil must follow to clear the market:

$$p_t = \left(\frac{\alpha r Q_0}{1 - e^{-\alpha r T}}\right)^{-\frac{1}{\alpha}} e^{rt}$$

There is an additional detail however: we don't yet know T, the moment when the oil is depleted.

To determine T, we can undertake a thought experiment: suppose that T is a finite date, July 20, 2091. At that moment, the price of oil will be determined by the flow of oil, and it will also be a finite rate of flow — to be concrete, we can posit that it is one barrel per day.

On the next day, July 21, the price will shoot to infinity because the oil is gone: $0^{-\alpha} = \infty$. This jump in the price violates our understanding that the price rises at the rate of interest. In our perfect foresight world, an arbitrageur could buy the last barrel of oil on July 20 and sell it on the 21st for an infinite profit. This just can't be an equilibrium.

The only way out of the conundrum is for T to be infinite. Then there is no price jump, and the solution for ξ_0 becomes more nuanced:

$$\xi_0 = (\alpha r Q_0)^{\frac{-1}{\alpha}}$$

and we can also solve for the price:

$$p_t = (\alpha r Q_0)^{\frac{-1}{\alpha}} e^{rt}$$

In the case of geometric demand, this price rise will continue indefinitely, and the quantity of oil pumped and used will ineluctably shrink. But it will never be fully depleted.

Exercises

Exercise 5.1. Consider the tree-cutting model with a growth function as follows:

$$\dot{X}_t = C X_t^{1-\alpha}$$

where C is a constant associated with the species of the tree. Note that we can express this as follows:

$$\frac{\dot{X}_t}{X_t} = C X_t^{-\alpha}$$

that is, the growth *rate* of the tree shrinks with its size. For saplings of size X_0, find the optimal harvest size for interest rate r.

Exercise 5.2 (Tree-cutting with re-planting). Consider the tree-cutting model but with re-planting of saplings after the harvest. Draw a phase diagram showing how the value at the harvest equals the profit from the harvest plus the value of replanting. This is an extension of the grain storage model, except there is no depletion of the grain during storage.

Exercise 5.3 (Monopoly oil extraction). In the initial oil extraction analysis, we took the price path as fixed and exogenous. With a monopoly, the price path is determined by the owner of the resource. Solve for the optimal depletion of the oil.

Exercise 5.4 (Extractible resource that is durable). If you mine diamonds or aluminum, the price is affected by the total mined. Intuitively, the price is reduced by the amount mined. This can be captured by making price a function of the cumulative amount mined:

$$p_t = \phi\left(\int_0^t q_s ds\right)$$

instead of

$$p_t = \gamma(q_t)$$

as with oil.

Bonus Material

What if government spending is beneficial?

Government spending can be beneficial. If in addition to the benefit the government's activities have externalities that cannot be internalised through markets, then a case can be made for undertaking them. National defense is the classic example of this: you can't really charge individuals for the benefit they get from an anti-missile defense system — it protects everyone at once. The system is costly to produce and must be financed via taxes; the question then becomes as follows: What is the optimal trade-off between the impairment of growth stemming from taxes — the distortion — and the benefits of the government spending? The generic term for this optimisation problem is Ramsey taxation, after the early 20th century economist, Frank Ramsey (1927).

There are myriad directions one could go with this extension of the taxation and growth model. The simplest is to presume that there is a separate element of utility, $v(g_t)$, that expresses the benefit of the anti-missile system, and also a cost function, $h(g_t)$. The utility function is increasing and concave in g_t, just as is the utility of consumption; the cost function is also increasing in the size of the anti-missile system. The objective for the representative individual becomes more complicated:

$$\max_{c} \int_0^\infty e^{-\rho t}(u(c_t) + v(g_t) - h(g_t))dt$$

The law of motion for capital remains the same. There are now two problems: the one solved by the representative individual as before, in the face of taxation on output, and the one solved by the government, which also strives to maximise the utility of the representative individual but with the choice of the public good:

$$\max_{g} \int_0^\infty e^{-\rho t}(u(c_t) + v(g_t) - h(g_t))dt$$

In addition to the regular state equation, there is an additional constraint reflecting the requirement that the tax revenue equal the cost of provision:

$$\tau f(k_t) = h(g_t)$$

Thus, choosing g_t is equivalent to choosing the tax rate τ.

The representative individual's problem will be unaffected by these embellishments because the additional terms $v(g_t)$ and $h(g_t)$ cannot be affected by individual action — he only controls consumption c_t as before, not the tax rate τ or government spending g_t. However, the government does control both variables, and so the relevant optimisation problem for the government has a different state equation:

$$\dot{k}_t = (1 - \tau)f(k_t) - c_t = f(k_t) - h(g_t) - c_t$$

In this equation, we removed the transfer of government revenue, as this is expressed in the utility function for the public good, $v(g_t)$, and we have substituted from the government budget constraint $\tau f(k_t) = h(g_t)$. This transforms the problem from choosing the tax rate τ to one choosing g. But there is an additional dimension to the problem: the representative individual is still going to solve his optimisation problem as before; the costate equation for this problem remains as before. If we proceed with the government's problem blindly, we will end up with a different costate equation: the government understands its effect on the tax rate τ and so it washes out of the state equation, and in turn the impact of the tax on the costate is removed. The representative individual's costate and the government's costate are therefore different.

The resolution of this conflict is for the government to add an additional state variable to its optimisation problem: the representative agent's costate variable. This new state variable is affected by the tax — to repeat, this costate equation is

$$\dot{\xi} = \left(\rho - (1-\tau)f'(k_t)\right)\xi_t$$

and it will have a nontrivial impact on the problem because τ appears in this equation. This makes it clear that the Ramsey problem in the growth model is fundamentally more difficult than the basic growth model.

Another approach to boundary conditions in the tree-cutting problem

It is useful to characterise the tree-cutting problem in terms of the boundary conditions associated with the differential equation for the value function $V(x)$.

When we cut the tree at T, the time at which the marginal value of the tree, $f'(k_T)$, is equal to the interest rate, we automatically satisfy the boundary condition that the market value of the wood from the tree at the harvest, x_T, is equal to the optimal value, $V(x_T)$. This is called the value-matching condition.

In addition, the marginal value condition is satisfied, $f'(x_t) = r$; this is called the smooth-pasting condition. Thus, the problem is solved with two boundary conditions. This is slightly unexpected: we wanted to find the solution for the optimal *time* T, but we did not explicitly solve for T; instead we find the optimal *state* x_T using the two boundary conditions: value matching and smooth pasting.

The conventional smooth pasting argument states $V'(x_T) = \frac{d}{dx}x_T = 1$; however, what we have is that the time derivatives satisfy the condition. We can use the chain rule to convert one to the other:

$$\frac{d}{dt}V = \frac{d}{dx}V\frac{dx}{dt}$$

At the harvest time, we have the equality

$$\frac{\dot{V}}{V} = r = \frac{\dot{x}}{x}$$

Cancelling the dts we have

$$\frac{dV_T}{dx_T} = 1$$

This is the smooth pasting condition. In addition, we have the value matching condition:

$$V_T = x_t$$

and the smooth-pasting condition is obtained by differentiating this equation with respect to X_T. Thus, we could start with the value-matching and smooth-pasting conditions and derive the tangency condition from them. This strategy continues to work when solving the stochastic models we later develop.

The tree-cutting problem with replanting

Consider the tree-cutting model as in Exercise 5.1 but with the re-planting of a sapling after harvesting the tree, and this cycle repeats indefinitely. (This is called the multiple rotation problem.) We would like to find the optimal cutting time for each cycle. Again assume a sapling size of X_0.

Things are a little more complicated because of the replanting. But there is some basic intuition that we can bring to the fore immediately: in the single-rotation problem, we harvest when the growth rate is equal to the interest rate. In the multiple rotation problem, by harvesting the tree when it is a little younger than in the single rotation case, we take advantage of the higher growth rate of the sapling.

At any moment of time, the tree has a size X_t and there is a value associated with the tree, $V(X_t)$. From the basic tree-cutting model, we know that before the moment of harvest, the value exceeds the tree size, and at the moment of harvest T, it is equal to the tree, that is, in the single rotation model we had the "value-matching" condition, $V(X_T) = X_T$. In the multiple rotation case however, the value includes the immediate payoff from selling the lumber from the tree we cut down, but also the value from planting the sapling and looking ahead to its harvest, and so on iteratively forever:

$$V(X_T) = X_T + V(X_0)$$

Since the process will be repeated exactly each time, so that the future harvest will also be X_T, it is more helpful to write

$$V(X_T) = X_T + e^{-rT}V(X_T)$$

We also understand from our previous efforts that the growth rate of the *value* must equal the interest rate. We can express this in the multiple rotation setting by first calculating $\frac{d}{dt}V(X_T)$:

$$\frac{d}{dt}V(X_T) = \frac{d}{dt}X_T + e^{-rT}\frac{d}{dt}V(X_T) - re^{-rT}V(X_T)$$

We want to find the optimal cutting size (and, equivalently, the optimal harvest time). To solve, we first note that both equations are recursive, in $V(X_T)$ and $\frac{d}{dt}V(X_T)$, respectively. Solving yields

$$V(X_t) = \frac{X_t}{1 - e^{-rT}}$$

$$\frac{d}{dt}V(X_T) = \frac{\frac{d}{dt}X_T - re^{-rT}V(X_T)}{1 - e^{-rT}}$$

Optimality requires that the growth of the value equal the interest rate

$$\frac{\frac{d}{dt}V(X_T)}{V(X_T)} = r$$

$$\rightarrow \quad \frac{\frac{d}{dt}X_T}{X_T} - \frac{re^{-rT}}{1 - e^{-rT}} = r$$

We can solve for the growth rate of the tree:

$$\frac{\dot{X}_T}{X_T} = \frac{r}{1 - e^{-rT}} > r$$

Thus, the intuition is borne out: in the multiple rotation problem, you cut the tree at a younger age than in the single rotation case.

Part II
Stochastic Models

Chapter 6

Brown and Bachelier

We want to introduce risk into the environment, especially focused on how risk affects the interest rate.

Pharaoh's Dream

In our deterministic control model of grain storage, we assumed that the farmers deciding how much grain to consume could see into the future perfectly. We motivated the idea using the story of Joseph: he was able to perfectly prophesy the future. We gave this a name: perfect foresight.

We also used perfect foresight in the growth model: Robinson Crusoe sees his future path perfectly. And when we calculated profits and the price of stock in Robinson Crusoe's goat farm, we assumed that the market can look into the future and exactly and correctly assess the profit flows in the future as well as the present. We saw that in general these profit flows change over time.

In the real world, of course, we cannot see into the future: there is risk. We can make educated guesses. We can decide how much grain to store over the season because we have a lot of information about how crops grow over the season. But there are random variations: there can be spates of good weather but also bad weather, infestations, floods, insects, and on. To account for these possibilities, especially the dire potential to use up all of the stored grain before the planting season begins, it makes sense to store a bit more grain in the silos as insurance.

We would like to quantify the decision process for insuring against risk so that the optimal decision can be mapped out, in the same spirit as with the grain storage model, that is, via an optimisation problem that we solve with calculus. As before, we need to develop some tools.

Brownian Motion

Robert Brown, a Scottish botanist, looked at pollen grains immersed in water under a microscope in 1827. You can see what he saw in this video: (Click for video). The reason for the movement of the grains in the video is the buffeting caused by the random motion of the water molecules in which they are suspended. (A question to ponder: What would the video look like if we raised the temperature of the water?)

Decades later, Louis Bachelier, a French mathematician, in his PhD thesis in 1900, hypothesized that stock market moved according to Brownian motion as well. We can motivate this insight very easily. If we view a stock as having a value that is determined by the integral of its discounted future profits — we already understand this from the growth model — then the only challenge is to correctly predict those profits. In a world with risk, that is not such an easy task: the traders who are buying and selling stocks are constantly uncovering new information about those future profit flows. When they receive new information, they do not announce it, but rather they attempt to exploit it by buying and selling the stock.

The result of those attempts to exploit information is that the stock price gets bid up or down in response to the purchases and sales. The prices are public knowledge in an open exchange, and so traders who do *not* have access to the new information might look at the price of the stock and attempt to predict its future movement so that they too can take advantage of it in trading.

A moment's thought establishes that this strategy — watching the pattern of prices and using to predict future prices, and concomitantly buying and selling so as to profit from them — cannot work: everyone will attempt it, given the vast sums that would accrue to success. Those attempts will bid the prices themselves up or down so that the predicted future prices then yield only normal and inconsequential returns. The pattern itself would be destroyed in the process, and what is left, the residual behaviour of stock prices, is entirely random. This is what Bachelier wanted to model.

The next step then is to characterise the random motion of prices in a technically concrete way. We begin with notation: Z_t denotes a random variable that evolves over time, that is, a stochastic process. The key characteristic of Z_t is that its *changes* over time are Gaussian (Normally distributed) with mean zero and variance dt, the increment of time over which we measure the change. Thus, dZ_t and dZ_s are Gaussian: $dZ_t \sim N(0, dt) \rightarrow E[dZ_t] = 0$, $E[dZ_t^2] = dt$.

The second key property is that the increments are independent:

$$\text{cov}(dZ_t, dZ_s) = \begin{cases} 0 & s \neq t \\ dt & s = t \end{cases}$$

And because they are independent, we can add them up with an integral, and the resulting object — Z_t — is also Gaussian (because the sum of Gaussians is Gaussian):

$$Z_t \equiv Z_0 + \int_0^t dZ_t$$

The process Z_t is called *Brownian motion* (named for Robert Brown).

We can figure out the mean and volatility of Z_t easily. First of all, we are adding up the increments — the dZ_ts — and the expected value of a sum is the sum of the expected values. So we can bring the expectation inside the integral. And then the expected value of each increment is zero — we assumed that. So, the whole integral is zero:

$$\begin{aligned} E[Z_t] &= Z_0 + E\left[\int_0^t dZ_s\right] \\ &= Z_0 + \int_0^t E[dZ_s] \\ &= Z_0 + \int_0^t 0 \\ &= Z_0 + 0 \end{aligned}$$

The variance of Z_t takes a little more work. The variance is the expected value of the square of the difference between Z_t and its mean. The square of the integral is the sum of all the cross products $dZ_s dZ_\tau$, where s and τ might not be the same. We again use the fact that the expectation of the sum is the sum of the expectations, so we integrate the expected value of all the cross products. But now we can bring in another rule: the expected value of a *product* is the product of the expectations if they are independent. But that's what we assumed. And the expectations are zero, so all of the cross products where t and s are different are zero. There is one exception however: when $s = \tau$, we assumed that $E[dZ_t^2] = dt$:

$$\begin{aligned}
\sigma_{Z_t}^2 &= E\left[\left(\int_0^t dZ_s - 0\right)^2\right] \\
&= E\left[\left(\int_0^t dZ_s\right)\left(\int_0^t dZ_\tau\right)\right] \\
&= E\left[\int_0^t dZ_s dZ_\tau\right] \\
&= \int_0^t E\left[dZ_s dZ_\tau\right] \\
&= \int_0^t E[dZ_s^2] \\
&= \int_0^t ds \\
&= t
\end{aligned}$$

The result is that we can fully characterise the distribution of Z_t: it is Gaussian but with a variance t, that is, the variance is not a constant:

$$Z_t \sim N(Z_0, t)$$

It seems intuitive that we could just carry on with Z_t like any other variable that changes over time, such as capital or consumption from our previous deterministic models. But that doesn't work: you cannot take the derivative of Z_t: it is too "crinkly," so it doesn't have a slope that we can define (see Figure 6.1). This means that if you want to do things like take a derivative and set it to zero in order to optimise something, it can't be done. We need a different set of tools.

Stochastic Differential Equations and Stochastic Calculus

There are two main steps in developing the tools we need for stochastic models. The first is to extend the idea of differential equations to the stochastic realm, and the second is to extend the idea of differentiation.

The extension of differential equations is stochastic differential equations. We generalise a differential equation by adding a stochastic process to the right-hand side of the equation, resulting in a stochastic differential equation, or diffusion process. (It is called a diffusion because the diffusion of molecules in a liquid or gas has this characteristic.)

The most basic diffusion would be the equation for the motion of a car but with a Brownian term added to it:

$$dX_t = adt + dZ_t$$

Note that we did not write the equation in the usual way: instead of

$$\frac{d}{dt}X_t = a$$

we write

$$dX_t = adt$$

and we are using the "dt" term as a regular algebraic object that multiplies other variables.

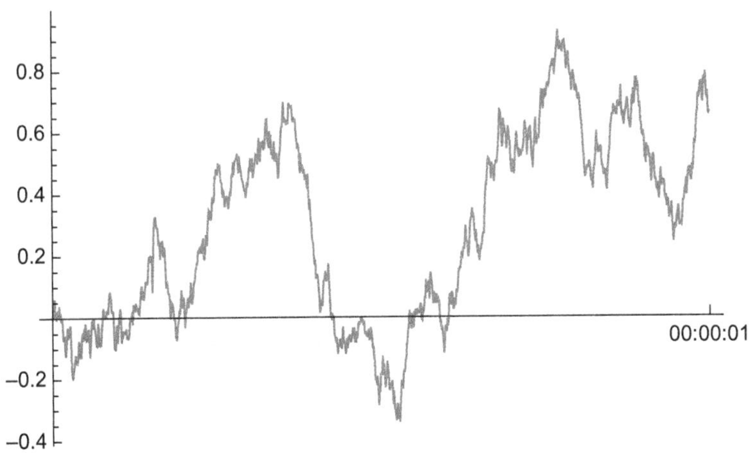

Figure 6.1. Z_t: Brownian path example.

We can write a general diffusion process as

$$dX_t = \mu(X_t, t)dt + \sigma(X_t, t)dZ_t.$$

This is a *stochastic differential equation*; $\mu(X_t, t)$ is called the *drift* and $\sigma(X_t, t)$ is the *volatility*. We can solve this equation: just integrate if (the drift and volatility are constants)

$$\begin{aligned} dX_t &= X_0 + \mu dt + \sigma dZ_t \\ \rightarrow X_t &= X_0 + \int_0^t \mu dt + \int_0^t \sigma dz_t \\ &= X_0 + \mu t + \sigma(Z_t - Z_0) \end{aligned}$$

In more complicated cases, you might be lucky, but, in general, this is the generalisation of ordinary differential equations and can be difficult to solve. But we are going to stick with examples that can, in fact, be solved, and fortunately these examples fit nicely with the economic situations we want to analyse.

Ito's Lemma

Even though we can't differentiate, we can still state the differential — that is the same thing in non-stochastic environments, but in stochastic environments they are different. The workhorse idea is Ito's lemma: if you take the differential of a function of a stochastic process that has its own stochastic differential equation, then you get another stochastic differential equation, and that new stochastic differential equation has a specific structure that looks sort of like the chain rule.

Theorem 6.1 (Ito's lemma). Let X_t be a diffusion process. Let f be a function of X_t, $f(X_t, t)$. Then $f(X_t, t)$ is also a stochastic process,

$$F_t \equiv f(X_t, t)$$

and F_t obeys the stochastic differential equation

$$dF_t = \left(f_t + \mu f_x + \frac{1}{2}\sigma^2 f_{xx}\right) dt + \sigma f_x dZ_t$$

It is in fact exactly the chain rule if we set the volatility to zero and eliminate the time dependence of F. With no volatility ($\sigma = 0$, so $dX_t = \mu dt$) and with F depending only on X_t, this just gives you the chain rule:

$$dF_t = \mu f_x dt$$

Divide by dt and you get the chain rule.

Aside on notation. In stochastic settings, we need to develop more nuanced notation. f_t is a derivative with respect to t, but X_t is a stochastic process at time t; for consistency, we distinguish between the process F_t and the function $f(X_t, t)$, with $F_t \equiv f(X_t, t)$.

Stochastic Differential Equation Examples

In our first example, we take a straight function of a pure Brownian motion process and determine its solution. Let

$$X_t = Z_t$$

so $\mu(X_t, t) = 0$ and $\sigma(X_t, t) = 1$. Define the function of X_t as the following exponential:

$$f(X_t, t) = F_t = F_0 e^{(\mu - \frac{1}{2}\sigma^2)t + \sigma Z_t}$$

We can verify that the conjectured solution is correct using Ito's lemma: write $F_t = f(X_t, t)$, where $X_t = Z_t$, that is,

$$dX_t = dZ_t$$

so $\mu(X_t, t) = 0$ and $\sigma(X_t, t) = 1$, and

$$F_t = f(X_t, t) \equiv Y_0 e^{(\mu - \frac{1}{2}\sigma^2)t + \sigma X_t}$$

Using Ito's lemma, we have

$$\begin{aligned} dF_t &= \left(f_t + \mu(X_t, t) f_x + \frac{1}{2}\sigma(X_t, t)^2 f_{xx}\right) dt + \sigma(X_t, t) f_x dZ_t \\ &= F_t \left(\left(\mu - \frac{1}{2}\sigma^2\right) + \sigma \times 0 + \frac{1}{2}(\sigma^2)\right) dt + F_t \sigma dZ_t \\ &= F_t(\mu dt + \sigma dZ_t) \end{aligned}$$

This is useful because we sometimes want to go the other way: starting with the stochastic differential equation $dF_t = F_t(\mu dt + \sigma dZ_t)$, we know that the solution is $F_0 e^{(\mu - \frac{1}{2}\sigma^2)t + \sigma Z_t}$.

Exercises

Exercise 6.1. Ito's lemma. Let

$$dY_t = \mu Y_t dt + \sigma Y_t dZ_t$$

The solution is

$$Y_t = Y_0 e^{(\mu - \frac{1}{2}\sigma^2)t + \sigma Z_t}$$

Re-verify the solution using Ito's lemma.

Exercise 6.2. Let

$$dX_t = \mu dt + \sigma dZ_t$$

Define the function

$$f(x,t) \equiv -e^{-\rho t} e^{Ax}$$

Characterise the process $F_t \equiv f(X_t, t)$ using Ito's lemma:

$$dF_t =$$

Exercise 6.3. Demonstrate that

$$E[e^{aZ_t}] = e^{\frac{1}{2}a^2 t}$$

where Z_t is a Brownian motion.
Hint: Take the expectation using the probability density explicitly and then complete the square.

Bonus Material

Non-rigorous derivation of Ito's lemma

Ito's lemma follows pretty intuitively from some familiar operations: the Taylor expansion and expected values. To begin, we remind ourselves that F_t is a function $f(X_t, t)$ of the process X_t that we know,

$dX_t = \mu dt + \sigma dZ_t$. Now take the Taylor expansion of f. As a reminder, the Taylor expansion of an abstract function f around a is

$$f(x) = f(a) + f'(a)(x-a) + \frac{f''(a)}{2!}(x-a)^2 + \frac{f'''(a)}{3!}(x-a)^3 + \cdots$$

$$2! = 2 = 2 \quad 3! = 3 \times 2 \times 1 = 6 \quad 4! = 4 \times 3 \times 2 \times 1 = 6 \quad \text{etc}$$

As an example, consider the Taylor expansion of the function $f(x) = x^2$:

$$\begin{aligned} f'(x) &= 2x \\ f''(x) &= 2 \\ f'''(x) &= 0 \end{aligned}$$

Expand around $a = 0$:

$$f(x) = 0 + 2 \times 0(x-0) + \frac{2}{2}(x-0)^2 + \frac{0}{6}(x-a)^3 + \frac{0}{24}(x-0)^4 + \cdots = x^2$$

Applying this to our function $F_t = f(X_t, t)$,

$$\begin{aligned} dF_t = f_t dt + \frac{1}{2}\left(f_{tt}dt^2 + f_x dX + f_{xt} dX dt + F_{xx} dX^2\right) \\ + \text{higher order terms} \end{aligned}$$

Now take the expectation of each differential term:

$$E[dt] = dt \quad E[dt^2] = 0$$

The dt^2 term approaches zero faster than dt; intuitively, $0.01^2 = 0.0001$, which is much smaller than 0.01; thus, and we only preserve terms that are "on the order of" dt.

To demonstrate Ito's lemma, dt and dZ_t will have the role of $(x-a)$. We only need the second and third terms:

$$\begin{aligned} f'(a)(x-a) &\sim f_t dt, f_x dX \\ \frac{f''(a)}{2!}(x-a)^2 &\sim f_{tt} dt^2, f_{xx} dX^2 \end{aligned}$$

The dX terms are as follows:

$$\begin{aligned} E[dX] &= E[\mu dt + \sigma dZ] = \mu dt + \sigma E[dZ] = \mu dt \\ E[dtdX] &= dtE[dX] = dt(E[\mu dt + \sigma dZ]) \\ &= dt(\mu dt + \sigma E[dZ]) = \mu dt^2 + \sigma E[dZ]dt) = 0 + 0 \\ E[dX^2] &= E[\mu^2 dt^2 + 2\mu\sigma dtdZ + \sigma^2 dZ^2] \\ &= \mu^2 dt^2 + 2\mu\sigma dtE[dZ] + \sigma^2 E[dZ^2]] = \sigma^2 dt \end{aligned}$$

A moment's thought results in the conclusion that following through on the "higher-order terms" in the Taylor expansion yields zero by this sort of algebra.

Gathering the results yields

$$\left(f_t + \mu f_x + \frac{1}{2}\sigma^2 f_{xx}\right) dt$$

This is not quite Ito's lemma — it is just the drift term.

Now we want to intuitively justify the volatility term $\sigma f_x dZ_t$. Consider the variance of df: square the Taylor expansion of f less the drift $dF_t - E[dF_t]$. Then, apply the same rules as above to the squared Taylor expansion. We end up with $\sigma^2 f_x^2 E[dZ^2] = \sigma^2 f_x^2 dt$ as the only surviving term in the expectation of $E[(dF_t - E[dF_t])^2]$.

Solving Ornstein–Uhlenbeck processes

An Ornstein–Uhlenbeck process has the form

$$dX_t = \mu X_t dt + \sigma dZ_t$$

where Z_t is a Brownian motion. The key aspect of the process is that the volatility is *not* multiplied by X_t as it would be in a geometric Brownian motion.

Define a new random variable

$$Y_t \equiv e^{-\mu t} X_t$$

The differential of this process is

$$dY_t = -\mu Y_t + e^{-\mu t} dX_t = -\mu e^{-\mu t} X_t + e^{-\mu t} dX_t = e^{-\mu t} \sigma dZ_t$$

because the drift terms cancel. Now integrate:

$$Y_t = Y_0 + \sigma \int_0^t e^{-\mu s} dZ_s$$

Now invert the change of variable:

$$X_t = e^{\mu t} X_0 + \sigma e^{\mu t} \int_0^t e^{-\mu s} dZ_s$$

Thus, we have an explicit solution for the process.

Solution with mean reversion

Suppose we have a mean-reverting process:

$$dX_t = \mu(\overline{X} - X_t)dt + \sigma dZ_t$$

so the drift is towards $\overline{X}$. The solution is

$$X_t = \overline{X} + (X_0 - \overline{X})e^{-\mu t} + \sigma e^{-\mu t} \int_0^t e^{\mu s} dZ_s$$

which is a generalisation of the basic Ornstein–Uhlenbeck process.

Solving stochastic differential equations with integrating factors

In this section, we show how to solve stochastic differential equations that have a particular structure. In our main discussions about stochastic differential equations, we noted that if an equation takes geometric form,

$$d\xi_t = \sigma \xi_t dZ_t$$

then it has an explicit solution,

$$\xi_t = e^{-\frac{1}{2}\sigma^2 t + \sigma Z_t} \tag{6.1}$$

It turns out that we can generalise this solution to cases with the following structure:

$$dX_t = \mu(X_t, t)dt + \sigma(t) X_t dZ_t$$

that is, where the volatility term still has the geometric structure but the drift can be more general. Note also that μ can be a function of time as well. As you might surmise there is a strategy that is very similar to the strategy of the Girsanov transformation that will enable us to explicitly solve the equation. The argument here is taken from the work of Rezaeyan and Baloui (2013).

The argument is simple: the solution for X_t is the product of two terms. The first term is a version of the formula in (6.1), and the second is the solution of an ordinary differential equation, for which explicit formulas exist.

To begin, posit that there are two artificial processes: F_t and G_t. The first is the artificial process

$$F_t = e^{\frac{1}{2}\sigma(t)^2 t - \sigma(t) Z_t}$$

that has the structure of (6.1) and has differential

$$dF_t = -\sigma(t) F dZ_t$$

that is, the sign is reversed.

The second is defined as a non-stochastic process, G_t, that is the product:

$$G_t = F_t X_t$$

We need to establish that G_t is, in fact, non-stochastic — we will do this in a minute. But let us pause for a second to note that this equation posits that we can soak up the stochastic part of X_t with the special function F_t.

Now take the differential of the product FX using Ito's lemma, using the ideas from the stochastic product rule that was part of the demonstration of the stochastic integration by parts formula from Appendix A:

$$\begin{aligned} dG_t = d(F_t X_t) &= F_t dX_t + X_t dF_t + dF_t dX_t \\ &= F_t \left(\mu(X_t, t)dt + \sigma(t) X_t dZ_t\right) - X_t \sigma(t) F_t dZ_t \\ &\quad - \sigma(t) X_t dZ_t \sigma(t) dZ_t \\ &= F_t \mu(X_t, t) dt \end{aligned}$$

The second and third terms cancel; this is where the assumption that the volatility of the X_t term is geometric becomes crucial. The final term disappears because our conjecture is that G_t is deterministic, so $\sigma_G = 0$.

Now restate the definition of G_t, yielding

$$X_t = F_t^{-1} G_t$$

This is the solution for X_t; all we have to do is fully flesh out the structure of G_t. But this can be done by writing

$$\frac{dG_t}{dt} = F_t \mu(X_t, t) = F_t \mu(F_t^{-1} G_t, t)$$

This is now an ordinary differential equation that has a known (although potentially very nonlinear) solution. With this solution in hand, we can substitute into $F_t^{-1} G_t$ and we have the solution for X_t. All of the stochastic structure has been folded into the F_t process; the rest can be handled with known methods.

It is also worth noting in passing that the F_t^{-1} factor is still stochastic — how can the G equation be an ordinary differential equation? The answer is we treat Z_t and therefore F_t as purely a function of time for the purposes of solving the ordinary differential equation for G_t.

As a strategic matter, if we start with an equation that does not have a geometric volatility term, it might be possible to reformulate the process so that this structure is followed. This is what Menoncin and Nembrini (2018) did in their stochastic growth model.

Transforming stochastic differential equations to achieve geometric volatility

In the previous section, we noted that an explicit solution can be found for a stochastic differential equation if the volatility term has geometric structure. There is no reason to expect this structure to hold generally but we can ask the following: is there a way to achieve the structure if we start with an arbitrary stochastic differential equation? The answer is yes, although there is another complication that may arise once we carry out the transformation — we will get to that at the end.

In the previous section, where we had

$$dX_t = \mu(X_t, t)dt + \sigma(t) X_t dZ_t$$

that is, the volatility separates into a volatility that is a function of time alone, and the coefficient X_t itself, so that the volatility has a geometric structure; we don't put restrictions on the drift $\mu(X_t, t)$, which can be a non-geometric function of X_t, for example, X_t^α or $\ln(X_t)$.

We want to be able to solve stochastic differential equations that have more general structure in the volatility as well:

$$dX_t = \mu(X_t, t)dt + \sigma(t)g(X_t)dZ_t$$

where $g(X_t)$ is not equal to X_t.

We can posit a transformed process, that is, a process $F_t = f(X_t)$ that is a function of X_t such that the transformed process has the geometric structure, that is,

$$dF_t = \mu_F(f(X_t), t)dt + \sigma_F(t)F_t dZ_t$$

and then solve it using the integrating factor method. To determine the function f, we can use Ito's lemma:

$$dF_t = (\mu(X_t, t)f'(X_t) + \frac{1}{2}\sigma(t)g(X_t)f''(X_t))dt + \sigma(t)g(X_t)f'(X_t)dZ_t$$

In order to achieve geometric structure, we require that the following condition holds:

$$f(X_t) = g(X_t)f'(X_t) \quad \rightarrow \quad f'(X_t) = \frac{f(X_t)}{g(X_t)}$$

This is an ordinary differential equation and therefore it has a known (although possibly very nonlinear) solution.

To solve for X_t, we then just compute the inverse of f:

$$X_t = f^{-1}(F_t)$$

This is where the extra complication might come: the inverse function f^{-1} might not be expressible in closed form. In the cases where it cannot be stated in closed form, you would use numerical methods to determine the solution for X_t.

Chapter 7

Stochastic Control

Stochastic Control

We're ready to talk about stochastic control. The main application will be how to choose an optimal portfolio when there is risk. We already saw that optimal consumption is not a trivial problem because you have to balance consumption now vs. consumption in the future in a nuanced way. With risk in the picture, you also have to balance consumption now against risk in the future.

The HJB Equation

We want to solve a problem like this,

$$\max_{\{a_t\}} E\left[\int_0^T f(a_t, X_t, t)dt\right] \tag{7.1}$$

subject to a law of motion for the state

$$dX_t = \mu(a_t, X_t, t)dt + \sigma(a_t, X_t, t)dZ_t \tag{7.2}$$

where we have some abstract objective, typically a utility function, that we want to optimise over some time span and taking the expected value.

Most of it is now familiar: the objective function and the integration. There is a constraint, but now we have to express it as a stochastic differential equation. We use notation to emphasise that the state variable is a stochastic process: X_t instead of x_t. The expected value is the other new wrinkle.

The drift and volatility functions, μ and σ, can be influenced by the state X_t and also by the control, a. As we saw in the earlier deterministic optimal control models, the control will typically be consumption.

This problem can be solved by solving the Hamilton–Jacobi–Bellman (HJB) equation — the same Hamilton as in the Hamiltonian:

$$-V_t = \max_a \left\{ f(a_t, X_t, t) + \mu(a_t, X_t, t)V_x + \frac{1}{2}\sigma(a_t, X_t, t)^2 V_{xx} \right\}$$

The HJB equation has derivatives of the function V, which did not appear in the statement of the problem in (7.1)–(7.2). This is the value function, and at this point, the agenda is to figure out V — it is an unknown function. The HJB equation is just a differential equation (a somewhat complicated one) that enables us to find V. Once we've done that, we can figure out the optimal action a and also characterise the evolution of the state variable X_t, as we see.

As with the Hamiltonian in the deterministic model, we have eliminated the integral, and in addition, we have also eliminated the stochastic term, Z_t. That means the derivatives in the HJB equation are the regular derivatives — we no longer need to worry about stochastic differential equations when solving the equation, although they will still show up later on.

The HJB equation is just Ito's lemma for *V*

To get the HJB equation, we can start by taking the differential of V using Ito's lemma:

$$\begin{aligned} dV = \max_a E\Bigg[& f(a, X_0, 0)dt + V(X_0, 0) \\ & + \left(V_t + \mu(a, X_0, 0)V_x + \frac{1}{2}\sigma(a, X_0, 0)^2 V_{xx} \right) dt + \sigma V_x dZ_t \Bigg] \end{aligned}$$

Then take the expected value. Since $E[dZ_t] = 0$, that term goes away and we are left with

$$0 = \max_a \left\{ f(a_t, X_t, t) + V_t + \mu(a_t, X_t, t)V_x + \frac{1}{2}\sigma(a_t, X_t, t)^2 V_{xx} \right\}$$

Now, bring the V_t term to the left-hand side and we have the HJB equation.

This derivation takes some shortcuts: specifically, (i) we did not explain why you should take the expected value after applying Ito's lemma, and (ii) why is it legitimate to carry along the maximisation operation with the Ito expansion? These questions require a bit more nuance, and this is covered in the Bonus Material at the end of the chapter.

Boundary conditions

In the discussion of differential equations, we took note that the statement of a differential equation is not enough to solve it: you also need some sort of boundary condition. In the differential equation for growth, you need to know the starting point before you can fully state where the equation will end up later at some time t. That is also the case for the HJB equation, and we will come back to this question.

Application: The Optimal Portfolio

Our first application of stochastic control is to choose an optimal portfolio, which is to say, choose optimal consumption, but now that there is risk, part of the decision-making process is how much risk to hold to buy a stock portfolio. As the first step, we can suppose that there are two assets: one is risky and the other is a bond.

The bond process

$$dB_t = rB_t dt$$

has no risk, and it will be an alternative investment beside the risky one. When we discussed investment in the deterministic model, there was only one asset, with an interest rate. The asset could be capital (goats, using the Robinson Crusoe story), where the owners get paid interest for lending them out. Note that we could write the bond process as a geometric growth differential equation, with growth rate r, since it has no risk.

There is also a risky stock with price process S_t which we describe by a stochastic differential equation:

$$dS_t = \mu S_t dt + \sigma S_t dZ_t$$

This is a special process: geometric Brownian motion, or GBM. We can write it as a rate of return, just as in the growth differential equation, except that the growth rate has a stochastic part:

$$\frac{dS_t}{S_t} = \mu dt + \sigma dZ_t$$

A key feature of this process is that because the rate of return has the stochastic part dZ_t, which has a Gaussian distribution, the rate of return can be negative. However, the process S_t itself cannot become negative; if it starts positive, it stays positive — although it can shrink to a level very close to zero if the return process is repeatedly negative.

It is also worth noting that (i) the drift μ can be considered a sort of average return and (ii) μ can be different from the bond rate of return r. Intuitively, it is going to make sense for μ to be bigger than r; higher average return will compensate for the risk that comes along with it via the σdZ_t term.

The consumer who is solving this problem is going to put a fraction of his wealth, which we index by α_t, into the risky asset and the remainder of his wealth, $1 - \alpha_t$, into the riskless bond; his portfolio consists of his holdings of the bond and the stock.

We can now formulate the portfolio optimisation problem as a stochastic control problem:

$$\max_{\{C_{(\cdot)}, \alpha_{(\cdot)}\}} E\left[\int_0^\infty e^{-\rho t} u(C_t) dt\right]$$

where wealth evolves according to

$$dW_t = \alpha_t W_t(\mu dt + \sigma dZ_t) + (1 - \alpha_t) W_t r dt - C_t dt$$

We again posit an infinitely lived individual solving the problem of optimising his discounted utility in expected value terms choosing both consumption c_t and also the portfolio share α_t and allowing both consumption and the portfolio share to vary over time. Wealth is going to evolve, driven by how much of the risky asset is held, and how much of the bond is held. We subtract off consumption again, noting as we have in our previous models, the growth model and the grain storage model, that we subtract consumption off from the state variable. This formulation of the problem was first posed by Merton (1971).

We can rearrange terms in the state equation, collecting the terms multiplying dt and the terms multiplying dZ_t:

$$dW_t = ((\alpha_t\mu + (1-\alpha_t)r)W_t - C_t)\,dt + \alpha_t W_t \sigma dZ_t$$

Note that this is all in proportional terms and so there's a W_t multiplying some of the terms, and that will turn out to help us to solve the model eventually.

We can now write down the corresponding Hamilton–Jacobi–Bellman equation, using the inputs that we saw a couple of paragraphs ago:

$$\rho V = \max_{\{c,\alpha\}} \left\{ u(c) + ((\alpha\mu + (1-\alpha)r)w - c)V_w + \frac{1}{2}(\alpha\sigma w)^2 V_{ww} \right\}$$

There's a detail on the left-hand side of the HJB equation: instead of $-V_t$, ρV appears. In fact, they are the same in this economic setting because of the discount factor $e^{-\rho t}$ in the objective. More detail is set out in the Bonus Material at the end of the chapter.

The other thing to remark about is the notation: instead of C_t, W_t, and so on, we have c and w. This is by way of emphasising that we want to determine the *function* $V(\cdot)$, and c, w, and α are, at this point, arbitrary variables that satisfy the optimality condition.

The optimisation problem is now straightforward: set the derivatives with respect to c and α to zero; these are the optimality conditions that we are familiar with for the deterministic control problem. Then we go in and start solving.

First of all, the optimality condition for consumption looks very familiar, involving the marginal utility of consumption:

$$u'(c) = V_w \tag{7.3}$$

This first derivative of V is going to be equivalent to a Lagrange multiplier eventually, and so this is actually a very familiar equation.

The optimality condition for α is new:

$$(\mu - r)wV_w + \alpha w^2\sigma^2 V_{ww} = 0$$

The solution for α is the product of two ratios, $\frac{\mu-r}{\sigma^2}$ and $\frac{V_w}{wV_{ww}}$:

$$\alpha = -\frac{\mu - r}{\sigma^2}\frac{V_w}{wV_{ww}}$$

The first ratio relates the average return of the risky asset that is in excess of the safe riskless rate of return, with the volatility, which is the parameter expressing the degree of risk. The second ratio is an elasticity: it expresses the percentage change in the value as a function of the percentage change in wealth. The product of the ratios can be interpreted as investment advice: keep a fraction of risky stocks in the portfolio, αW_t, with this fraction determined in part by the return to risk ratio $\frac{\mu-r}{\sigma^2}$.

The optimal portfolio with geometric utility

We can do an example by extending the geometric (CRRA) utility example that we explored in the deterministic growth model:

$$u(c) = \frac{1}{1-\gamma}c^{1-\gamma}$$

The geometric formulation has two advantages. The first advantage is that risk aversion is expressed by a single number, the constant relative risk aversion (CRRA) parameter, γ.

The second advantage is that the HJB equation can be solved explicitly, in closed form, just by making an educated guess. The guess is that the value function V has exactly the same form as utility function that we've seen before, except that W appears instead of C:

$$V(w) = \frac{B}{1-\gamma}w^{1-\gamma}$$

There is a constant, B, and we don't know what B is yet, but we're going to figure it out later.

We can easily take the derivatives V_w and V_{ww} of the guess for V and substitute into the solution we already worked out for the Merton portfolio problem:

$$-\frac{V_w}{wV_{ww}} = \frac{1-\gamma}{\gamma(1-\gamma)} = \frac{1}{\gamma}$$

$$\to \alpha = \frac{\mu - r}{\sigma}\frac{1}{\gamma\sigma}$$

The solution for α is again the product of two ratios. The first ratio is the net return to risk ratio, which is known as the Sharpe ratio. The second ratio, the elasticity, is simply the inverse of the product of the volatility with the risk aversion. As we already discovered when we used this utility function in the growth model, the risk aversion parameter expresses the curvature of the utility function, and thus the resistance to intertemporal substitution; increases in γ here *reduce* the risky portion of the portfolio.

Thus, the product of the ratios expresses how the individual optimising his portfolio relates his subjective distaste for risk, $\frac{1}{\sigma\gamma}$, against the price of risk as expressed in the market opportunities embodied in the Sharpe ratio, $\frac{\mu-r}{\sigma}$.

So, (i) the more risk averse you are, the less you hold of the risky asset; (ii) risk drives you away from risky assets, but (iii) return drives you to hold more.

Using this utility function and using the derivatives, we can then substitute into the HJB equation and end up with a somewhat complicated equation, but it has an interesting feature, that wherever there's a $w^{1-\gamma}$ term, it's the same everywhere after we consolidate terms like $ww^{-\gamma}$:

$$\rho\frac{B}{1-\gamma}w^{1-\gamma} - \frac{1}{1-\gamma}c^{1-\gamma} \\ + ((\alpha\mu + (1-\alpha)r)w - c)w^{-\gamma} - \frac{1}{2}(\alpha\sigma)^2\gamma w^{1-\gamma} \tag{7.4}$$

Consumption is also going to be solvable because of our guess of the form of the utility function. Consumption is the inverse of the u' function; u' is equal to V_w; we have a guess for V, so we can calculate the V_W:

$$\begin{aligned} c &= (u'(c))^{-\frac{1}{\gamma}} = (V_W)^{-\frac{1}{\gamma}} \\ &= B^{-\frac{1}{\gamma}}\left(w^{-\gamma}\right)^{-\frac{1}{\gamma}} = B^{-\frac{1}{\gamma}}w \end{aligned}$$

Substituting this solution into the HJB equation (7.4), it is apparent that we can then divide $W^{1-\gamma}$ from the equation, yielding an *algebraic* equation in B:

$$\rho\frac{B}{1-\gamma} = \frac{B^{-\frac{1-\gamma}{\gamma}}}{1-\gamma} + (\alpha\mu + (1-\alpha)r)B - B^{-\frac{1-\gamma}{\gamma}} - \frac{1}{2}(\alpha\sigma)^2\gamma B$$

Substituting the solution for α and simplifying, we obtain a solution for B:

$$B^{-\frac{1}{\gamma}} = \frac{\rho}{\gamma} - \frac{1-\gamma}{\gamma}\left(r + \frac{1}{2}\frac{(\mu - r)^2}{\gamma\sigma^2}\right) \tag{7.5}$$

Remember that we pointed out that the solution for the portfolio risky asset share α was the product of two ratios, one of which is the Sharpe ratio $\frac{\mu - r}{\sigma}$, expressing the *market* price of risk. How does this market work? That is the subject of the following chapter.

Exercises

Exercise 7.1. Consider the Merton portfolio model.

(i) What does it mean if $\mu < r$? What happens?

Exercise 7.2. Art lovers' optimal portfolio. An individual solves an optimal portfolio problem as follows:

$$\max_{\{\alpha(\cdot)\}} E\left[\int_0^\infty e^{-\rho t}\frac{W_t^{1-\gamma}}{1-\gamma}dt\right]$$

where his wealth evolves according to

$$dW_t = W_t(\alpha_t(\mu dt + \sigma dZ_t) + (1 - \alpha_t)rdt)$$

Note that c_t does not appear in the utility function or on the right-hand side of the wealth equation.

(i) Write down the consolidated wealth process dW_t.
(ii) Write down the HJB equation.
(iii) State the optimality condition for the portfolio holding α.
(iv) Conjecture a form for V, and also state the derivatives V_w and V_{ww} for the conjectured form. Your conjecture might have one or more constants; because this is an exam, I do not expect you to solve for the constant(s) — just carry them forward to this and later questions in abstract form:

$$V(w) =$$
$$V_w =$$
$$V_{ww} =$$

(v) State the solution for the optimal holding of the risky asset α using the conjectured form (leaving the unknown constant(s) undetermined for now).
(vi) Substitute the conjectured form of the value function V into the HJB equation, along with the actual utility function and simplify (but again you do not need to solve for the abstract constant(s)).

Exercise 7.3. Art lovers' optimal portfolio with exponential utility.

- Let the price of a stock change according to the equation

$$dS_t = \mu dt + \sigma dZ_t$$

  Note that S_t does not appear on the right-hand side, so this is not a returns equation.
- A riskless bond grows as interest rate r:

$$dB_t = rB_t dt$$

- Define the utility function

$$u(w) = \frac{1 - e^{-\gamma w}}{\gamma} \to u'(w) = e^{-\gamma w}$$

  where γ is a measure of risk aversion. Note that the utility function is a function of wealth w rather than consumption. One can think of this as a person who holds their wealth in the form of valuable paintings and whose consumption consists of looking at the paintings.

An individual solves an optimal portfolio problem, that is, he chooses the holdings of the risky asset α to solve

$$\max_{\{\alpha(\cdot)\}} E\left[\int_0^\infty e^{-\rho t} u(W_t) dt\right]$$

where his wealth evolves according to

$$dW_t = \alpha_t(\mu dt + \sigma dZ_t) + (1 - \alpha_t) r dt$$

Note that

- W_t does not appear on the right-hand side.
- c does not appear on the right-hand side.

(i) Write down the consolidated wealth process dW_t.
(ii) Write down the HJB equation. Don't substitute the utility function yet.
(iii) State the optimality condition for the portfolio holding α.
(iv) Conjecture a form for V, and also state the derivatives V_w and V_{ww} for the conjectured form. Your conjecture might have one or more constants that are determined later.
(v) State the solution for the optimal holding of the risky asset α using the conjectured form (leaving the unknown constants undetermined for now).
(vi) Substitute the conjectured form of the value function V into the HJB equation, along with the actual utility function.
(vii) Solve for the constants. Gather the constant terms and the coefficients of $e^{-\gamma w}$ to generate two equations.

Exercise 7.4. An individual solves an optimal portfolio problem as follows:

$$\max_{\{\alpha(\cdot)\}} E\left[\int_0^\infty e^{-\rho t}\ln(\gamma W_t)dt\right]$$

where his wealth evolves according to

$$dW_t = W_t(\alpha_t(\mu dt + \sigma dZ_t) + (1-\alpha_t)r dt)$$

Note that c_t does not appear in the utility function or on the right-hand side of the wealth equation.

Repeat the steps of Exercise 7.3.

Exercise 7.5. An individual solves an optimal portfolio problem as follows:

$$\max_{\{\alpha(\cdot)\}} E\left[\int_0^\infty e^{-\rho t}\left(-\frac{1}{2}(-W_t)^2\right)dt\right]$$

where his wealth evolves according to

$$dW_t = W_t(\alpha_t(\mu dt + \sigma dZ_t) + (1 - \alpha_t)rdt)$$

Note that consumption c_t does not appear in the utility function or on the right-hand side of the wealth equation.

Repeat the steps of Exercise 7.3.

Bonus Material

Details of the HJB derivation

To get the HJB equation Hamilton–Jacobi–Bellman equation, we use the strategy of taking the original object and chopping it into pieces and then taking expectations of those pieces; when you're done with that process, you use Ito's lemma.

Chop the objective into a current part and a future part:

$$\begin{aligned} V(X_0, 0) &= \max_a E \int_0^T f(a, X_t, t)dt \\ &= \max_a E \int_0^{\boxed{dt}} f(a, X_s, s)ds + \max_a E \int_{\boxed{dt}}^T f(a, X_s, s)ds \\ &\approx \max_a E \left(f(a, X_0, 0)dt + V(X_{\boxed{dt}}, dt) \right) \end{aligned}$$

- In the second line, the first integral is approximated by the product $f(a, X_0, 0)dt$.

You end up with a drift term involving V, but we still don't know what V is.

We could expand the future value $V(x_{dt}, dt)$, but it is easier just to use Ito's lemma:

$$V\left(X_{\boxed{dt}}, dt\right) = V(x_0, 0) + dV_0$$

Using Ito's lemma, the optimisation problem then becomes

$$\begin{aligned} V(x_0,0) &= \max_a E\left[f(a,X_0,0)dt + V(X_0,0) + dV_t\right] \\ &= \max_a E\Bigg[f(a,X_0,0)dt + V(X_0,0) \\ &\quad + \left(V_t + \mu(a,X_0,0)V_x + \frac{1}{2}\sigma(a,X_0,0)^2 V_{xx}\right)dt + \sigma V_x dZ_t\Bigg] \end{aligned}$$

We can simplify this equation:

(i) The $V(X_0,0)$ terms subtract out.
(ii) The expectation $E[\sigma V_x dZ_t] = 0$.
(iii) We can divide by dt, leaving the HJB equation.

This reasoning works for any time t, not just $t = 0$.

How to go from $-V_t$ to ρV

In the main text, it was asserted that the left-hand side of the HJB equation for the portfolio problem was ρV, not the time derivative $-V_t$. Here is the proof.

Lemma 1.

$$-V_t = \rho V$$

Proof. Begin by positing that the value function V has a form similar to the utility function form *including the discounting*:

$$e^{-\rho t}V(w)$$

Now calculate V_t:

$$-\rho e^{-\rho t}V(w)$$

Now e^{-rt} multiplies every term in the HJB equation:

$$\begin{aligned} \rho e^{-\rho t}V &= \max_{\{c,\alpha\}} e^{-\rho t}u(c) \\ &\quad + ((\alpha\mu + (1-\alpha)r)w - c)e^{-\rho t}V_w + \frac{1}{2}(\alpha\sigma w)^2 e^{-\rho t}V_{ww} \end{aligned} \tag{7.6}$$

and it divides out. □

Standard economics problems with discounting have this property.

A reminder about elasticity

We saw that the optimal fraction of the risky asset in the portfolio, α, was driven by two terms: the return to risk ratio $\frac{\mu-r}{\sigma^2}\frac{V_w}{wV_{ww}}$ and the elasticity term $\frac{V_w}{wV_{ww}}$. It is helpful to remind ourselves why the elasticity term takes this form. Remembering that we could express the ratio $\frac{\dot{x}}{x}$ as $\frac{d\ln(x)}{dt}$, we can write this as

$$\frac{d\ln(w)}{d\ln(V_w)} = \frac{\frac{dw}{w}}{\frac{V_{ww}dw}{V_w}} = \frac{\frac{1}{w}}{\frac{V_{ww}}{V_w}}$$

which is the inverse of the elasticity expressing the percent change in the value relative to the percent change in wealth w.

Chapter 8

Equilibrium

The solution of the optimal portfolio problem is a value function, with α giving the percentage or fraction of assets in the risky asset. In this chapter, we want to specialise this as follows: to state and solve the stochastic control problem for the whole economy, and the attendant elements of the model.

Equilibrium with a Representative Agent

We call the economy-as-a-whole approach the representative agent economy, in which every individual is going to solve the same stochastic control problem, the optimal portfolio problem that we already have in hand. But because it is the whole economy, the economy has to hold all of the risky assets that exist and none of the bonds; it can hold none of the bonds if all individuals are identical as with Robinson Crusoe in our deterministic control model. There is no one to sell you a bond, if you want to buy a bond, that is, there's no one to borrow from you, because everyone else is in the same boat, also attempting to buy. Equivalently, if you want to lend, no one wants to borrow at the interest rate you are offering.

To express this situation, we can specialise our model by adjusting the interest rate so that the representative individual decides on his own to hold only the risky asset and none of the bonds.

The interest rate that we adjust is the risk-free rate, which is the bond interest rate: we have to move it downwards to make bonds unattractive. We have a starting point for this adjustment: in the growth model, we saw that capital grows towards the steady state, so the steady state is a reasonable benchmark, and at the steady state, the interest rate equalled the subjective rate of time discount, ρ. So intuitively, this is the starting benchmark interest rate and we need to go below it.

The tree economy

It is helpful to think of the economy in terms of a story, similar in spirit to the Robinson Crusoe story: the "tree" economy of Lucas.[1]

The economy has trees that exogenously produce physical dividends — fruit — that stochastically fluctuate. There are firms that own the trees, very much in the vein of the firms that operated the goat farms in the Robinson Crusoe economy. However, there is no production, so consumption must equal the dividends that are paid to the shareholders. We can then price assets with the pricing induced by the intertemporal marginal rates of substitution induced by the resulting consumption pattern.

The riskless asset must be in zero net supply, so we must establish the condition that will ensure that only the risky asset is held by the representative agent in equilibrium. In the notation of the model, $\alpha = 1$ must hold:

$$\alpha = \frac{\mu - r}{\gamma\sigma^2} = 1$$

Now, we can do a search for a risk-free rate, that is, the bond interest rate, that is so low that nobody wants to hold the bonds because it's not remunerative enough. Once we find that interest rate, we can say we have an equilibrium: not just an optimum where people have chosen the optimal portfolio but an equilibrium where the interest rates dictate that people hold such a portfolio.

If we impose this idea, then we get that the expected rate of return on the risky asset has to obey a certain rule: $\alpha = 1$ requires that the return on the risky asset satisfies

$$\mu = r + \gamma\sigma^2 \tag{8.1}$$

---

[1]See the work of Lucas (1978). Stokey *et al.* (1989), p. 300, also set out a discrete-time version of the model.

With this restriction, μ has to be the risk-free rate plus what's called a risk premium, which is a product of γ and σ^2, and so we capture the interaction of risk aversion and actual risk by σ in that term.

This is something that we have the potential to test empirically. We can observe the risk-free rate r if we're willing to accept very low-risk bonds as the exemplar of the risk-free rate, such as the interest on US Treasury securities. And we can observe σ^2 because if we think of this as the economy as a whole, holding the risky portfolio, we can just look for an actual risky portfolio that is that resembles it. There is such a portfolio, to a rough approximation: the S&P500, which is traded on the New York Stock Exchange. The index has 500 stocks in it, designed to be as inclusive as possible for companies, representing the economy as a whole.

We can estimate σ^2 by estimating the variance of the returns on the risky portfolio as represented by the S&P500. The estimation of γ is a little harder. You can't observe γ directly, but later in the book we circle back and talk about how to estimate γ as well. In a preview of that discussion, there is a huge literature observing that the empirical rate of return on stocks seems to be quite big relative to what the model, when calibrated with reasonable values for the parameters, would predict.

When we set $\alpha = 1$, we can then simplify the elements of the model that we've already discussed and, in particular, we can simplify the formula for B; if we do a little bit of algebra, then we end up with answering the question that we didn't actually answer yet, which is as follows: What risk-free rate do we need to deter people from holding the riskless bond?

Deriving the value of the risk-free rate

Since the riskless asset must be in zero net supply, we must establish the condition that ensures that only the risky asset is held by the representative agent in equilibrium. In the notation of the model, $\alpha = 1$ must hold:

$$\alpha = \frac{\mu - r}{\gamma\sigma^2} = 1$$

This is assured by the following expected return on the risky asset:

$$\mu = r + \gamma\sigma^2 \tag{8.2}$$

The excess return over the risk-free rate, $\gamma\sigma^2$, is the *risk premium* — note that it is proportional to both risk and risk aversion.

With $\alpha = 1$, we can solve for the stochastic process of wealth, which is the same as the stock of capital in the economy:

$$dW_t = (\mu W_t - C_t)dt + \sigma W_t dz_t$$

Substituting from the solution for consumption,

$$C_t = B^{-\frac{1}{\gamma}} W_t$$

we obtain

$$\frac{dW_t}{W_t} = (\mu - B^{-\frac{1}{\gamma}})dt + \sigma dZ_t$$

Thus, the drift is reduced by consumption.

For consumption to equal expected income from the portfolio — that is, the representative agent consumes all the fruit — it requires

$$C_t = \mu W_t$$

In that case,

$$\mu = B^{-\frac{1}{\gamma}}$$

Substituting into the equilibrium wealth process,

$$\frac{dW_t}{W_t} = (\mu - \mu)dt + \sigma dZ_t = \sigma dZ_t$$

eliminating the drift, so wealth grows purely at a random rate — there is no systematic wealth accumulation.

In that case, we can compute the risk-free rate: substituting into the equation for $B^{-\frac{1}{\gamma}}$ from equation (7.5) and remembering that we have the assumption $\alpha = \frac{(\mu - r)}{\gamma\sigma^2} = 1$:

$$\mu = \frac{\rho}{\gamma} - \frac{1-\gamma}{\gamma}\left(r + \frac{1}{2}\frac{(\mu - r)^2}{\gamma\sigma^2}\right) = \frac{\rho}{\gamma} - \frac{1-\gamma}{\gamma}\left(r + \frac{1}{2}\gamma\sigma^2\right)$$

We also have continued the assumption that $\mu = r + \gamma\sigma^2$, so substituting this on the left-hand side yields

$$r + \gamma\sigma^2 = \frac{\rho}{\gamma} - \frac{1-\gamma}{\gamma}\left(r + \frac{1}{2}\gamma\sigma^2\right)$$

yielding

$$\boxed{r = \rho - \frac{1}{2}(1+\gamma)\gamma\sigma^2} \tag{8.3}$$

Thus, increased risk aversion induces an increased desire for safe bonds, but to deter this extra demand for bonds, the riskless rate must be reduced so that net bond holdings are zero. And so, risk aversion induces a desire for safe bonds, but you can deter the holding of those bonds by pushing the risk-free rate much lower than ρ.

So, in equilibrium, we have the formula for the risk-free rate, equation (8.3), and

$$\begin{aligned} \alpha = 1 &\implies \mu = r + \gamma\sigma^2 \\ &\implies \boxed{\frac{\mu - r}{\sigma} = \gamma\sigma} \quad \text{Hub's equation} \end{aligned} \tag{8.4}$$

The Sharpe ratio is therefore related to this product $\gamma\sigma$. This is so central to our subsequent agenda that we have given the equation a name: Hub's equation.

Additional implications for consumption and growth. We can also characterise consumption and growth in the representative agent economy. Recall the solution for consumption:

$$C_t = B^{-\frac{1}{\gamma}} W_t$$

Substituting for the solution of α, μ, and the risk-free rate in equilibrium into the solution for $B^{\frac{1}{\gamma}}$ in the HJB equation (7.5),

$$\begin{aligned} B^{-\frac{1}{\gamma}} &= \frac{\rho}{\gamma} - \frac{1-\gamma}{\gamma}\left(r + \frac{1}{2}\frac{(\mu - r)^2}{\gamma\sigma^2}\right) \\ &= \frac{\rho}{\gamma} - \frac{1-\gamma}{\gamma}\left(r + \frac{1}{2}\frac{(\gamma\sigma^2)^2}{\gamma\sigma^2}\right) \end{aligned}$$

$$
\begin{aligned}
&= \frac{\rho}{\gamma} - \frac{1-\gamma}{\gamma}\left(r + \frac{1}{2}\gamma\sigma^2\right) \\
&= \frac{\rho}{\gamma} - \frac{1-\gamma}{\gamma}\left(\rho - \frac{1}{2}\gamma\sigma^2 + \frac{1}{2}\gamma\sigma^2 - \frac{1}{2}\gamma^2\sigma^2\right) \\
&= \frac{\rho}{\gamma} - \frac{1-\gamma}{\gamma}\left(\rho - \frac{1}{2}\gamma^2\sigma^2\right) \\
&= \rho + \frac{1}{2}\gamma(1-\gamma)\sigma^2
\end{aligned}
$$

Thus, in equilibrium, consumption is

$$
C_t = \left(\rho + \frac{1}{2}\gamma(1-\gamma)\sigma^2\right) W_t
$$

This is very similar to the steady state consumption in the growth model. There, we found (for CRRA utility and for geometric production with $f(K) = \frac{k^\alpha}{\alpha}$) that

$$
c = \rho \frac{\overline{k}^\alpha}{\alpha}
$$

In the model we have developed here, we have implicitly assumed linear production — the productivity parameter $\alpha = 1$ — so in the absence of risk, we have an exact match with the deterministic growth model.

Exercises

Exercise 8.1 (Continuation of Exercise 7.2).

(vii) Write down the W_t process under the assumption that $\alpha = 1$.

Exercise 8.2 (Continuation of Exercise 7.3).

(vii) Write down the W_t process under the assumption that $\alpha = 1$.

Exercise 8.3 (Continuation of Exercise 7.4).

(vii) Write down the W_t process under the assumption that $\alpha = 1$.

Exercise 8.4 (Continuation of Exercise 7.5).

(vii) Write down the W_t process under the assumption that $\alpha = 1$.

Chapter 9

The Capital Asset Pricing Model

There is no alpha. Only beta. — Yoda

We covered the optimal portfolio problem in general equilibrium and uncovered the equilibrium interest rate with risk, and we have an actual formula for it. Now, we're ready to do the Girsanov theorem, the risk-neutral measure, and the capital asset pricing model.

The Measure Associated with a Process

We start with a now-familiar setting: we suppose that there is a risky stock that has the price process S_t, described by the same equation we saw previously, except we're now specialising S_t to be the market portfolio.[1] We base this on our discussion of the general equilibrium portfolio model, where we have an equilibrium interest rate for the risky asset and an equilibrium riskless rate of return, r, as well. The market portfolio process is

$$dS_t = S_t(\mu_M dt + \sigma_M dZ_t)$$

We can now identify the portfolio that we're talking about as the market portfolio — the portfolio for the whole economy. But we're

[1]This chapter draws extensively from a passage in the work of Ewald and Taub (2022).

going to suppose that there is another asset, such as a single stock, which is not the market portfolio but which might be a constituent of it that we consider separately. We call the price of this stock X_t:

$$dX_t = X_t(\mu_X dt + \sigma_X dZ_t)$$

It has the same geometric structure as the S_t process but possibly different values for its drift μ_X and for its volatility σ_X.

We want to be able to value the stock at some arbitrary time and we're going to discount the stock, according to this formula for some future time τ, which is some distance ahead of this time t given where X_t is at the moment:

$$V(x) = E[e^{-r(\tau-t)}X_\tau | X_t = x]$$

To do this in general would be quite difficult, however, we are going to be able to help with this process by undertaking the so-called Girsanov transformation, otherwise known as a measure change.

To begin, have another look at Figure 6.1. By looking at this picture, can you tell what the drift of that process is? You actually cannot: it's possible that more than one drift generated this picture same volatility, but you can't go backwards and figure it out from the picture. This reflects a property that is more general; we can rationalise different drifts for that process by adjusting the measure.

Suppose that we have a stochastic process where instead of $\frac{dX_t}{X_t}$ equals this right-hand side, we're just going to start with dX_t, so this is what you could call a level process:

$$dX_t = \mu_X dt + \sigma_X dZ_t$$

Before proceeding further, we need the concept of a *measure*. Due to the assumption that Z_t is normal (AKA Gaussian) $\mathcal{N}(0, t)$, there is a probability density function, the normal density, which has an associated cumulative normal cumulative distribution function. We are going to label this cumulative distribution function as $\mathbb{P}$ but refer to it as the $\mathbb{P}$ *measure*. Thus, measure is just a fancy word for probability distribution, and later on we see that $d\mathbb{P}$ is the notation for the probability density.

If we integrate the level process X_t, that is, take its expectation using that probability measure, in the case of the level process, we obtain

$$X_t = \mu_X t + \sigma_X Z_t.$$

Remember that we assume that Z_t — the stochastic part of this equation — is Gaussian with zero and mean and variance t. There's an associated probability density function that we're going to identify and the associated probability distribution function or cumulative distribution function.

Eliminating the drift: Girsanov transformation

Let's start out with just the practical use of Girsanov's theorem or the measure change: it enables you to alter the drift of the stochastic process.

For our level process X_t from the previous paragraphs, define a new Z-process, Z_t^*. The Z_t^* process is the old Z_t process, plus the mean divided by the volatility times t. As an example we can convert the drift of X_t to zero:

$$\begin{aligned} Z_t^* &= Z_t + \frac{\mu}{\sigma} t \\ \implies X_t &= \mu t + \sigma \left(Z_t^* - \frac{\mu}{\sigma} t \right) = \sigma Z_t^* \end{aligned}$$

Now go back to our earlier equation for X_t and substitute Z_t using the formula relating Z_t and Z_t^*. We have σ times Z_t^*, and then we subtract off σ times the ratio; after cancellations the drift has been eliminated. This is a completely legal operation: we haven't fundamentally altered the stochastic process — it is the same process — we are just altering the direction from which we look at the process.

This might seem a bit strange: we can just decide that we don't like the drift and eliminate it. But actually we have to balance this with an additional change.

Risk-Neutral Measure

By converting from Z_t to Z_t^*, we also at the same time change the measure $\mathbb{P}$ to something else which we're going to call $\mathbb{Q}$, which we refer to as the $\mathbb{Q}$ measure. This conversion to $\mathbb{Q}$ has to be done to legalise the alteration of the drift that we've done up to here, but it can stay in the background; we don't have to actually make it very explicit, although we start to do that in subsequent chapters. The first step in this so-called measure change operation or the application of Girsanov's theorem is that we do this substitution and eliminate or alter the drift.

We can note in passing that if there is no drift, then X_t becomes a martingale, which is to say that its expected value in the future is the same as its actual value today:

$$E[X_t] = X_0 + \sigma E[Z_t^*] = X_0$$

under $\mathbb{Q}$.

We can do the same thing if there's a geometric diffusion and that's of interest to us because we've been expressing stochastic processes in our portfolio models in terms of these geometric diffusions where it's $\frac{dY_t}{Y_t}$, instead of just dY_t equals the right-hand side, and we saw in an earlier chapter that we can actually solve for Y_t.

Summary

- We can construct a new measure, $\mathbb{Q}$, so that Z_t^* is normal $\mathcal{N}(0, t)$ under $\mathbb{Q}$.
- By converting Z_t to Z_t^* and $\mathbb{P}$ to $\mathbb{Q}$ simultaneously we've converted X_t into a driftless process under $\mathbb{Q}$; that also makes X_t a martingale under $\mathbb{Q}$.

Measure change for the stock price process S_t

Recall this ratio

$$\theta \equiv \frac{\mu_M - r}{\sigma_M},$$

the Sharpe ratio for the market, that we discussed in the previous chapter, where we remind ourselves that the drift μ_M and volatility σ_M are for the whole market; we denote it by θ.

If we mechanically replace dZ_t by the equivalent process dZ_t^* under the $\mathbb{Q}$ probability measure,

$$Z_t^* = Z_t + \frac{\mu - r}{\sigma}t$$

then

$$
\begin{aligned}
dS_t &= S_t(\mu_M dt + \sigma_M(dZ_t^* - \theta dt)) \\
&= S_t((\mu_M - \sigma_M\theta)dt + \sigma_M)dZ_t^*) \\
&= S_t(rdt + \sigma_M dZ_t^*)
\end{aligned}
$$

redefining Z_t, generating Z_t^* but using θ instead of $\frac{\mu_X}{\sigma_X}$. We end up with a geometric Brownian motion or geometric diffusion but which has drift rX_t rather than zero drift.

The discounted *market* portfolio price process $e^{-r(T-t)}S_t$ is a martingale under the $\mathbb{Q}$ measure. Using Ito's lemma,

$$
\begin{aligned}
de^{-rt}S_t &= -re^{-rt}S_t + e^{-rt}dS_t \\
&= -re^{-rt}S_t dt + e^{-rt}(rS_t dt + \sigma_M S_t dZ_t^*) \\
&= e^{-rt}\sigma_M S_t dZ_t^*
\end{aligned}
$$

Thus, if you pre multiply S_t by e^{-rt}, you get a martingale — a process with zero drift — but S_t itself is not a martingale.

What happens if we do the same thing to X_t, the single stock we are analysing? θ was defined as ratio $\frac{\mu_M - r}{\sigma_M}$, but where the drift and volatility μ_M and σ_M are for the market portfolio. If we substitute for dZ_t as before, what we end up with doesn't have a cancellation, in general, because μ_X and σ_X aren't necessarily the same as μ_M and σ_M.

The dynamics of X_t under the measure $\mathbb{Q}$ is given by

$$
\begin{aligned}
dX_t &= X_t(\mu_X dt + \sigma_X(dZ_t^* - \theta dt)) \\
&= X_t((\mu_X - \sigma_X\theta)dt + \sigma_X)dZ_t^*)
\end{aligned}
\tag{9.1}
$$

While μ_X and μ_S, and σ_X and σ_M, are not assumed to be identical in general, if their ratios are the same, that is if they have the same Sharpe ratios, then you do get something to happen. In particular, when you do this measure change operation where you exchange Z_t for Z_t^*, the cancellation that we developed in the previous paragraphs does take place, and, after multiplying by e^{-rt}, you end up with the drift of zero.

Thus, the new drift term is equal to r only if

$$\frac{\mu_X - r}{\sigma_X} = \frac{\mu_M - r}{\sigma_M}$$

To see this, calculate the drift:

$$\begin{aligned}\mu_X - \sigma_X\theta &= \mu_X - \sigma_X\frac{\mu_M - r}{\sigma_M} \\ &= \mu_X - \sigma_X\frac{\mu_X - r}{\sigma_X} = r\end{aligned}$$

So, we don't need equality between the drift and the volatility between a particular stock X in the market, but we do need the Sharpe ratio to be the same in order to get that same drift as the risk-free rate.

As the next step we suppose that we have some function $V(\cdot)$ of that stock X_t, and we're going to impose the requirement that V_t is a martingale under $\mathbb{Q}$, that is, under this new measure it has drift r. We're going to see what happens with the function as we characterise it using Ito's lemma and other tools.

Note that we want V to be some generalised function of X_t, but because it's general, it could just be X_t itself. But to keep track of things, we can call it V_t, remembering that the letter V is suggestive of the value function as we saw in our earlier developments, so it could come from V being the value function for some optimisation problem, but we're leaving the optimisation problem in the background for the moment.

We require that V_t have drift r under the $\mathbb{Q}$ measure (because we are obeying the ratio condition $\frac{\mu_X - r}{\sigma_X} = \frac{\mu_M - r}{\sigma_M}$). So, the expected value of dV_t under the $\mathbb{Q}$ measure is

$$E_t^{\mathbb{Q}}[dV_t] = rV\,dt$$

We can expand dV_t using Ito's lemma:

$$E_t^{\mathbb{Q}}[dV_t] = \left((\mu_X - \sigma_X\theta)xV_x + \frac{1}{2}\sigma_X^2x^2V_{xx}\right)dt$$

(Since V is a function of X_t, but not of time t, there is no $\frac{\partial V}{\partial t}$ term in this application of Ito's lemma.)

Using $\frac{\mu_X - r}{\sigma_X} = \frac{\mu_M - r}{\sigma_M}$,

$$\begin{aligned} (\mu_X - \sigma_X\theta)xV_x + \frac{1}{2}\sigma_X^2 x^2 V_{xx} &= rV \\ \rightarrow \quad \mu_X x V_x + \frac{1}{2}\sigma_X^2 x^2 V_{xx} &= rV + \sigma_X \theta x V_x \end{aligned} \tag{9.2}$$

Equating the drift that we get under Ito's lemma with the right-hand side, we get this relationship involving the derivatives of V_t and rV.

The CAPM

Apply Ito under $\mathbb{P}$ rather than $\mathbb{Q}$:

$$E_t^{\mathbb{P}}[dV_t] = \left(\mu_X x V_x t + \frac{1}{2}\sigma_X^2 x^2 V_{xx}\right) dt$$

Now, substitute dV_t under $\mathbb{P}$ into the right-hand side of dV_t under $\mathbb{Q}$ from (9.2), yielding

$$E_t^{\mathbb{P}}[dV_t] = (rV + \sigma_X \theta x V_x)dt$$

Under the $\mathbb{P}$ measure, we get this drift, which is different from the drift under the $\mathbb{Q}$ measure.

Next, divide the combined equation by V and also substitute the definition of θ:

$$\mathbb{E}_t^{\mathbb{P}}\left(\frac{dV}{V}\right) = \left(r + \frac{V_x X \sigma_X}{V \sigma_M}(\mu_M - r)\right) dt \tag{9.3}$$

And so when we do some algebraic manipulation, dividing by V in particular, we get that $\frac{dV}{V}$ in expectation, which is the expected return of V for the stock, is the risk-free rate plus this coefficient times the excess return $\mu_M - r$ for the market portfolio.

This formula is very suggestive: it says the expected return is the risk-free rate plus some coefficient times the excess return. We have seen the CAPM before, and this is exactly what's going on, so let's make that explicit. We get the capital asset pricing model out of this equation. (See the Bonus Material for further development.)

Beta

We can give the ratio $\frac{V_x X \sigma_X}{V \sigma_M}$ a name, beta ("β"), and it is actually the beta from the capital asset pricing model. What it says is that the return on any asset, which we have labeled V here, is the risk-free rate plus beta times the excess return over the risk-free rate of the market.

When you see the capital asset pricing model in a more standard setting, you see the ratio of the covariance to the variance; this is actually a regression coefficient of the return of the stock on the market stock and the riskiness of that stock can then be indexed by β.

No arbitrage

The next thing to say is that the relationship (9.3) has to hold for all stocks in equilibrium. That is to say, all stocks must in the end obey the relationship which we actually assumed for V, that their Sharpe ratios are the same as the market Sharpe ratio. If that does not hold, then arbitrage would be possible.

To understand the arbitrage argument it helps to tell a couple of stories.

In the first story, you could go to a casino in Monaco, head for the roulette wheel, and use the following strategy:

- Place a bet of €1 on red.
- If the wheel comes up red, you win €1 and you walk away with €1 as profit.
- If the wheel comes up black, you've lost your bet; you place a bet of €2 on red.
- If the wheel comes up red, you walk away with a profit of €1.
- If the wheel comes up black, you've lost €3; place a bet of €4 on red.
- If you keep doubling your bet, the wheel will eventually come up red and you will walk a way with €1 as profit.

Some essential points to make are as follows:

- You have to completely commit to walking away when you win; your winnings are limited to €1.

- You have to have enough money to be able to double for every outcome; although unlikely, it is possible that a very long string of black outcomes can occur that uses up your funds.

Example 9.1. Suppose you have €1M to start: how long can you go with black outcomes? $2^n = 10^6$ gives n of about 20 — would you risk that sum to win €1?

The story of the peasant, the princess, the rice, and the chessboard

To understand why you should agree that the doubling strategy is doomed to fail, consider the following story.[2] A young man, a peasant, was walking from his village to the nearby city, carrying a sack of grain that he had harvested from his mother's farm that he intended to sell there. While walking along, he suddenly heard someone screaming in terror from beyond the top of the next hill. Running towards the sound, he saw two brigands attacking a young woman. He ran towards them, and using his staff, he hit them, knocking them over. Since he was obviously ready for more fighting, the brigands ran away.

After saving the young woman, he asked her if she was injured. Fortunately, she was not injured. She told the peasant, "Thank-you for saving my life. I am a princess and I would like you to follow me to the city so that my father, the king, can reward you." The young peasant agreed, as he could see that the princess was beautiful and he wanted to be in her company.

When they reached the city, the princess related how the young man had saved her. The king immediately said, "Young man, my gratitude to you for saving my daughter has no bound; please name any reward and I will give it to you."

The young man continued to be struck by the beauty of the princess, so he said, "Your highness, I can think of only one gift I desire: the hand of your daughter in marriage."

The king was taken aback: he said, "You are a peasant; you cannot marry a royal person. Please name another reward."

[2]This is one of many versions of this story. An earlier version can be found in the work of Gamow (1988), pp. 7–9.

The young man was angry that the king had gone back on his promise. He said, "Very well. Instead of your daughter's hand, I ask that you agree to this wager: give me only a few grains of rice; enough to fit on a chessboard but in a pattern that I will explain to you. If you can fulfill the pattern I will take the grains of rice and leave. But if you cannot provide the rice, then you must give me your daughter's hand."

"Here is the pattern. You should take the royal chessboard and place one grain of rice on the first square of the chessboard. And on the second square, place two grains. And on the third square, place four grains. And on the fourth square, place eight grains. Please continue doubling the grains until you have filled up the chessboard. Do you agree to the wager?"

The king immediately agreed. "This is a modest request. I will fulfill it immediately. Are you sure this will be enough?" And then he commanded that the chessboard be brought in, and the grains placed as the young peasant had requested.

After several of the squares had been covered, the amounts needed began to grow. Soon the servants who were bringing the rice began to bring the rice in large sacks; once one sack was brought in, two more were needed for the next square, then four more. Soon more servants were needed, and eventually the head servant told the king, "Your highness, to fill the next square, we will need all the rice in your granary. And there are still many more squares left after that!"

The king realised that there would not be enough rice in his entire kingdom to fill the chessboard. At that moment, he also realised that he had lost the wager. Yet he was pleased because he understood that the peasant was intelligent as well as brave and would make a great husband for his daughter. (And the fact that he now owned all the rice in the kingdom didn't hurt.) He smiled and gave the young man her hand in marriage.

The rice story and the casino strategy have in common that if you don't have infinite resources, your wager will ultimately fail.

The stock market is like a casino. Going to the stock market is like going to a casino, where you have a stock that pays a return, on average, which is greater than the risk-free bond interest rate r.

Suppose the stock price rate of return evolves according to

$$\frac{dX_t}{X_t} = \mu dt + \sigma dZ_t$$

and $\mu > r$ under $\mathbb{Q}$. (We are going to show that this can't be right.) Here is how an arbitrage scheme could work:

- Borrow the money for the purchase; because the debt will then compound at the riskless rate, you will owe $e^{rt}X_0$ when you cash in your winnings at time t.
- Set a target level for the stock price $\overline{X} > X_0$ so that $e^{rt}\overline{X} > e^{rt}X_0$: when the stock price hits it, sell it and repay the loan (this will eventually happen because $\mu > r$).
- The present value of the profit would be $e^{-rt}(e^{rt}\overline{X} - e^{rt}X_0) = \overline{X} - X_0 > 0$, that is, it doesn't matter how long you have to wait, the present value is the same.

You just have to decide how much profit you willing to wait for. But that fact means that it can't happen because everybody would want to do it, and in so doing, and in attempting to do that, they would buy the stock which has this feature of having a drift greater than r. And they would drive the price up, but that would alter the return characteristics of the stock and the attempted to buy it would continue until its expected return equalled r.

This is actually a very powerful and important result: it says that every stock in the market can be described using the beta. And every stock in the market has a drift equal to r under the $\mathbb{Q}$ measure. And that means in in addition that when you making decisions about what portfolio to hold it becomes very simple: you just decide how much of the market portfolio you want to hold vs. how much of the riskless bond that you want to hold. And that is the end of your decision-making. If you are willing to take on risk in exchange for a higher expected return, you can hold more of the market portfolio; if you don't like risk, you can hold less, but in the end, that's all you need to do. And we know, also from our previous reasoning, that the average person decides to hold zero bonds and exactly the right amount of the market portfolio so that the market portfolio gets held by the average person.

How would you test this empirically? We mentioned in passing that the beta is actually a regression coefficient. You could run regressions of the returns of any stock on the market portfolio returns and estimate the beta that way. Economists have been doing that for decades now. There is an econometric issue attached to that history of empirical tests, which has been under dispute for those same decades. But as a theoretical matter, this is a very compelling result.

The ability to characterise the return on assets using beta means that you can use the capital asset pricing model as a tool to decide on investments. When you make an investment, you anticipate the future returns, but you have to discount those future returns using an interest rate; the capital asset pricing model allows you to decide which interest rate that applies, based on the risk characteristics of your returns from the investment, so it's a useful tool.

Now, we also found that the risk-free rate came from our equilibrium considerations. The risk-free rate from the equilibrium "tree" model in equation (8.3) was

$$r = \rho - \frac{1}{2}(1+\gamma)\gamma\sigma^2$$

and is thus a function of the underlying parameters that we saw in the portfolio optimisation model and, in particular, it is a function of ρ, it is a function of γ, the risk aversion, and it is a function of the volatility σ.

The Sharpe ratio shows up in the capital asset pricing model, but in our earlier analysis, when we converted the portfolio optimisation model to the general equilibrium portfolio model by setting $\alpha = 1$, we discovered that there is an equality between the Sharpe ratio for the market and these two parameters, γ and σ:

$$\frac{\mu_M - r}{\sigma_M} = \gamma\sigma_M$$

We can observe the Sharpe ratio in the market because we can observe all three of the quantities: μ_M, σ_M, and r. And also, we can observe one of them on the right-hand side: σ_M. What we cannot observe directly is γ, but we might have another way to estimate γ, and so the remainder of the book is going to go through the process of developing a way to estimate γ as well.

Intuitive meaning of the Sharpe ratio

It is important at some point to ponder the intuitive meaning of the Sharpe ratio. It is a price: the price of return in terms of risk. If you increase the expected return $\mu - r$ of the asset you are purchasing, you have to pay with an increase in the risk — the volatility — so as to obey the market Sharpe ratio.

Empirical Returns and Volatility

Table 9.1 displays the index and annual returns for the NASDAQ, which is a very broad stock index in the USA, from 1972 through 2020. It is evident that the returns fluctuate.

We can then ask what the mean return is and view that as an estimate of the expected return for the market portfolio and we can also look at the volatility of these returns.

The mean return is about 0.12. That means, if you had invested in NASDAQ stocks this broad index, starting in around 1971 you would have received in a return of about 12%/year, which is much better than the return you would get by buying bonds as keeping your money in a savings account. There is volatility, however, which is about 19%.

We can immediately calculate the Sharpe ratio if we remember that the risk-free rate is very tiny — it's on the order of 1% or 2%, plus or minus a percentage point.[3] And so we can ignore it, so if you calculate the Sharpe ratio just by looking at the ratio of the mean return to the market portfolio to the volatility, you get about 0.64. This is the ballpark Sharpe ratio that people accept.

We can look at these numbers predicted by the model empirically, but we still have this issue of what γ is, if we want to fully flesh out the model empirically so that's going to be part of our future agenda.

---

[3]We can be a little more precise. The US Treasury sells inflation adjusted bonds, called TIPS ("Treasury Inflation Protected Securities"), that eliminate the inflation component of the interest rate — a detail that we have swept under the rug in this book. Since US Treasuries are viewed as very safe assets, it is commonly accepted to use the yield on these bonds as a proxy for the risk-free rate of return, r. The yield on TIPS has hovered around 2% for many years now. However, one must account for taxes as well as inflation and this pushes the true riskless rate even lower.

Table 9.1. Returns to Nasdaq.

Year	Nasdaq index	Return	Year	Nasdaq index	Return
1971	107.44	—	2000	3783.67	38.69
1972	128.53	19.62	2001	2035.00	−46.22
1973	109.95	−14.45	2002	1539.73	−24.34
1974	76.29	−14.45	2003	1647.17	6.98
1975	77.20	1.20	2004	1986.53	20.60
1976	89.90	16.44	2005	2099.32	5.68
1977	98.71	9.80	2006	2263.41	7.82
1978	117.53	19.06	2007	2578.47	13.92
1979	136.57	16.21	2008	2161.65	−16.17
1980	168.61	23.46	2009	1845.38	−14.63
1981	203.15	20.49	2010	2349.89	27.34
1982	188.98	−6.98	2011	2677.44	13.94
1983	285.43	51.04	2012	2965.56	10.76
1984	248.89	−12.80	2013	3541.29	19.41
1985	290.25	16.62	2014	4375.10	19.41
1986	366.97	26.43	2015	4945.55	13.04
1987	402.57	9.70	2016	4987.79	0.85
1988	374.43	−6.99	2017	6235.30	25.01
1989	437.80	16.92	2018	7425.96	19.10
1990	409.18	−6.54	2019	7940.36	6.93
1991	491.69	20.16	2020	10201.51	28.48
1992	599.26	21.88			
1993	715.16	19.34			
1994	751.65	5.10			
1995	925.19	23.09			
1996	1164.95	25.91			
1997	1469.49	26.14			
1998	1794.91	26.14			
1999	2728.15	51.99			

Source: NASDAQ OMX Group, NASDAQ Composite Index [NASDAQCOM], retrieved from FRED, Federal Reserve Bank of St. Louis; https://fred.stlouisfed.org/series/NASDAQCOM.

How to Make Money in the Stock Market

We can put our ideas to practice. Consider the picture in Figure 9.1(a).

The figure shows points on a scatter-plot relating two things on a long series of dates. Thus, in the upper-right part of the picture, both things were simultaneously large and positive. The two quantities are obviously correlated.

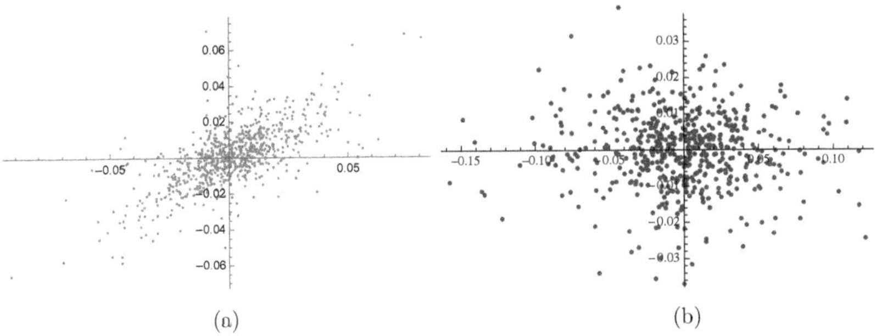

Figure 9.1. Cross-stock return residuals. (a) CAT vs. GE raw returns. (b) CAT vs. GE return residuals.

The plots show the relationship between the returns to Caterpillar Corporation stock and the returns to GE stock, over the three years from 2010 to 2012. (A reminder that a return is the percentage net payoff from holding a stock, which comes from two sources: the appreciation of the stock price and the dividend you get, if any, during the period you hold the stock.) Each dot is the return from holding the stock for a single day, but annualized.[4]

It is obvious from the figure that the returns are correlated: what affects the returns to one of the companies is affecting the other as well. You can easily calculate the actual correlation: it is 0.69, a large positive value.

This is not very surprising: both companies are engaged in manufacturing heavy industrial equipment: Caterpillar makes bulldozers, loaders, steam shovels, and similar heavy equipment for mining and construction; GE makes steam turbines and jet engines.

This might translate into a trading strategy. You would think that the relationship between GE and Caterpillar would be extremely strong: if you know one you know the other. Specifically, if you have some sort of inside dope on GE, you might be able to use that information to some degree to forecast how the price of CAT would move and trade CAT at the same time.

Now, look at Figure 9.1(b). That figure also shows a scatter plot of daily returns for CAT vs. GE but after we have subtracted out a factor from the returns — we can call this factor the "secret sauce." Figure 9.1(b) seems to show that there is *no* relationship between the returns of CAT and GE.

[4]Specifically, you take the daily return r and calculate $(1 + r)^{365} - 1$.

The picture shows what is left over after removing the part that GE and Caterpillar have in common. This common part is the secret sauce that would let you predict Caterpillar if you knew something about GE.

Here is the reveal of the secret sauce. It is amazingly simple. You don't have to have a degree in physics, computer science, or mathematical finance to understand it and to use it yourself. There is only one number — no square roots, exponentials, or logarithms.

Along with this one number, each stock has a partner number. Once you know that partner number for each of the stocks, you can then relate the stocks to each other. Thus, GE has a partner number, n_{GE}, and CAT has its own separate partner number, n_{Cat}. Once you know those two numbers, along with the secret sauce number, then you pretty much know the relationship between the two stocks.

Here is how Figure 9.1(b) was generated. First, figure out the returns for GE with the secret sauce number and the partner number for GE, then do the same for CAT. In each case, there is a leftover part of the return; pair up the leftover parts — the residuals — on each date.

If the secret sauce didn't catch everything that GE and CAT have in common, the picture would be different: it would have a shape, like a line sloping up, for example. The fact that the picture is so random is convincing evidence that the secret sauce is everything. Once you have that, you have everything that relates the two companies.

It would be pretty cool if we had discovered this incredibly simple relationship between the two companies. After all, both are huge, global, complicated companies doing complicated and very different things. It is surprising that there is such a simple relationship between them. But it gets more amazing. You can take a whole list of companies; take out the returns explained by the single secret sauce number and the company partner number. And if you then plot the relationships between the leftover parts of the returns against each other in pairs, you again get randomness in *every* case — this is illustrated in Figure 9.2. (The figures on the diagonal are plots of GE leftovers vs. GE leftovers, CAT vs. CAT, and so on — by definition they are on a 45° line.)

We can calculate the correlation of the residuals explicitly in Table 9.2: You can see that the off-diagonals are pretty small — statistically, we can't be sure they aren't zero. This is just expressing

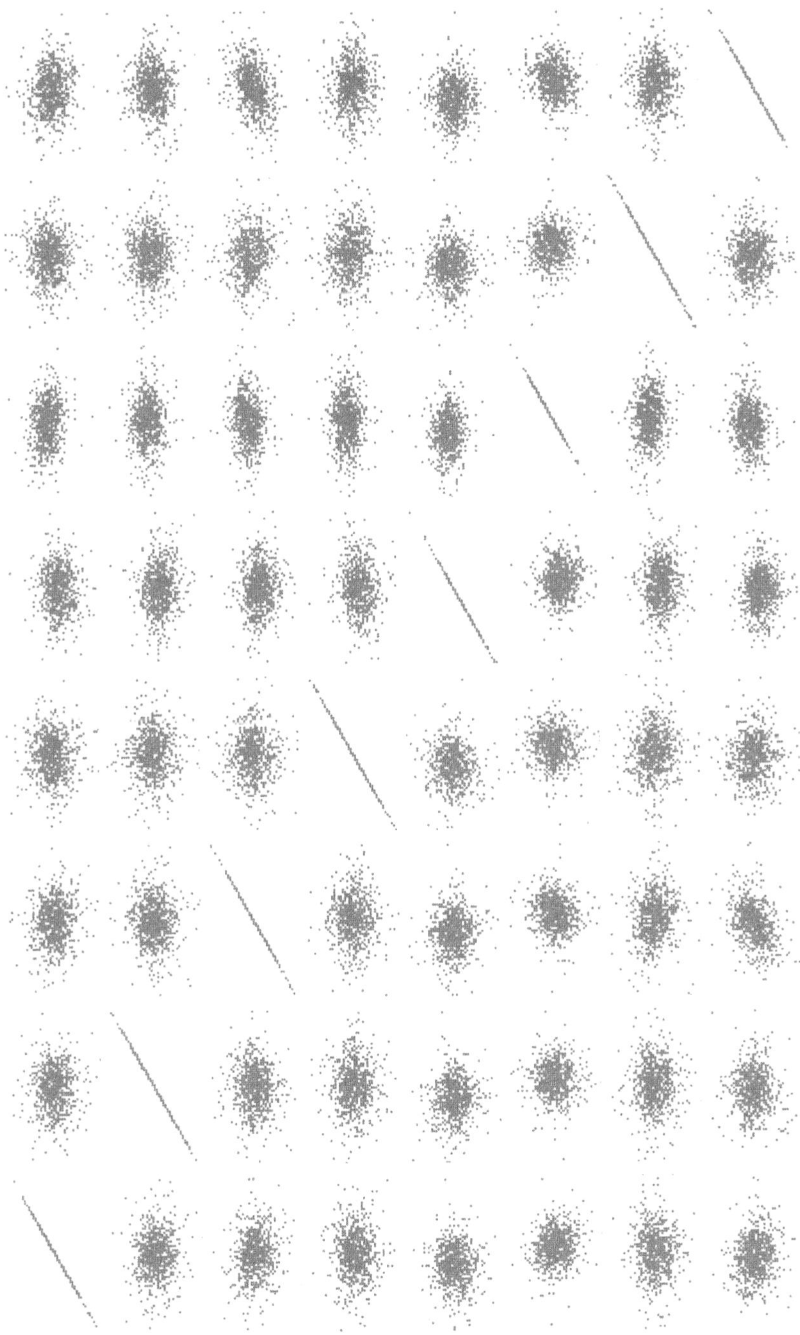

Figure 9.2. Multiple stock return cross-residuals.

Table 9.2. Cross-correlations of residuals.

1.0	0.00251509	−0.0870173	0.0147913	0.0585452	−0.138614	−0.0137177	−0.138996
0.00251509	1.0	0.0199643	−0.0578784	−0.0901144	0.00520261	−0.0209976	0.0428176
−0.0870173	0.0199643	1.0	−0.00247675	−0.0866395	0.144573	−0.0876528	0.388044
0.0147913	−0.0578784	−0.00247675	1.0	0.133648	0.0138451	−0.0874187	−0.0114093
0.0585452	−0.0901144	−0.0866395	0.133648	1.0	−0.0420609	−0.0238268	−0.0314687
−0.138614	0.00520261	0.144573	0.0138451	−0.0420609	1.0	−0.10288	0.14837
−0.0137177	−0.0209976	−0.0876528	−0.0874187	−0.0238268	−0.10288	1.0	0.0011671
−0.138996	0.0428176	0.388044	−0.0114093	−0.0314687	0.14837	0.0011671	1.0

what is in the pictures (Figure 9.2: there isn't any cross-correlation of returns after we take out the secret sauce number.)

You are probably dying to hear what the secret sauce number is. Is it $\sqrt{\pi}$? Is it $\ln(e)$? Well, not so simple. It is the return of the whole stock market, and that changes from day to day. But if you know that return, and the special partner number, you know *everything* about *every* company, except for the stuff on the scatter plots.

Sadly, the secret sauce numbers in the plots are from the *past*, not the future. If they were from the future, we would have it made, and we could apply this special knowledge just like so many authors promise to do. Predicting the secret sauce number isn't so easy, and we're going to leave this for a separate discussion.

What about this partner number? Each company has its own special partner number, and you have to do a little bit of work to find it. But you can do it on a laptop computer, using Excel. Once you have it, you multiply the overall stock market return (the secret sauce number) and that is the common part of the return for that stock. (Well, you also have to add the Treasury bill rate on top of that.) Thus, the special partner number is essentially an *amplification* factor of the secret sauce number. *Every* company essentially amplifies the stock market in this way.

Ticker	β	R-squared	Cumulative return	Residual autocorrelation
CAT	1.43689	0.688447	0.642485	−0.0485246
GE	1.16926	0.692231	0.499888	0.0421692
MRK	0.727807	0.466651	0.266343	0.104668
EQT	1.24138	0.487181	0.454765	0.0837896
EGY	1.78097	0.364898	0.84435	−0.0903266
DUK	0.453198	0.35945	0.466686	−0.0902971
CHH	0.956885	0.479829	0.47874	−0.0912128
PFE	0.760601	0.496294	0.504467	−0.0190431

So, if you know the secret sauce number — the current or future overall stock market return number — then you know the expected return (aside from the amplification factor) of *every company in the world.* The leftover part of each company is specific to *that company only* and no other company in the world — we know that from the pictures. Thus, if you know something about the leftover part, then you cannot use it to make money on any other company.

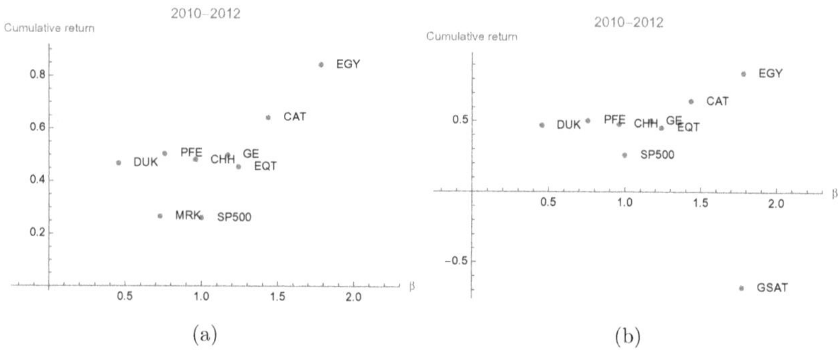

Figure 9.3. Cross-stock return residuals. (a) β vs. return 2010–2012. (b) β vs. return 2010–2012.

Table 9.2 displays the list of the other companies, labelled by their stock market ticker symbol, and the secret sauce partner number.

So it appears that all you need to do to make money in the stock market is to either (i) predict what the *overall* stock market's return will be or (ii) know something specific to a single company. Let's talk about that next.

The partner number is the "beta" (β) — it is the amplification factor that we already found from the theoretical model — it is the ratio of the covariance of the return of the ticker with the overall market return as proxied by the S&P500.

The plot in Figure 9.3(a) shows that the bigger the β, the bigger the return — the β just amplifies the market return (or damps it for stocks with β below 1.0).

A company that doesn't fit the pattern

There is a ticker that was left out of Figure 9.3(a), GSAT, that has a high β of 1.78 but which had a negative return for 2010–2012, −0.68, not as predicted by theory; Figure 9.3(b) includes it.

Ticker	β	R-squared	Cumulative return	Residual autocorrelation
GSAT	1.77675	0.125823	−0.675532	−0.100511

Does this mean the theory is wrong?

No! There is another dimension to the return to GSAT: the residual. This residual is also stochastic — we saw that the residuals aren't correlated with the residuals of other tickers, but we should also note that the residual itself has a variance. The fraction of the variance of the return that is not explained by the systematic return via the β is $1 - R^2$. This means that even though GSAT amplifies the market return due to the systematic return, the volatility of the return is still very high because the R^2 is small. The interpretation is that GSAT had some bad outcomes in 2010–2012 that were due to things affecting GSAT alone, not the entire market.

What Portfolio Should You Hold?

We're now ready to look at the question of practical investment advice. We can begin by recalling that consumption in our baseline equilibrium model is linear in wealth,

$$C_t = \mu W_t$$

and μ is the return to risky stocks. The utility of consumption (using our geometric utility construct) is

$$u(\mu W_t) = \frac{(\mu W_t)^{1-\gamma}}{1-\gamma}$$

If the consumption is in the future — a moment later, at $t + dt$ — then the return has the form $e^{\mu dt + \sigma dW_t}$ so expected utility is

$$E\left[\frac{\left(e^{\mu dt + \sigma dW_t} W_t\right)^{1-\gamma}}{1-\gamma} \mu W_t\right]$$

Now we can use our rules of exponents to separate the elements of utility:

$$= \frac{(\mu W_t)^{1-\gamma}}{1-\gamma}\left(\frac{\left(e^{\mu dt}\right)^{1-\gamma}}{1-\gamma}\right) E\left[\frac{(e^{\sigma dW_t})^{1-\gamma}}{1-\gamma}\right]$$

We can use our rules about the expected value of an exponential to solve the expectation:

$$E\left[\frac{(e^{\sigma dW_t})^{1-\gamma}}{1-\gamma}\right] = \frac{(e^{-\frac{1}{2}(1-\gamma)^2\sigma^2 dt})}{1-\gamma}$$

The negative sign is key: $e^{-\frac{1}{2}\sigma^2 dt}$ is less than 1.0.

In the argument so far, we've harked back to our Merton model, but in actual practice, we would choose a portfolio of actual tickers. We know the characteristics of those tickers from the analysis we've just done.

Suppose we wanted to put all of our eggs in one basket. Reasoning that the demand for construction equipment will never wear out because of increasing globalisation of the world economy, we could put all of our investment into CAT. What is the return to CAT? It is the return we estimated above (well that is from 2010 to 2012, so we would redo the analysis with more recent dates). The return would be

$$\beta_{\text{CAT}} R_M + e_{\text{CAT}}$$

where R_M is $\mu_M dt + \sigma_M dW_t$ and $e_{\text{CAT}} = dZ_t^{\text{CAT}}$. Some explanation is needed here: the residual is labelled as dZ_t^{CAT}, which is the increment of a Brownian motion, because it is independent of dW_t, the market return, and as we already saw in our empirical investigation above, it is also independent of all the other tickers' residual returns.

Now we can look at the expected utility of the portfolio:

$$= \frac{(\mu W_t)^{1-\gamma}}{1-\gamma}((e^{\beta_{\text{CAT}}(1-\gamma)R_M dt}))e^{-\frac{1}{2}\beta^2_{\text{CAT}}(1-\gamma)^2\sigma^2_M dt)}$$
$$\times\ e^{-\frac{1}{2}(1-\gamma)^2\sigma^2_{e_{\text{CAT}}} dt)}$$

Now suppose you read this book and say to yourself, "Maybe I shouldn't put all my eggs in one basket; I'll split my portfolio between CAT and GE." In that case, the return will be

$$= \frac{(\mu W_t)^{1-\gamma}}{1-\gamma}(e^{\frac{1}{2}(\beta_{\text{CAT}}+\beta_{\text{GE}}(1-\gamma)R_M dt})$$
$$\times\ e^{-\frac{1}{2}\frac{1}{4}\beta^2_{\text{CAT}}(1-\gamma)^2\sigma^2_M dt)}e^{-\frac{1}{2}\frac{1}{4}\beta^2_{\text{GE}}(1-\gamma)^2\sigma^2_M dt)}$$
$$\times\ e^{-\frac{1}{2}\frac{1}{4}(1-\gamma)^2\sigma^2_{e_{\text{CAT}}} dt)}e^{-\frac{1}{2}\frac{1}{4}(1-\gamma)^2\sigma^2_{e_{\text{GE}}} dt)} \tag{9.4}$$

The $\frac{1}{4}$ weights come from squaring the weights of $\frac{1}{2}$ when calculating the expected value; as we already saw, the expected value of an exponential normal gives you the exponential of the variance, so the coefficients are squared — $\frac{1}{2}(1-\gamma)\sigma$ is the new volatility.

It is an important detail that the dW_t is common to both tickers, so the volatility term for dW_t, $(1-\gamma)\frac{1}{2}(\beta_{\text{CAT}} + \beta_{\text{GE}})\sigma_M dW_t$, when squared, yields $\frac{1}{4}(1-\gamma)^2\left(\beta_{\text{CAT}}+\beta_{\text{GE}}\right)^2\sigma_M^2 dt$ so that the ratio $\frac{(\beta_{\text{CAT}}+\beta_{\text{GE}})^2}{4}$ is simply the square of the average β — it isn't much affected by splitting the portfolio. The β for CAT and GE are about the same, so we just get the average β. This is because these terms are picking up the same process dW_t.

But the volatility term from the residual term e_t is different: each residual is independent of all the others:

$$e^{-\frac{1}{2}\frac{1}{4}(1-\gamma)^2\left(\sigma^2_{e_{\text{CAT}}}+\sigma^2_{e_{\text{GE}}}\right)dt}$$

is definitely a *bigger* number than $e^{-\frac{1}{2}(1-\gamma)^2\sigma^2_{e_{\text{CAT}}}dt)}$ because the exponent has gotten *smaller* because of the negative sign. If we add a third ticker, say EQT to the portfolio so that each stock has weight $\frac{1}{3}$, then this term will become

$$e^{-\frac{1}{2}\frac{1}{9}(1-\gamma)^2\left(\sigma^2_{e_{\text{CAT}}}+\sigma^2_{e_{\text{GE}}}+\sigma^2_{e_{\text{EQT}}}\right)dt}$$

The $\frac{1}{4}$ has become $\frac{1}{9}$, that is, the square of $\frac{1}{3}$. Since there are three of these volatility terms, the weight on the residuals exponent becomes $\frac{1}{9}\times 3=\frac{1}{3}$.

We can keep going: with N stocks, the residual volatility exponent shrinks by $\frac{1}{N}$, so the exponential term increases towards 1.0 as N gets larger.

This is a free lunch: we didn't have to pay anything, we just split the portfolio. This is the effect of diversification.

So there is an obvious next step: keep diversifying until you run out of tickers. You do that when you have split your portfolio among all of the tickers in the S&P500. And the exponents involving the residual terms shrink down to zero.

So the advice here is simple: just buy the S&P500 (unless you have some inside dope on a company that no one else has). Diversify.

And if our representative agent follows this advice, then our assumption that he holds the market portfolio is validated!

Exercises

Exercise 9.1. Let

$$dS_t=\mu_M S_t dt+\sigma_M S_t dZ_t \quad dX_t=\mu_X X_t dt+\sigma_X X_t dZ_t t$$

Let

$$V(x) = Bx^A$$

The "physical" measure is $\mathbb{P}$.

Now consider a measure change to $\mathbb{Q}$, such that the S_t process has drift r under $\mathbb{Q}$:

(i) State the derivatives V_X, V_{XX}.
(ii) State the V process under the $\mathbb{P}$ measure using Ito's lemma.
(iii) State the V process under the $\mathbb{Q}$ measure.
(iv) Now make an additional assumption: that the Sharpe ratio for the X_t process is the same as the Sharpe ratio for the S_t process. Is $e^{-rt}V_t$ a martingale under the $\mathbb{Q}$ measure?
(v) Continuing with the Sharpe ratio assumption, find the β of the V_t process. (You might find it easier to do this question before undertaking questions (ii) and (iii).)
(vi) Interpret.

Exercise 9.2. Measure change and related quantities. Let

$$dS_t = \mu_M S_t dt + \sigma_M S_t dZ_t$$
$$dX_t = \mu_X X_t dt + \sigma_X X_t dZ_t$$

Let

$$V(x) = -\frac{1}{2}(-x)^2$$

The "physical" measure is $\mathbb{P}$. Consider a measure change to $\mathbb{Q}$, such that the S_t process has drift r under $\mathbb{Q}$:

(i) State the derivatives V_x, V_{xx}.
Note: Be careful about positive and negative signs.
(ii) State the $V(X_t)$ process under the $\mathbb{P}$ measure using Ito's lemma.
(iii) State the Sharpe ratio for the the S_t process. Assume the $\mathbb{Q}$-measure is constructed from this Sharpe ratio. Using a Girsanov transformation, show that $e^{-rt}S_t$ is a martingale under the $\mathbb{Q}$-measure.
Note: You do not have to write down the $\mathbb{Q}$-measure explicitly.
(iv) What condition must hold for $e^{-rt}V(X_t)$ to be a martingale?
(v) Assume that the Sharpe ratio condition is met for the $V(X_t)$ process. Find the β ("beta") of the $V(X_t)$.

Bonus Material

More on the CAPM

We can look at the covariance of the return to the asset dV_t with the return to the portfolio process dS_t, remembering that V_t is a function of the X_t price process for a stock other than the market portfolio, and which is driven by the same Z_t process.

Calculating the expected value of the product of the volatility terms (the drifts are means and therefore we subtract them out), we obtain the covariance, using the stochastic calculus rule $dZ_t dZ_t = dt$:

$$\begin{aligned}\mathrm{cov}^{\mathbb{P}}\left(\frac{dV}{V}, \frac{dS}{S}\right) &= E^{\mathbb{P}}\left(\sigma_X \frac{xV_x dZ_t}{V} \sigma_M dZ_t\right)\\ &= \sigma_X \frac{xV_x d}{V} \sigma_M dt\end{aligned}$$

Similarly, the variance of $\frac{dS_t}{S_t}$ is

$$\mathrm{var}^{\mathbb{P}}\left(\frac{dS}{S}\right) = E^{\mathbb{P}}(\sigma_M dZ_t) = \sigma_M^2 dt$$

The correlation of the option returns and the market returns (that is, the regression coefficient) can then be computed:

$$\beta_V(x) = \frac{\mathbb{E}_t^{\mathbb{P}}\left(\frac{dV}{V}\frac{dS}{S}\right)}{\frac{1}{dt}\mathbb{E}_t^{\mathbb{P}}\left(\left(\frac{dS}{S}\right)^2\right)} = \frac{\frac{xV_x}{V}\sigma_X \sigma_M}{\sigma_M^2}$$

This is the same ratio we have in the equation for $\frac{dV}{V}$ that we derived in the main text using completely different reasoning. Therefore, we can express the expected return of the asset in classic CAPM form. Usually, you see this in discrete-time or static form, but this emphasises that the CAPM relationship holds in continuous time:

$$\mathbb{E}_t^{\mathbb{P}}\left(\frac{dV}{V}\right) = (r + \beta_V(\mu_M - r))dt$$

As we already established via the arbitrage argument, this has to hold for *all* stocks in equilibrium. And we have the following corollary:

Corollary 1. *No-arbitrage requires that all stocks have the same Sharpe ratio:*

$$\frac{\mu_X - r}{\sigma_X} = \frac{\mu_M - r}{\sigma_M}$$

A simple no-arbitrage argument

We have set out a somewhat formal argument that establishes the no-arbitrage result, namely that all equities must have the same Sharpe ratio, in Appendix B. However, there is a simpler and less formal argument. The argument reaches a contradiction by proposing the construction of a self-financing portfolio as follows. From an initial position of zero financial assets, borrow an initial quantity of bonds, which we record as a negative bond holding $-B_0$. Use the funds from this loan to purchase an initial quantity of the risky asset S_0, noting that $S_0 = B_0$.

We then note that the value of the bonds will evolve such that $B_t = B_0 e^{rt}$, and under $\mathbb{Q}$, the stock will evolve such that $S_0 = E^{\mathbb{Q}}[e^{-rt} S_t]$. Any expected profit is $E^{\mathbb{Q}}[e^{-rt}(S_t - B_t)] = S_0 - B_0 = 0$. Thus, no arbitrage is possible in expected value terms.

Chapter 10

State Prices

In the previous chapters, we developed the notion of a Lagrangian in dynamic settings in which we discovered that we can have separate Lagrange multipliers for each period of the model and that those Lagrange multipliers have a dynamic structure that relates to the interest rate. We have also developed and applied the risk-neutral measure. In this chapter, we bring these ideas together in the state-price model.

The State Price

The target of this chapter is to understand the empirical tests we are ultimately going to undertake, using the framework that we have developed. There are many papers in this literature, but two papers that we highlight would be the paper by Hansen and Jagannathan (1991), which is has had a huge influence on how people think about macro finance, and second, the paper by Barone-Adesi *et al.* (2020). The Barone-Adesi *et al.* paper is very recent, but it has a nice way of looking at the issues that we have been developing.

Early in the book we were thinking about Lagrangians, and we started out with very simple models, but we very soon went to models with two goods. And we learned how to set up a Lagrangian and learned what the first-order conditions would be like. We learned that for the two-good model, there would be three equations and we could solve the three equations for the three things we're interested in, namely consumption for each type of good and then also the

Lagrange multiplier. And we had an interpretation of the Lagrange multiplier as the marginal value of income. And finally we reinterpreted the two goods as consumption at two different times, and found that the constraint could be split into two subconstraints, each with its own multiplier, and these multipliers were related to each other by the interest rate. In this chapter, we are going to extend this idea to the infinite horizon setting.

We're going to take inspiration from an example that is in the He and Pages (1993) paper. He and Pages' agenda is to analyse the continuous time optimal consumption problem, but with the extra proviso that the consumer who is solving the problem cannot borrow beyond a certain point. He faces a borrowing constraint, so he is not allowed to let his wealth or his borrowing fall below a certain level. As a technical matter, that's actually a really hard problem, much harder than the one we're going to think about, but related to the one we're going to think about.

The objective for the infinite-horizon optimal consumption problem starting from time t is

$$\max_{\{(C_s)_0^\infty\}} E^{\mathbb{P}}\left[\int_t^\infty e^{-\rho(s-t)}u(C_s)ds\middle|Y_t\right]$$

Note that we're integrating forward through time, taking the discounted value of utility discounted by the subjective rate of time discount ρ. Consumption can change from period to period, and we're integrating starting at time t. The letter s denotes the index of integration, which can signify any period after time t any moment after time t. As in our previous models, we're not just choosing consumption at time t, we choose consumption all the way into the future somehow, and we now know that that's actually quite subtle. What does it mean to choose consumption into the future in a stochastic setting? We made significant progress on that question using the stochastic control with the HJB equation, but we will use a more direct approach in this chapter.

Note that the expectation is with respect to the $\mathbb{P}$ measure. Usually, we don't even think about the $\mathbb{P}$ measure; it's just there. But in this chapter we are going to use a measure change. Another key thing to note here is that we are conditioning on information as a time t; Y_t is income as of time t. But into the future, Y_{t+s} is stochastic.

There is a notational issue to raise. In He and Pages' example, they use a geometric utility function, otherwise known as Cobb Douglas utility function, $\frac{c^\alpha}{\alpha}$. But we've also now seen models where instead of α, we have $1-\gamma$; the $1-\gamma$ approach is better because γ has an interpretation as the risk aversion coefficient, and this is the formulation we use:

$$\max E\left[\int_0^T e^{-\rho t}\frac{C_t^{1-\gamma}}{1-\gamma}dt\right]$$

There is a risky stock, similar to the Merton portfolio model, and the price of the stock evolves according to

$$dS_t = \mu S_t dt + \sigma S_t dZ_t$$

that is, a geometric Brownian motion.

There is a budget constraint or budget process; to make the notation consistent with the Merton model notation and budget process, we would write

$$dW_t = Y_t dt + ((\alpha_t\mu + (1-\alpha_t)r)W_t - C_t)\,dt + \alpha_t W_t \sigma dZ_t$$

where W_t is the consumer's wealth process. Integrating the constraint yields

$$\int_0^t C_s ds + W_t = W_0 + \int_0^t Y_s ds + \int_0^t ((\alpha_s\mu + (1-\alpha_s)r)W_s)ds + \int_0^t \alpha_s W_s \sigma dZ_t$$

$$\to \int_0^t C_s ds + W_t = W_0 + \int_0^t Y_s ds + \int_0^t (1-\alpha_s)rW_s ds + \int_0^t \alpha_s dW_s$$

The budget constraint has four elements: the wealth from your discounted actual income process, Y_t, added up, which He and Pages assume is somehow given from the outside, plus your income from your holdings of bonds — fraction $(1-\alpha)$ of your wealth — added up over time, plus your income from your holdings of the risky stock — fraction α of your wealth — added up over time, plus any initial wealth W_0 that you started out with. That has to equal your consumption added up over time, but also it gives you the current wealth;

this allows for the possibility that you might end up with more wealth than you started with. This holds for every t, so we're integrating from zero to t rather than from t to infinity. That is, we are adding up retrospectively, rather than in anticipation of the future, so there is no expectation operator.

The equation is always true for every t, so there is no expectation under the $\mathbb{P}$ measure; it's always true; anything that is left over from the income that's generated from the portfolio holdings and the actual income process gets put into wealth if it's not consumed. And we're already familiar with that sort of thing with the growth models. And where does the wealth come from? Ultimately, it comes from the holdings of the assets.

He and Pages impose an extra constraint, that wealth can never be negative, and that prevents people from saying, "Well, I'm going to borrow some money today, and I promise I'll pay it back in the future," and actually, one way you can borrow is you can use your Visa card. If you're not in Russia, that is, you can use your Visa card to pay for goods and services. But then when you get your monthly Visa bill, you could just pay it with your Visa card and just keep doing that. And you know, I tried that, but they said, No, you're not allowed to do that. However we are not going to impose this constraint of no negative wealth, as it creates significant complications technically. We're going to assume that the person we are modelling commits to repaying any debts, and that the debts are commensurate with his income.

More on the risk-neutral measure $\mathbb{Q}$

We now use the measure change ideas we developed in the previous chapter. First, some notation. He and Pages define

$$\kappa \equiv \frac{\mu - r}{\sigma}$$

We've seen κ many times now: it is the Sharpe ratio, which we have also denoted by θ. We define a new process Z_t^*, using κ:

$$dZ_t^* = dZ_t - \kappa dt$$

After a bit of algebra as we did in Chapter 9, we end up with the S_t process having a drift of r, the risk free rate, but otherwise looking the same, except that the stochastic term is dZ_t^* instead of dZ_t:

$$\begin{aligned} dS &= \mu S dt + \sigma S_t dZ_t = \mu S dt + \sigma S_t \left(dZ_t^* + \kappa dt\right) \\ &= r S dt + \sigma S_t dZ_t^* \end{aligned}$$

under the $\mathbb{Q}$ measure. We need to be careful to say that now that we've done this, this equation holds under the $\mathbb{Q}$ measure.

We can now say a little more about the $\mathbb{Q}$ measure. Previously, we limited ourselves to noting that there is a measure in the background and focussed on the algebra when you substitute for dZ from the definition of dZ^*. We now want to expand our focus to encompass $\mathbb{Q}$ itself. There is an algebraic character to $\mathbb{Q}$ that is a little bit surprising and useful. The algebraic property is that you can you can get $\mathbb{Q}$ by multiplying the original measure, $\mathbb{P}$, by a specific coefficient function, ξ_t, the Radon–Nikodym derivative:

$$\mathbb{Q} = \xi_t \mathbb{P}$$

where ξ_t is defined as

$$\xi_t \equiv e^{-\frac{1}{2}|\kappa|^2 t + \int_0^t \kappa dZ_s} \tag{10.1}$$

The formula for ξ_t looks familiar: it is the solution of a geometric diffusion process.

The practical use of it is here. Suppose you have a function $f(\cdot)$. We want to take the expected value of the discounted value of $f(s)$ integrated under the new measure, the algebraic fact works like this: you can just multiply by ξ_t. The expectation of a function f in the budget constraint under $\mathbb{Q}$ is equivalent to expectation of the function multiplied by ξ_t under $\mathbb{P}$:

Theorem 10.1.

$$\boxed{E^{\mathbb{Q}}\left[\int_0^t e^{-rs} f(s) dt\right] = E^{\mathbb{P}}\left[\int_0^t \xi_s e^{-rs} f(s) ds\right]}$$

We already have an explicit expression for this discounted function for this same integral under $\mathbb{Q}$. But now we can take the expectation under $\mathbb{P}$. That is often more comfortable because that's the measure we start with.

So this very esoteric thing, the measure change, turns out to have a couple of very nice properties that go with it. One of them is you can change the dZ_t in a clever way so that the drift of the process you're interested in changes. But there's a second nice payoff, which is that you can go back and forth between the two measures and just have to multiply by a function that we can state explicitly.

You might ask, is the product of ξ_t with the original normal probability density still a probability density? Yes; because it is has this special exponential form, it actually has the structure needed to keep the property of something being a probability distribution. Specifically, it has to integrate to one to be a probability: the ξ_t function actually does that. Actually, ξ_t is also a probability density. And it is a martingale as well.

Back to the budget constraint

Let's go back to the budget constraint from the consumer problem. We're adding up consumption and we also have wealth at time t. There's some initial wealth or some income that's been coming in that we add up. And there are inflows from the holdings of assets, the bonds and the stocks.

Write the budget constraint in differential form,

$$C_t dt + dW_t = Y_t dt + (1 - \alpha_t) dB_t + \alpha_t \left(\mu S_t dt + \sigma S_t dZ_t \right)$$

We are going to consolidate a little bit. At any time t, consumption, plus the change in wealth, is the current income, plus the increment of bonds from any interest from the bonds, plus the drift from the risky asset, plus the payoff from random events, from the risky asset of this relationship. Now do the measure change: substitute for dZ_t, $dZ_t^* + \kappa dt$. And when we do that we kill off the drift term. Here. So we end up with this equation:

$$C_t dt + dW_t = Y_t dt + (1 - \alpha_t) dB_t + \alpha_t \sigma S_t dZ_t^*$$

The drift term for the risky asset has dropped out.

There is one additional step, which is to pre-multiply everything in the equation by e^{-rt}:

$$e^{-rt} C_t dt + e^{-rt} dW_t = e^{-rt} Y_t dt + e^{-rt} (1 - \alpha_t) dB_t + e^{-rt} \alpha_t \sigma S_t dZ_t^*$$

Now integrate from zero to t, so we're going to get our original constraint back but in slightly modified form:

$$\int_0^t e^{-rs}C_s ds + \int_0^t e^{-rs}dW_s$$
$$= \int_0^t e^{-rs}Y_s ds + \int_0^t e^{-rs}(1-\alpha_s)dB_s + \int_0^t e^{-rs}\alpha_s\sigma S_s dZ_s^*$$

If we take the expectation of this under the $\mathbb{Q}$ measure, the Brownian term disappears as it has expectation zero:

$$E^{\mathbb{Q}}\left[\int_0^t e^{-rs}\alpha_s\sigma S_s dZ_s^*\right] = E^{\mathbb{P}}\left[\int_0^t \xi_s e^{-rs}\alpha_s\sigma S_s dZ_s^*\right]$$
$$= 0$$

Explicitly expressing the Radon–Nikodym derivative, ξ, in the expectation (so that, invoking Theorem 10.1, we are taking the outside expectation under $\mathbb{P}$ not $\mathbb{Q}$) and keeping in mind that in this benign setting we can bring expectations inside the integral, we have the expectation of that under $\mathbb{Q}$, the expected value of dZ_t^* is zero. This rests on the fact that the increments dZ_t^* have mean zero, are independent of each other, and also that they are independent of the other elements of the integrand, ξ_s, α and S_s. Our budget constraint therefore simplifies to

$$E^{\mathbb{Q}}\left[\int_0^t e^{-rs}C_s ds + \int_0^t e^{-rs}dW_s\right]$$
$$= W_0 + E^{\mathbb{Q}}\left[\int_0^t e^{-rs}Y_s ds + \int_0^t e^{-rs}(1-\alpha_s)dB_s\right]$$

Now we restate the budget constraint, again invoking Theorem 10.1:

$$E^{\mathbb{P}}\left[\int_0^t e^{-rs}\xi_s C_s ds\right] = W_0 + E^{\mathbb{P}}\left[\int_0^t e^{-rs}\xi_s Y_s ds\right]$$

Consolidating what we've already done, the budget constraint has been reduced to discounted expected values of consumption and income, but pre-multiplying by the ξ_t factor, and initial wealth. We are taking the expectation, but with respect to the $\mathbb{P}$ measure.

What happened to the $(1-\alpha_t)dB_t$, the $\alpha_t S_t$, and the W_T terms? They have disappeared due to the requirement of no arbitrage, which we saw in Chapter 9, is equivalent to the requirement that a self-financing portfolio cannot exist under the $\mathbb{Q}$ measure.

Let's talk about that intuitively. Let's start out with no wealth at all and no income either. In the risk-neutral measure world, we could go to a bank and say, I want to borrow some money. And I'll pay you back in six months and then we could take that money and we could go and invest it in the stock market, and wait for the drift of the return on the stock market to develop over those six months. And by the way, we know from the work we did in Chapter 9 that we don't need to make complicated decisions about which stocks to invest in. We now know that the only thing that matters from the point of view of risky investments is the overall stock market, which for intuitive purposes is just the S&P 500. We don't need to worry about other stocks because we can diversify our holdings of our stocks. Diversification will average out the stochastic fluctuations in those other stocks and leave only the stochastic fluctuation that's correlated with the overall stock market as the thing that matters. So not a complicated decision, but we also figured out that the drift of the return that you get from the market portfolio is such that under $\mathbb{Q}$, it is r, the risk-free rate. Since the expected return under $\mathbb{Q}$ is r, we are cannot actually make any money in expectation so as to repay the loan in six months with certainty and have something left over, because the bank lending rate is also going to be r. It just can't work. So a self-financing portfolio that would operate according to this story can't happen in equilibrium.

Here is another way to think about it. Under the $\mathbb{Q}$ measure, the self-financing portfolio would have to have a negative $(1-\alpha)$, the bond weight, because you are borrowing. And in addition, under $\mathbb{Q}$ the drift of the risky asset would be bond-like, that is, rdt, so α, the weight on the risky asset, would necessarily equal $(1-\alpha)$, so they would cancel because the bond equals the risky asset — that's how you are acquiring the risky asset. The dZ_t^*s cancel due to the expectation operator. So if we start with zero bonds and zero wealth, everything cancels, and the expected profit from the self-financing portfolio is zero.

There are lots of ads on the internet telling you how to do the equivalent of a self-financing portfolio, but as we now understand, it can't really work systematically. So if we start with zero wealth, which is a kind of convenient assumption, because then we can forget about this W_0 term, we can also forget about the the new drift of the portfolio, which is r times B_t, and just dispense with it. The following paragraph references this idea:

> For the above securities price system to be reasonable, it is necessary that something cannot be created from nothing through dynamic trading using the strategies specified above. The securities price system is said to admit an arbitrage opportunity if there exists $c \in \mathcal{C}$ financed by some $\alpha, \theta) \in \mathbf{H}$ with $W_0 = 0$ and $Y = 0$ such that c, $W(T) > 0$ and either $c \neq 0$ or $W(T) \neq 0$. [He and Pages, 1993, p. 9]

The upshot of this is that you can't end up with more wealth than your initial wealth, using asset purchases and sales, and because all the stochastic terms are wiped out by the expectation, the net result, the cumulated drifts of the bonds and stocks just balance the final wealth W_T due to the absence of arbitrage — no self-financing allowed — all these terms disappear. The budget constraint then reduces to

$$E^{\mathbb{P}}\left[\int_0^T e^{-rs}\xi_s C_s ds\right] = E^{\mathbb{P}}\left[\int_0^T e^{-rs}\xi_s Y_s ds\right] \tag{10.2}$$

When we were solving the deterministic optimal control problem, the technical problem that we faced was we wanted to take the derivative with respect to C_t to find the optimal consumption C_t. But we saw in the original way the problem was structured that there were C_s in the future, and they somehow have to relate to each other. So we carried out a bookkeeping maneuver, integration by parts. This enabled us to rearrange the problem so that we could take the derivative in a consistent way at each time t. Our re-characterisation of the budget constraint will enable us to do that here as well.

We originally took the expectation under $\mathbb{Q}$, but now we've gone back to the $\mathbb{P}$ measure using this trick of multiplying by ξ_t, but taking the expectation under $\mathbb{P}$; this is the relevant equation now. And when we took the expected value of utility discounted over time, that was also under the $\mathbb{P}$ measure. So now we've got the expectation of utility and the expectation of the budget constraint under the same measure. However, the budget constraint is modified because it has the ξ_t terms.

The ξ_t terms kind of look like Lagrange multipliers the way they're interacting with both the Y_t part and the C_t part. And that observation is correct.

Now we can write down a Lagrangian using the reduced budget constraint in (10.2):

$$\max_{\{C_s\}} E^{\mathbb{P}}\left[\int_0^T e^{-\rho t}u(C_t)dt\right] + \lambda\left(E^{\mathbb{P}}\left[\int_0^T e^{-rs}\xi_s Y_s ds\right] - E^{\mathbb{P}}\left[\int_0^T e^{-rs}\xi_s C_s ds\right]\right) \quad (10.3)$$

Taking the derivative with respect to C_t, we obtain the first-order condition:

$$e^{-\rho t}u'(C_t) = \lambda e^{-rt}\xi_t$$

This is essentially the same first-order condition as in the two-period model of Chapter 2: the derivative of utility with respect to consumption is equal to a Lagrange multiplier multiplying a price; the price is the price of consumption period-by-period, the discount factor. We can then solve for C_t.

Now let us remind ourselves that when we were doing these ultra simple Lagrangians with only two goods, there were three ways we went at them.

The first way was to have a general utility function of two goods. Then we said suppose that utility function is the sum of two separate utility functions good 1 and good 2. In the third approach, there were two goods, but we specifically linked them to consumption at a particular time rather than of a particular good. So instead of consumption of wine and cheese as goods one and two, it was consumption of wine at a time $t = 1$ and consumption of wine at time $t = 2$. And we also introduced saving into that model. Due to the way it was restructured, when you have saving, there were actually two budget constraints, each with a Lagrange multiplier. When you solve out the problem, what we saw was the Lagrange multipliers attached to those two constraints had a relationship with each other, and that relationship was the interest rate. One was a function of the other, multiplied by an interest rate factor. We have a similar situation here: we can interpret ξ_t as a Lagrange multiplier and attach the discount term to it.

We also saw this in the deterministic growth model: the costate, which we established is essentially a Lagrange multiplier, is a function of the interest rate.

By imposing the requirement that consumption equal income as in the Merton equilibrium setting with $\alpha = 1$,

$$C_t = Y_t$$

and inverting the first order condition, we obtain the state price:

$$\xi_t = \lambda^{-1} e^{-(\rho - r)t} u'(Y_t)$$

This defines ξ_t in terms of preferences and endowments.

We view the consumer who solving this optimisation problem as the representative consumer but with the risk-free rate and the return on the stock rigidly determined by the relationships that have to hold because that representative consumer is representing the behaviour of the entire economy. And just to remind you because of what we did in developing the capital asset pricing model and the no-arbitrage side of the capital asset pricing model, this representative consumer is a completely fine construct in the sense that we don't need to worry about other people in the economy who are not like the representative consumer, because everybody is going to be driven by the Sharpe ratio of the market portfolio at the margin, that is, the generalisation of the requirement that the ratio $\frac{u'(c_1)}{u'(c_2)} = \frac{p_1}{p_2}$.

We can therefore think about there being a representative consumer. And when we look at empirical tests, which we're going to do in a later chapter, we are able to do that safely as it were because of the connections we've developed. And just to say, again, something we hinted at earlier, suppose that we force people to consume their income — in the macro economy, the income is the consumption. It's possible that we don't know ξ_t, but we do know the income process Y_t or the consumption process C_t — for our purposes the same thing, we can estimate ξ_t. (And we also need to determine λ.)

It is worth pointing out that that ξ_t started out as the measure change coefficient — the Radon–Nikodym derivative. We got it by putting in the Sharpe ratio, which got us eliminating the drift or converting the drift to the risk-free interest rate. So that was the sort of technical purpose it had, but it has turned out to be the same as the Lagrange multiplier in the optimal consumption problem. This is unexpected and surprising. Let's try to say more about that connection.

Why is it called the state price?

Let's summarise. We transformed the basic budget constraint as follows: We transformed the budget constraint to $\mathbb{Q}$ and Z_t^* for the risky asset (with drift r). Then we argued using a self-financing argument that if we start with W_0 and $B_0 = 0$ then the bond and risky asset terms when we extend the budget constraint out to the terminal time T, S_T and B_T, along with wealth W_T can be dropped, additionally, taking the expectation under $\mathbb{Q}$, eliminates the Z_t^* terms which have expectation zero.

We then use Theorem 10.1 where we convert back to $\mathbb{P}$ but we have the ξ_t multiplying consumption and income inside the integral of the budget constraint, $e^{-rt}\xi(Z_t^*)p(Z_t^*)$ ($p(Z_t^*)$ is the normal density), in equation (10.2); this enables us to take the first order condition for each t, just as in the deterministic models.

But what happened to the stochastic element? It is embodied in the multiplier ξ_t, which is a random process; there is one multiplier for each t but also for each state — that is, each realisation of the Z_t^*; you could also interpret it as the price — this is why it is called the state price. We could combine the $\xi(Z_t^*)$ with the probability $p(Z_t^*)$ and now it looks exactly like a price in a continuum of constraints, just as in the two-good model.

Thus, $e^{-rt}\xi(Z_t^*)p(Z_t^*)$ is called the state price because each possible value of Z_t^* that can be reached at each time t is referred to as a "state" by economists. One can think of "it is raining next Sunday" and "it is sunny next Monday" as states in this sense. Each of those states has a probability — that's the probability $p(Z_t^*)$ from the normal density; we then attach the product of the values of ξ and the probability of the state to each of them. That product behaves exactly like the prices in the two-good model, hence it is appropriate to think of it as a price.

The State Price in the Merton Portfolio General Equilibrium Model

In the He–Pages model, we defined $\mathbb{Q}$ via the Sharpe ratio

$$\kappa \equiv \frac{\mu - r}{\sigma}$$

In the Merton model with $\alpha = 1$ (therefore no bonds held in equilibrium), we can solve for μ, and we then can reformulate the model in terms of the same κ:

$$\mu = r + \gamma\sigma^2$$
$$\implies \kappa = \gamma\sigma$$

Therefore, preferences (via the risk aversion parameter γ) determine $\mathbb{Q}$ in equilibrium.

We converted the Merton model to a macro model by saying zero bonds are held and that translated into the Merton α, the Merton portfolio weight on the risky stock being 1. Then we ended up with $\alpha = 1$, further implying that κ, which is the Sharpe ratio, equals $\gamma\sigma$.

Recall Hub's equation (8.4). The left-hand side, the Sharpe ratio $\frac{\mu-r}{\sigma}$, is about how the stock market relates the return on stocks to the risk-free rate and the riskiness of the stock. But what's in the expression on the right-hand side? γ, a preference parameter, something that's even more fundamental in the model because it's about the structure of utility, and that structure is somehow related to the Sharpe ratio and equilibrium.

We want to explore that relationship even more. So we're going to take the value function from the Merton model $V(W_t)$, for which we conjectured a closed form solution when utility is geometric, and for which it is easy to compute the derivatives. Suppose utility is geometric (CRRA):

$$u(c) = \frac{c^{1-\gamma}}{1-\gamma}$$

Then we established that the value function V is also geometric:

$$V(w) = B\frac{w^{1-\gamma}}{1-\gamma}$$

where γ as a risk aversion coefficient, as in the earlier Merton model where utility was geometric, and where B is a complicated function of the parameters of the model. But then when we solve the model, we made this guess about what V was going to look like and it looked like this and it worked. And this ratio, $\frac{V_W}{wV_{WW}}$, is of interest, and in particular, if you solve it out, you get that this ratio is $\frac{1}{\gamma}$. Now, $\frac{1}{\gamma}$ came up in our growth model, no stochastic aspect to it, just the pure deterministic growth model. We had a utility function like the one we've been using in the Merton model and found that as γ gets bigger, growth slows down. So γ is capturing something about utility, the dislike of intertemporally substituting consumption. But it is, of course, also directly capturing the idea of risk aversion[1]: in the Merton model, we saw directly that an increase in volatility reduced the holding of the risky asset. And at the optimum we also had that the marginal utility of consumption is the first derivative of the value function, $V_W(W_t)$ in equation (7.3):

$$V_w = u'(c) \tag{10.4}$$

We can manipulate this a little bit. First of all, we can solve for consumption by using the geometric form of utility. Using the solution of the value function, we can solve for consumption, and we get that consumption is a straight line function of wealth, that is, consumption is the product of a coefficient B with wealth W_t. We're just going to carry it around without the explicit solution for the innards of the coefficient B, and we can go the other way: we can solve for W as a function of consumption, just by dividing consumption by $B^{-\frac{1}{1-\gamma}}$.

[1]So γ is doing double duty. One can separately capture the dislike of intertemporal substitution and the dislike of risk with more complicated utility functions.

What is the interpretation of γ that we're interested in now? Well, in our earlier work, we have that this ratio

$$\frac{1}{\gamma} = \frac{u'(c)}{cu''(c)}$$

is actually an elasticity; it is the intertemporal elasticity of substitution, capturing the reluctance to substitute intertemporally, and it is also capturing risk aversion. So more explicitly, we can express this thing on the right-hand side, as the time derivative of the logarithm of consumption, the percentage change over time of consumption with respect to the risk-free rate.

In a simplified version of what we saw in the previous development, we can say that the marginal utility is equal to ξ_t. From the He–Pages consumption problem,

$$u'(C_t) = e^{(\rho-r)t}\lambda\xi_t$$

For the Merton CRRA model,

$$u'(C_t) = V_w = BW_t^{-\gamma}$$

The first equality followed from (7.3); the second equality follows from the solution of the geometric utility value function.

We can embark on characterising the state price process ξ_t in terms of the fundamentals of the model with this relationship as the starting point. To calculate $d\xi_t$ we just need to calculate dV_w:

$$\begin{aligned} d\xi_t &= dV_w = B\,dW_t^{-\gamma} \\ \Longrightarrow \frac{d\xi_t}{\xi_t} &= -\gamma\sigma dZ_t \end{aligned}$$

Equating the two expressions for $u'(C_t)$ and using the equilibrium structure of the risk-free rate $r = \rho - \frac{1}{2}(1+\gamma)\gamma\sigma^2$, we have

$$e^{\frac{1}{2}(1+\gamma)\gamma\sigma^2 t}\lambda\xi = Bw^{-\gamma}$$

so to find $d\xi_t$ we just need to calculate

$$d\xi = d\,e^{-\frac{1}{2}(1+\gamma)\gamma\sigma^2 t}V_w = d\,e^{-\frac{1}{2}(1+\gamma)\gamma\sigma^2 t}\lambda^{-1}Bw^{-\gamma}$$

using Ito's lemma. Dropping $\lambda^{-1}B$, using the solution for dW_t above and Ito's lemma with

$$\begin{aligned} f(t,w) &\equiv e^{-\frac{1}{2}(1+\gamma)\gamma\sigma^2 t} w^{-\gamma} \\ f_t(t,w) &\equiv -\frac{1}{2}(1+\gamma)\gamma\sigma^2 e^{-\frac{1}{2}\gamma(1+\gamma)\sigma^2 t} w^{-\gamma} \\ f_W(w) &= -\gamma e^{-\frac{1}{2}(1+\gamma)\gamma\sigma^2 t} w^{-\gamma-1}, \\ f_{WW}(w) &= \gamma(1+\gamma) e^{-\frac{1}{2}(1+\gamma)\gamma\sigma^2 t} w^{-\gamma-2} \end{aligned}$$

Applying Ito's lemma,

$$\begin{aligned} d\xi_t &= \left(f_t + \mu_W f_W + \frac{1}{2}\sigma_W^2 f_{WW}\right) dt + \sigma_W f_W dZ_t \\ &= \left(-\frac{1}{2}(1+\gamma)\gamma\sigma^2 + 0 + \frac{1}{2}\sigma_W^2 \gamma(1+\gamma)\right) dt - \gamma\sigma dZ_t \\ &= -\gamma\sigma dZ_t \end{aligned}$$

Therefore,

$$\frac{d\xi_t}{\xi_t} = -\gamma\sigma dZ_t$$

We can consider ξ_t to be stochastic process now, note that it has a time subscript — it's not a constant — and because it has this time subscript, we can actually characterise it using Ito's lemma, restating the fact that consumption is a linear function of wealth, and we can also write down the solution for wealth using Ito's lemma. Wealth evolves as a stochastic process, according to the portfolio holdings. And in that model, there was the portfolio holdings of the risky assets, so that was the weight α on the risky asset, and $1-\alpha$ on the risk-free asset.

This is huge. There is no drift. We already know the solution of this stochastic differential equation:

$$\xi_t = e^{-\frac{1}{2}\gamma^2\sigma^2 t - \gamma\sigma Z_t}$$

But we earlier established that (for $\alpha = 1$ in the Merton model)

$$\boxed{\frac{\mu - r}{\sigma} = \gamma\sigma}$$

We are done: the risk-neutral measure (which is a function of $\frac{\mu-r}{\sigma}$) has been connected to the state price (which is a function of $\gamma\sigma$); *they are the same thing.*

Something to remind ourselves is that when we convert every asset using the measure change so that the drift is the risk-free rate r so that there can be no arbitrage, we're also using the r that comes out of the $\alpha = 1$ in the Merton model. And that r is itself a function of the fundamentals of the model. Those fundamentals are ρ, the subjective time discount rate, γ, the risk aversion of the representative agent, and σ, the riskiness of the fundamental economy-wide asset, the riskiness of the S&P 500, if you want to think about it concretely. And so the term "risk-free rate," actually, is a bit misleading; it is a function of the volatility of the economy and of the risk aversion in the economy.

There are some things in these models that we can observe. We can observe consumption in the aggregate. Of course, there are lots of measurement issues, but basically we can observe it. We can observe simulacra of the risk-free rate in the form of safe government bonds. We've noted that we can observe the expected return of the systematic part of the market, the overall market, approximated by the S&P 500. And we can observe the volatility of that return, σ, as well. We can therefore test the model. That is the agenda for Chapter 12.

But there is one other thing we need to do in preparation, which is the theory of options. We're going to talk about options and we're going to develop the Black–Scholes formula for option pricing, and we are going to go at it in a way that's different from the standard approach, which entails establishing the behaviour of an equivalent portfolio comprised of the underlying stock and riskless bonds. This approach leads to a partial differential equation whose solution is the option price. Rather than the partial differential equations approach, we're going to use the risk-neutral measure approach, which is conceptually much more straightforward.

A little more intuition

The state price approach alters the intuition we laboriously built up, where we showed that the holdings of the risky asset are determined by the interaction of risk aversion and the volatility of the stock. With the state price approach we went back to a much simpler view, the Lagrangian in the two-good model. Intuitively, if the expected return for all discounted assets is the risk-free rate r, why would we care about the riskiness of any asset? Any asset gets you that expected return.

The answer to this conundrum is that the effect of risk is now fully embodied in the state price: we would shy away from risky assets because their price is higher given the expected return. Thus, if we were to ask how to construct a portfolio under the risk-neutral measure $\mathbb{Q}$ in actual practice, the answer would be to first of all estimate the $\mathbb{Q}$ measure, then estimate the state prices, including those for the individual stocks we might consider holding in our portfolio. In the following chapters, we touch on how to carry out these estimates.

Exercises

Exercise 10.1. Recall that

$$\kappa(t) \equiv -\frac{(\mu - r)}{\sigma}$$

Show that the state price process

$$\xi_t \equiv e^{-\frac{1}{2}\int_0^t |\kappa|^2 ds + \int_0^t \kappa dZ_s}$$

is the solution of the stochastic differential equation for the driftless process

$$\frac{dS_t}{S_t} = \sigma dZ_t$$

Exercise 10.2 (Continuation of Exercise 7.3).

(ix) In this chapter, we discovered that the state price ξ_t is equal to the first derivative of the value function V_w; set $\xi_t \equiv V_w$. Using Ito's lemma, state the stochastic process for $d\xi_t$, *under the assumption that* $\alpha = 1$. [Note that no measure change has been imposed.]

Exercise 10.3 (Continuation of Exercise 7.4).

(ix) Using Ito's lemma, state the stochastic process for $d\xi_t$, *under the assumption that* $\alpha = 1$.

Exercise 10.4 (Continuation of Exercise 7.5).

(ix) Using Ito's lemma, state the stochastic process for $d\xi_t$, *under the assumption that* $\alpha = 1$.

Chapter 11

Options

In this chapter, we discuss option theory. In addition to the intrinsic interest of options, we need them as a tool in our empirical analysis for two separate reasons. First, we use the concept of implied volatility. Second, we use the surprising relationship between options and the risk-neutral measure.

In the standard approach, you solve a partial differential equation to obtain the price of an option, but this requires knowing how to solve partial differential equations. We use a less standard approach to the pricing of options, but one which fits perfectly into the risk-neutral measure framework and which is very intuitive.

Options under $\mathbb{Q}$

We begin by reminding ourselves that the environment consists of the riskless bond and a risky stock, called the "underlying," which could be the market portfolio:

$$\frac{dB_t}{B_t} = rdt \quad \frac{dS_t}{S_t} = \mu dt + \sigma dW_t$$

To begin, there is a very basic and fundamental type of option, a European call, the payoff of which has the following form:

$$\Phi[S_T] = \max\{S_T - K, 0\}$$

where K is the *strike* and T is the *maturity*, denoting the time at which the option pays out; see Figure 11.1. The function Φ is a

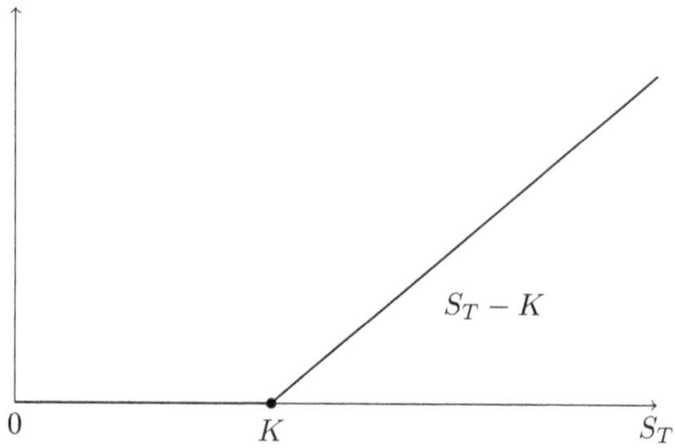

Figure 11.1. European call payoff.

function of the price of the stock at maturity, but it is not a simple function: there is a kink. In this discussion, we focus on the European call, but other payoffs functions are allowable. On the horizontal axis, we have S_T, the price of the stock at time T, the maturity date, and K is the strike price. To determine the payoff, you take the value of the stock at maturity and you subtract the strike price K, which has been determined at the purchase of the option, from it. If the difference is positive, the payoff is the difference; if the stock price is less than K, you get zero.

The value of the option in the market — its price C, is simply going to be the discounted expected value of this function:

$$C = e^{-rT} E^{\mathbb{Q}} \left[\max\{S_T - K, 0\}\right]$$

under the $\mathbb{Q}$ measure.

We would like to obtain a formula for C that uses the ingredients we have: K, T, S_t, μ, and σ. When deriving the formula we keep in mind that the purchaser of the option wants a fair price, but we also need to establish the correct price for the seller of the option. Since option sellers compete with each other, the correct price will give sellers zero expected profit.[1]

Figuring out the price is actually non-trivial because the payoff function has that kink. So how are we going to go at it? Well, the

[1]In fact, their profit is zero not just in expectation, as we would anticipate if an option seller sold options repeatedly, but with certainty, using so-called delta hedging.

first thing we can do is to note that by taking e^{-rT} times this object, we kind of already know that this has to be a martingale under $\mathbb{Q}$, because of no arbitrage. And because it is a martingale, the future value of it is going to be driven by the normal distribution, because the underlying stock process is driven by a Brownian motion. Once we know that, taking the expected value is just about taking the expected value of a normal random variable because there's no drift term we have to worry about. This is the approach used by Norstad (1999).

Deriving the pricing formula proceeds in several steps. There is a preliminary step, which is to slightly redefine the problem as follows. Take the expected value of the stock but only in the case where the stock exceeds the strike price. The option price can then be chopped into two parts:

$$C = e^{-rT}(E^{\mathbb{Q}}[S_T|S_T > K] - K)\mathbb{Q}[S_T > K]$$

The vertical bar means we are taking the conditional expected value of this object, where the conditioning is on S_t being greater than K. If that's true, we subtract K: that is the payoff. Then we weight this payoff by the probability that S_T is greater than K, $\mathbb{Q}[S_t > K]$.

There's a little bit of additional terminology for the first term. It is the payoff conditional on the fact that the option is "in the money," which means S_T is greater than K. And if S_T less than K, you would say it was out of the money, which means it pays zero. Now we can figure out what these two terms are using the $\mathbb{Q}$-measure approach.

As the underlying asset must have drift r due to the no-arbitrage requirement under $\mathbb{Q}$, the underlying process follows the geometric process:

$$dS_t = rS_t dt + \sigma S_t dZ_t$$

Recalling that we have an explicit solution for a geometric Brownian motion, this has solution

$$S_t = S_0 e^{(r-\frac{1}{2}\sigma^2)t+\sigma Z_t} \tag{11.1}$$

The solution has this exponential function form, but the drift is not zero; under the $\mathbb{Q}$ measure, it is r.

With this solution in hand we can analyse the probability that S_T is greater than K. The probability of the option being in the money at time t is

$$\begin{aligned}\mathbb{Q}[S_t > K] &= 1 - P[S_t < K] \\ &= 1 - P[S_0 e^{(r-\frac{1}{2}\sigma^2)t+\sigma Z_t} < K]\end{aligned}$$

We now use a standard argument to solve for the probability. Take logs and solve for Z_t:

$$\ln(S_0) + \left(r - \frac{1}{2}\sigma^2\right) t + \sigma Z_t < \ln(K)$$

$$\rightarrow \quad Z_t < \frac{-\ln\left(\frac{K}{S_0}\right) + \left(r - \frac{1}{2}\sigma^2\right) t}{\sigma\sqrt{t}}$$

This isolates the Z_t term, which is normally distributed. Therefore,

$$1 - P[S_0 e^{(r-\frac{1}{2}\sigma^2)t+\sigma Z_t} < K] = \mathcal{N}\left(\frac{-\ln\left(\frac{K}{S_0}\right) + \left(r - \frac{1}{2}\sigma^2\right) t}{\sigma\sqrt{t}}\right)$$

Denoting the complicated constant on the right-hand side by a in Figure 11.2(a), we see that the probability is the shaded area to the right of a. A key thing to note is that if we keep the reference

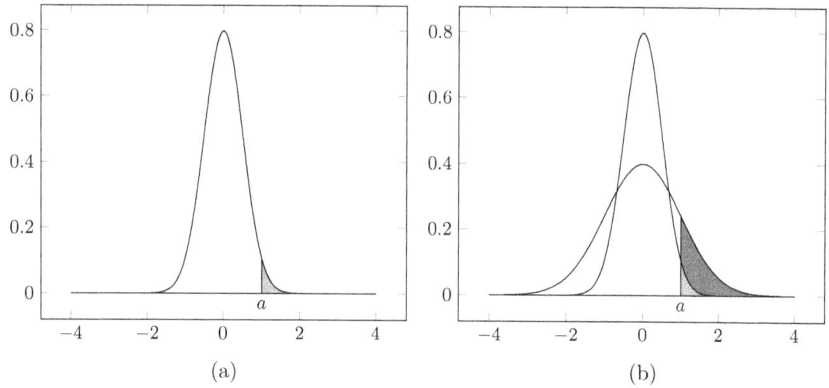

Figure 11.2. Option value. (a) Gaussian density with $P(x \geq a)$ for low σ. (b) Gaussian density with $P(x \geq a)$ for high σ.

point fixed (point a in Figure 11.2(a)) but increase the volatility of the underlying, σ, as in Figure 11.2(b), then the total area to the right of a — the probability $P(x \geq a)$ — increases. This is the key observation: as volatility increases, the probability of ending up to the right of a increases, and so the price of the option increases. The fact that the option increases in value with higher volatility is called "upside risk."

The next task is to calculate other element of the option price, the conditional expected value:

$$E^{\mathbb{Q}}[S_t|S_t > K]$$

We can express the expectation directly, using the solution for the price process:

$$\int_{z \text{ s.t. } S_0 e^{(r-\frac{1}{2}\sigma^2)t+\sigma Z_t}>K}^{\infty} (S_0 e^{(r-\frac{1}{2}\sigma^2)t+\sigma Z_t}) p(z) dz$$

where $p(z)$ is the normal density, keeping in mind that $z \sim \mathcal{N}(0, \sigma^2 t)$. This integral is a bit more complicated than the one we worked out above, so the details are set out in the bonus material.

Assembling the results from the bonus material, we can assemble the two terms, yielding the option price:

$$C = S_0 \mathcal{N}\left(\frac{-\ln\left(\frac{K}{S_0}\right) + (r - \frac{1}{2}\sigma^2)t}{\sigma\sqrt{t}} + \sigma\sqrt{t}\right)$$
$$- K\mathcal{N}\left(\frac{-\ln\left(\frac{K}{S_0}\right) + (r - \frac{1}{2}\sigma^2)t}{\sigma\sqrt{t}}\right) \tag{11.2}$$

This is the Black–Scholes formula for the price of a European option.

Puts

A put option works the other way; it pays you if the price of the stock goes *below* the strike price, by a certain date. It's more intuitively clear that in that situation, it's a kind of insurance. You're worried about a very bad outcome and it protects you against that bad outcome. It insures against the losses, but if the stock improves in value, you don't get any of that increase. So, a put option insures against your losses but limits your gains, whereas a call option allows you to cash in on gains and limits your losses.

Implied Volatility

Options have a property that is not at all intuitive but which is of great interest for us. Let's go back to formula (11.2) for a minute and note that it has several ingredients: the strike price K, the maturity date T, and the risk-free rate r. These are all things that can be directly observed. When you buy an option, you know the current price of the underlying stock, S_t, and you know the maturity date because that's built into the option; you know the risk-free rate r more or less, we can think of it as the US Treasury bill rate because treasuries are viewed as very safe assets. You know the maturity T that's built into the contract as well.

It is not immediately obvious what σ is however; it is not directly observable, and so you might have to estimate it by looking at the historical volatility of the stock. However, economists noted many decades ago that once you know the Black–Scholes formula, and once you have trust in the market's ability to correctly assess what the volatility σ is through the interactions of thousands and thousands of market traders, all of whom are very interested in the value of σ because they use options in their portfolio constructions, you can then infer σ by looking at the price of the option: this is the implied volatility. The option price is also immediately and directly observable in the options markets, and you can back out the σ that makes that option price the correct price according to the Black–Scholes model. That's a straightforward process. Since the normal cumulative distribution function is so nonlinear you can't write a formula for the implied volatility using algebraic manipulation; you have to use a computer, but it's otherwise very straightforward. The calculation is built in to hand-held calculators, apps, and is reported as a standard quantity in websites, such as Yahoo Finance.

Options in the Real World

We can have a look at the Yahoo Finance page, putting in the S&P 500, which has a ticker symbol itself, GSPC, and it is currently at around 5,375.32 as of the writing of this book. This ticker symbol doesn't have options because it is an index rather than something that you can buy and sell. However, there is an equivalent of the S&P500, an index fund or "spider" that you can buy and sell as if it were an equity: the SPX. It is explicitly constructed to exactly mimic the S&P 500.[2] There are various things you can click on for the SPX, one of which is options.

Clicking the options button, we see a list of many, many options just on this one asset, each associated with a different maturity and strike price. We can scroll down the page to where the colours go from blue to white, that is, the at-the-money point, where the strike price is equal to the current price of the underlying. The price of the underlying asset, SPX, was for \$5,375. So at 5,375, we are at the at-the-money point and if the strike price is very close to this, and also it the maturity date is soon — one day from the initiation of the option — then we can see the prices so that this column is the last price right next to the strike price. And we see that the option price, \$26.70, is pretty close to zero (relative to the underlying — 26.70/5375 = 0.0049) because the probability of going well above the current price of the underlying is tiny. On the other hand, if we go way down to a strike price of \$5,275, the difference between the underlying and the strike of \$5,275 in one day is almost certainly going to be about \$100, and we see that the option price is around \$97.27. Alternatively, if we look at a strike that is \$100 higher than the at-the-money price, \$5,475, the option price is tiny — \$0.20.

If we change the maturity to one month, things change. The options at the money have gone up in price, to \$80.30. The risk that the issuer of this option is taking has gone way up because it's quite possible that you would end up above this price. And the options with a lower strike price, \$5,275, have increased a bit in price, to \$132.93. And for the higher strike, \$5,475, the price has increased to \$32.42. Thus, a longer maturity flattens the price over the strikes.

Now we get to the punchline for us. By substituting the maturity T (one month), the interest rate r (the low-risk treasury rate, roughly

[2]You can also buy the more digestible SPY spider; as of this writing, the SPY is selling for \$537.5. (That is, the GSPC divided by 10 so that the SPY shares have a more digestible unit price.)

0.05), the strike price K (\$5,375 if at the money), and the current price of the underlying (again, \$5,375) into the Black–Scholes pricing formula, noting the market's price of the option (\$80.30), one can then compute the value of the volatility σ is required to obtain an equality. And note that it's more or less in agreement right at around 13% (that is, 0.13 in fractional form). That's the thing we're after.

The theory we have in hand predicts that the implied volatility should be the same, regardless of the maturity or strike price, and it is clear that there is wide variation in the implied volatility as we move away from the at-the-money strike price; this is called the volatility smile. We need more theorizing to explain this — it is beyond the scope of this book.

Since the implied volatility of the SPY is so important, there is a second way of finding it: the VIX. This is an index constructed from the implied volatilities of the options of the constituent stocks of the S&P500 index. As of this writing, this number also comes in at around 13% (0.13 in fractional form).

Getting $\mathbb{Q}$ from the SPY option

A fact that is not at all intuitive, but which is going to be a fantastically useful, is that if you take the second derivative of this option price for the SPY with respect to the strike price, K, it gives you the risk-neutral measure $\mathbb{Q}$. It's actually fairly straightforward to show that — see the Bonus Material.

Empirical estimation of $\mathbb{Q}$. As a practical matter, you can estimate the second derivative from empirical option data by looking at option prices for different strike prices. You take the list of option prices for a broad panel of strike prices (fixing the maturity date T) and calculate the differences of the prices for changes in the strike price, that is, $\frac{C(K_i)-C(K_{i-1})}{K_i-K_{i-1}}$, letting i range over all the available strikes K_i for a fixed maturity T. This give you a list of estimated first derivatives; repeat the process with this list, giving you the estimated second derivatives — this is your estimated $d\mathbb{Q}$. This recipe can be found in the work of Malz (2014).

You can also estimate the physical measure $d\mathbb{P}$: it is the probability density of the return process of the SPX. You can look at the mean and variance of the historical returns for the SPX directly to obtain this.

With the estimates of $d\mathbb{Q}$ and $d\mathbb{P}$ in hand you can then immediately estimate the state price ξ_t: because $d\mathbb{Q} = \xi d\mathbb{P}$, the ratio of the estimates $\frac{d\mathbb{Q}}{d\mathbb{P}}$ gives you ξ_t. We make use of this idea in the following chapter.

Exercises

Exercise 11.1. In the discussion of the Black–Scholes formula, we looked at actual market data for the SPY, finding that increasing the maturity spread the option price away from the extremes of zero (very short maturity at the money) and the difference between the strike and the current price for strikes far from the at-the-money value of the underlying. Consider the following experiments with the parameters:

(i) What happens if the maturity T becomes infinite?
(ii) What happens if the volatility σ becomes infinite?
(iii) What happens if the volatility σ is zero?

Bonus Material

Details of the derivation of the European option value under $\mathbb{Q}$

We set out additional details of the derivation of the Black–Scholes formula here.

First, calculate the conditional expectation:

$$E^{\mathbb{Q}}[S_t | S_t > K] \tag{11.3}$$

We can calculate the expectation directly:

$$\int_{z \text{ s.t. } S_0 e^{(r-\frac{1}{2}\sigma^2)t+\sigma Z_t} > K}^{\infty} (S_0 e^{(r-\frac{1}{2}\sigma^2)t+\sigma Z_t})\phi(z)dz$$

where ϕ is the normal density because $z \sim N(0, \sigma^2 t)$.

Lemma 11.1. *If z is normal $N(0,t)$, the mean of $e^{\sigma z(t)}$ is $e^{\frac{1}{2}\sigma^2 t}$.*

Proof. Complete the square as follows:

$$\begin{aligned}
E[e^{sz}] &= \frac{1}{(2\pi t)^{1/2}}\int e^{\sigma z}e^{-\frac{z^2}{2t}}dz \\
&= \frac{1}{(2\pi t)^{1/2}}\int e^{-\frac{1}{2}\left(\frac{z^2}{t}-2z\sigma+\sigma^2 t\right)+\frac{1}{2}\sigma^2 t}dz \\
&= e^{+\frac{1}{2}\sigma^2 t}\frac{1}{(2\pi t)^{1/2}}\int e^{-\frac{1}{2}\left(\frac{z^2}{t}-2z\sigma+\sigma^2 t\right)}dz \\
&= e^{+\frac{1}{2}\sigma^2 t}\frac{1}{(2\pi t)^{1/2}}\int e^{-\frac{z^2-2zt\sigma+\sigma^2 t^2}{2t}}dz \\
&= e^{+\frac{1}{2}\sigma^2 t}\frac{1}{(2\pi t)^{1/2}}\int e^{-\frac{(z-\sigma t)^2}{2t}}dz \\
&= e^{+\frac{1}{2}\sigma^2 t}
\end{aligned}$$

The key step is in the second line: we add and subtract $\frac{1}{2}\sigma^2 t$ in the exponent, allowing us to write the bracketed term. The bracketed term is a square, which means we can treat it as a normal density for a random variable with variance $\sigma^2 t$. The last equality follows because we are integrating a probability density, yielding 1.

We need to calculate the expectation

$$\frac{1}{\sqrt{2\pi t}}\int_a^\infty (e^{\sigma z-\frac{1}{2}\sigma^2 t})e^{-\frac{z^2}{2t}}dz = e^{-\frac{1}{2}t}\frac{1}{\sqrt{2\pi t}}\int_a^\infty e^{\sigma z}e^{-\frac{z^2}{2t}}dz$$

that is, the same object we examined in Lemma 11.1 but with a limit of integration, a. Using the reasoning of Lemma 11.1, we can write

$$\begin{aligned}
e^{-\frac{1}{2}t}\frac{1}{\sqrt{2\pi t}}\int_a^\infty e^{\sigma z}e^{-\frac{z^2}{2t}}dz &= e^{-\frac{1}{2}t}e^{+\frac{1}{2}\sigma^2 t}\frac{1}{(2\pi t)^{1/2}}\int_a^\infty e^{-\frac{(z-\sigma t)^2}{2t}}dz \\
&= \frac{1}{(2\pi t)^{1/2}}\int_a^\infty e^{-\frac{(z-\sigma t)^2}{2t}}dz
\end{aligned} \tag{11.4}$$

The limit of integration a follows from the inequality

$$S_0 e^{(r-\frac{1}{2}\sigma^2)t+\sigma Z_t} > K \to Z_t > \frac{\ln\left(\frac{K}{S_0}\right)-(r-\frac{1}{2}\sigma^2)t}{\sigma} = a$$

It is key that Z_t is not a standard normal but rather $Z_t \sim N(0,t)$.

If we define a standard normal random variable $\tilde{z} \equiv \frac{(z-\sigma t)}{\sqrt{t}}$, then

$$z = a \to \frac{(z-\sigma t)}{\sqrt{t}} = \tilde{z} = \frac{(a-\sigma t)}{\sqrt{t}} \equiv \tilde{a}$$

and

$$d\tilde{z} = \frac{dz}{\sqrt{t}} \to dz = \sqrt{t}d\tilde{z}$$

so we can write the integral (11.4) as

$$\frac{1}{(2\pi t)^{1/2}} \int_{\tilde{a}}^{\infty} e^{-\frac{\tilde{z}^2}{2}} \sqrt{t}d\tilde{z} = \frac{1}{(2\pi)^{1/2}} \int_{\tilde{a}}^{\infty} e^{-\frac{\tilde{z}^2}{2}} d\tilde{z} \tag{11.5}$$

The limit of integration a is

$$a = \left(\frac{\ln\left(\frac{K}{S_0}\right) - (r - \frac{1}{2}\sigma^2)t}{\sigma} \right)$$

and therefore

$$\begin{aligned} \tilde{a} &= \frac{\left(\left(\frac{\ln\left(\frac{K}{S_0}\right) - (r-\frac{1}{2}\sigma^2)t}{\sigma}\right) - \sigma t\right)}{\sqrt{t}} \\ &= \left(\left(\frac{\ln\left(\frac{K}{S_0}\right) - \left(r - \frac{1}{2}\sigma^2\right)t}{\sigma\sqrt{t}}\right) - \sigma\sqrt{t}\right) \end{aligned}$$

The expected value is therefore

$$\begin{aligned} 1 - \mathcal{N}&\left(\frac{\ln\left(\frac{K}{S_0}\right) - (r - \frac{1}{2}\sigma^2)t}{\sigma\sqrt{t}} - \sigma\sqrt{t}\right) \\ &= \mathcal{N}\left(\frac{-\ln\left(\frac{K}{S_0}\right) + \left(r - \frac{1}{2}\sigma^2\right)t}{\sigma\sqrt{t}} + \sigma\sqrt{t}\right) \end{aligned}$$

(To calculate the integral, we have gone from

$$\frac{1}{\sqrt{2\pi\sigma^2 t}} \int_{a}^{\infty} (e^{\sigma z - \frac{1}{2}\sigma^2 t}) e^{-\frac{z^2}{2\sigma^2 t}} dz$$

to

$$\frac{1}{\sqrt{2\pi\sigma^2 t}}\int_{-\infty}^{-a}(e^{\sigma z-\frac{1}{2}\sigma^2 t})e^{-\frac{z^2}{2\sigma^2 t}}dz$$

using the symmetry of the normal distribution.)

We also need to calculate the probability

$$\mathbb{Q}[S_t > K]$$

The conditional expectation in (11.3) implicitly has $\mathbb{Q}[S_t > K]$ in the denominator as a normalization, so these terms cancel. The net result is

$$S_0\mathcal{N}\left(\frac{-\ln\left(\frac{K}{S_0}\right)+(r-\frac{1}{2}\sigma^2)t}{\sigma\sqrt{t}}+\sigma\sqrt{t}\right)$$

Assembling the results yields

$$\begin{aligned} C = S_0\mathcal{N}&\left(\frac{-\ln\left(\frac{K}{S_0}\right)+(r-\frac{1}{2}\sigma^2)t}{\sigma\sqrt{t}}+\sigma\sqrt{t}\right)\\ -K\mathcal{N}&\left(\frac{-\ln\left(\frac{K}{S_0}\right)+(r-\frac{1}{2}\sigma^2)t}{\sigma\sqrt{t}}\right) \end{aligned} \tag{11.6}$$

Inferring $\mathbb{Q}$ and the state price from options

In practical applications, we would consider the index fund for the S&P500, which has ticker symbol SPX, as a proxy for the market portfolio process S_t. Consider a European option on S_t. We can state two interesting results by considering this option.

The first result is that the second partial derivative of the option price with respect to the strike price K is equal to the risk-neutral density

$$\frac{\partial^2}{\partial K^2}C(S_t,t,T,K)=\xi_t d\mathbb{P}(S_t)=d\mathbb{Q}_t=e^{-rT}p(K)$$

which is the risk neutral density of the stock under the $\mathbb{Q}$ measure. This formula is known as the Breeden and Litzenberger (1978) formula.

Derivation of the Breeden–Litzenberger formula. Starting with the price of the option,

$$C(t,K,T) = E^{\mathbb{Q}}\left[\max\{S_T - K, 0\}\right] = e^{-rT}\int_K^{\infty}(s-K)p(s)ds$$

take the derivative w.r.t. K. There are two terms, $e^{-rT}\int_K^{\infty} sp(s)ds$ and $-\int_K^{\infty} e^{-rT}Kp(s)ds$. For the first term, we use the fact that the derivative of an integral with respect to the limit of integration is just the integrand evaluated at that limit:

$$-e^{-rT}Kp(K)$$

with the minus sign stemming from the fact that we subtract the lower limit of integration. The anti-derivative at the upper limit of integration (∞) is not a function of K so it has derivative zero.

We can use the product rule for the second term:

$$+e^{-rT}Kp(K) - \int_K^{\infty} e^{-rT}Kp(s)ds$$

Putting the two terms together, we obtain a cancellation:

$$-e^{-rT}Kp(K) + e^{-rT}Kp(K) - \int_K^{\infty} e^{-rT}p(s)ds = -\int_K^{\infty} e^{-rT}p(s)ds$$

Taking the second derivative yields

$$\frac{\partial^2}{\partial K^2}C(t,X,T) = e^{-rT}p(K)$$

which, after dividing by e^{-rT}, is the risk neutral density of the strike price, $d\mathbb{Q}(K)$.

When do you cut down a tree in a stochastic setting?

In Section 5, we explored the problem of when to cut down a tree in a deterministic setting. We found that the optimal time to cut the tree was the moment at which the growth rate of the tree was equivalent to the interest rate. At a technical level, we established that the value of the firm owning the tree was the discounted value of the tree when harvested optimally, that is, at the right moment, and also that the right moment was when the time derivative of the logarithm of the value of the firm was equal to the time derivative of the growth rate of a bond's value, that is, the interest rate.

We then went to the trouble of showing that the time derivative condition was equivalent to a derivative with respect to the state of the tree — the mass of the wood. This condition has a name: smooth pasting ("smooth" denoting a derivative).

Things are more complicated in a stochastic setting: if the tree grows randomly, then when the tree is mature and you are tempted to cut the tree, you will hesitate because, due to the stochastic nature of the growth of the tree, there is a possibility that the tree will grow fast in the next few weeks or months and provide a greater return than you would obtain by cutting the tree immediately. This reasoning should sound familiar: it is the same idea as a European option in that there is a possibility that the option will go into the money by the maturity date, and this probability increases in the volatility of the underlying asset, and so increases the value of the option. The tree therefore embodies a so-called "real option."

There is a key difference between the real option embodied in the tree-cutting problem and a European call: the maturity date is determined by the forester rather than being fixed in advance. Financial options for which the owner of the option can decide to execute the option are known as American options.

The price of lumber also fluctuates stochastically, and because the profit from felling the tree stems from the product of the price and the mass of the tree when felled, the same reasoning applies when pondering whether to cut the tree now or later.

There is a better way to frame the question. We can view the company that owns the tree as issuing equity and we can then ask what the value of the equity will be. We know that this will entail a present value analysis using the CAPM. Specifically, before the harvest, and at the moment of harvest, the value of the firm will obey the no-arbitrage requirement of the CAPM, and we can characterise the value at the harvest using this idea.

To keep our model tractable we will suppose that the value (that is, incorporating the price) of the mass of the tree, X_t, is a stochastic process in which the drift of the value is a function of the value, that is,

$$dX_t = \mu(X_t)dt + \sigma(X_t)dZ_t$$

under the "physical" measure $\mathbb{P}$. To be a little more specific, the drift function $\mu(X_t)$ is an increasing but concave function of the mass of the tree: the tree grows on average but the growth slows down as the tree increases in size.

We begin by stating the value of the firm as an expected present value of the tree when it is harvested:

$$V(X_t) = \max_T E^{\mathbb{P}} e^{-rT} X_T$$

We can write down the HJB for the value as follows. First, we note that the value is a function of the state of the tree before it is harvested, so it will not be time-dependent. Second, because this is not a fruit tree, there is no flow of valuable fruit from the tree before it is harvested. Third, we again use the time dependency that is expressed in discounting, so the term rV appears instead of the time derivative V_t. The resulting HJB equation is

$$rV = \mu(x)V_X + \frac{1}{2}\sigma(x)V_{XX}$$

The problem as stated is to find the optimal time of harvest, but it is not so clear how to find the optimal time in a direct analytical way. However, we can find it in an indirect way using the idea of smooth pasting that we saw in passing in the deterministic tree-cutting problem. The mechanics of this are straightforward: you begin by noting that the value function $V(X_t)$ takes on the same value at the moment of the harvest as the value of the tree itself:

$$V(X_T) = X_T$$

This equation has a somewhat eponymous name: "value matching." The smooth pasting condition is simply the derivative of this condition; you just take the derivative of both sides of the value matching condition:

$$V'(X_T) = 1$$

Since the HJB equation has both first and second derivatives, we need two boundary conditions to solve it; the value matching and smooth pasting conditions provide exactly these two equations. We also need a third condition to solve for the optimal X_T at the harvest.

The interesting thing from the mechanical point of view is that we don't need to solve for the optimal harvest time T explicitly, we just need to solve for the optimal size of the tree, X_T; this size is reached at a random time. When we cut the tree at that time we have implicitly chosen T. This is what we saw in the deterministic tree-harvesting problem: the marginal conditions were expressed in terms of finding the optimal time, but we established that this had an equivalence with the marginal conditions with respect to the size of the tree.

An example

The HJB equation in this case has, by the nature of the problem, a drift coefficient, $\mu(X_t)$, that reflects the growth of the tree, which by construction shrinks as the tree increases in size, and so is inherently nonlinear. This makes solving the HJB equation difficult in general. By judiciously choosing the growth function, we can nevertheless devise an explicit solution, although the solution is complicated. We can solve an example.

The example works as follows: the drift coefficient $\mu(X_t)$ of the tree is represented by the following function:

$$\mu x^{-\alpha}$$

where μ is a parameter. The volatility is

$$\sigma x^{-\alpha}$$

where σ is a parameter; that is, it has the same form as the drift.

In the absence of risk, the growth process for the tree would be an ordinary differential equation with the growth rate equal to

$$\frac{\dot{x}}{x} = \frac{\mu X_t^{-\alpha}}{X_t} = X_t^{-(1+\alpha)}$$

which is positive but which shrinks as the size of the tree increases.

The HJB equation is then

$$rV = \mu x^{-\alpha} V_X + \frac{1}{2}\sigma^2 x^{-2\alpha} V_{XX}$$

Since the growth process has this particular geometric structure, we can solve the HJB equation using differential-equation solving software. Using Mathematica for this purpose, the solution is

$$2^{\frac{\alpha}{2(\alpha+1)}} c_1 (x^{\alpha+1})^{\frac{\alpha}{2(\alpha+1)}} x^{-\alpha/2} \exp\left(-\frac{x^{\alpha+1}\sqrt{\mu^2+2r\sigma^2}}{\sqrt{\alpha^2\sigma^4+2\alpha\sigma^4+\sigma^4}} - \frac{\mu x^{\alpha+1}}{(\alpha+1)\sigma^2}\right)$$

$$\times U\left(\frac{\alpha\mu^2 + \frac{\alpha^2\sigma^2\sqrt{\mu^2+2r\sigma^2}\mu}{\sqrt{(\alpha+1)^2\sigma^4}} + \frac{\alpha\sigma^2\sqrt{\mu^2+2r\sigma^2}\mu}{\sqrt{(\alpha+1)^2\sigma^4}} + 2r\alpha\sigma^2}{2(\alpha\mu^2+\mu^2+2r\sigma^2+2r\alpha\sigma^2)},\right.$$

$$\left.\frac{\alpha}{\alpha+1}, \frac{2x^{\alpha+1}\sqrt{\mu^2+2r\sigma^2}}{\sqrt{\alpha^2\sigma^4+2\alpha\sigma^4+\sigma^4}}\right) + 2^{\frac{\alpha}{2(\alpha+1)}} c_2 (x^{\alpha+1})^{\frac{\alpha}{2(\alpha+1)}} x^{-\alpha/2}$$

$$\times \exp\left(-\frac{x^{\alpha+1}\sqrt{\mu^2+2r\sigma^2}}{\sqrt{\alpha^2\sigma^4+2\alpha\sigma^4+\sigma^4}} - \frac{\mu x^{\alpha+1}}{(\alpha+1)\sigma^2}\right)$$

$$\times L^{\frac{\alpha}{\alpha+1}-1}_{-\frac{\alpha\mu^2 + \frac{\alpha^2\sigma^2\sqrt{\mu^2+2r\sigma^2}\mu}{\sqrt{(\alpha+1)^2\sigma^4}} + \frac{\alpha\sigma^2\sqrt{\mu^2+2r\sigma^2}\mu}{\sqrt{(\alpha+1)^2\sigma^4}} + 2r\alpha\sigma^2}{2(\alpha\mu^2+\mu^2+2r\sigma^2+2r\alpha\sigma^2)}}$$

$$\times\left(\frac{2x^{\alpha+1}\sqrt{\mu^2+2r\sigma^2}}{\sqrt{\alpha^2\sigma^4+2\alpha\sigma^4+\sigma^4}}\right) \tag{11.7}$$

where U is the hypergeometric U function and L is the Laguerre L function. The hypergeometric function and the Laguerre function are special functions that arise in differential equation solutions, which do not have explicit formulas except in specific instances, but which can be appropriately approximated using numerical methods.

The solution procedure proceeds in several steps. In the first step, we determine which of the two constants, c_1 or c_2, will be set to zero. We then solve for the second constant by using the first of the boundary conditions, $V(X_T) = X_T$, and substitute this solution into the solution for the value function. Finally, we determine the optimal tree-harvesting size X_T by solving the second boundary condition, the smooth pasting condition, $V'(X_T) = 1$. The formula for the derivative $V'(X_T)$ is extremely complicated but, again, we can calculate it using equation-solving software. We can then analyze the solution numerically by substituting values for the parameters μ, σ, α, and r.

In the first step, it is evident that if the constant c_1 is non-zero, the solution will explode and will in general lead to negative values of the value function. We therefore go forward with $c_1 = 0$. The second and third steps are then straightforward.

The results of these approximations are presented in Figure 11.3. The key results of interest are the impact of volatility and the interest rate on the harvest time. Based on the intuition we developed in the deterministic tree-cutting problem, we should expect that the harvest size will be a decreasing function of the interest rate, and this intuition is borne out; see Figure 11.3(a).

It is also evident that as the volatility increases, the optimal harvest size increases — it is optimal to wait to harvest in order to take advantage of the "upside risk" of the tree, viewing it as an option — see Figure 11.3(b). With real options such as the tree-harvesting problem, there is an additional dimension to upside risk: one can delay the harvest and in so doing take advantage of the possibility of future positive growth. This is evident in the numerical analysis: an increase in the volatility delays the harvest.

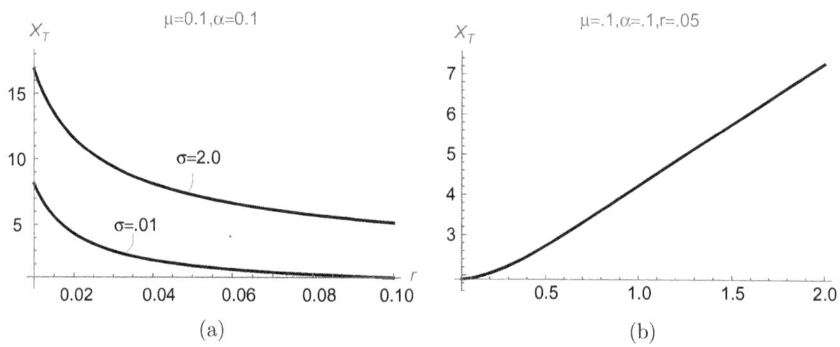

Figure 11.3. Optimal tree harvest size response to interest rate and volatility. (a) Optimal tree harvest size response to interest rate. (b) Optimal tree harvest size response to volatility.

A generalisation

We carried out the analysis of the optimal harvest under the $\mathbb{P}$ measure, but we have already established that because it is an asset, it would also be appropriate to discount the harvest value under the risk-neutral measure $\mathbb{Q}$, and the value of the tree prior to the harvest — V_t, not the physical value X_t — must obey the market Sharpe ratio at all times prior to the harvest due to the requirement of no arbitrage. Therefore, at the moment of the harvest, the physical tree, because it is obeying the value-matching and smooth-pasting conditions, also obeys the Sharpe ratio. Thus, another way to decide when to harvest the tree is to simply wait for the moment that the tree obeys the market Sharpe ratio and harvest it then.

Chapter 12

Empirical Tests

We've developed a list of tools, particularly the models of optimisation under constraints, and the equilibrium version of those of those problems, specifically the Merton portfolio model with α equal to one which we then interpreted as a model of the macro economy, and the He and Pages consumption optimisation problem, which we saw ended up being essentially equivalent to the portfolio problem. The solutions of those problems boiled down to expressions involving a very short list of parameters: μ, σ, r, γ, and ρ. Some of these parameters are directly observable — μ, σ, r — but γ and ρ, which are preference parameters, are not. And we have seen that the risk aversion parameter γ is key. If the model is correct, then we should be able to estimate γ from observables in multiple ways, and these estimates should agree with each other.

Estimating γ: What "Micro" Studies Show

There is a long literature by labour economists on estimating the elasticity of labour supply: how workers (that means everyone in the country who works for a living, not just factory workers) respond to changes in wages, that is, the percent change in hours worked for a given percent change in wages (broadly defined so as to include salaries, not just hourly wages).

Just to give a preview, the estimated elasticities are small, on the order of 0.1: an increase in wages of 10% will result in an increase in hours of 1%.

The issue is more complicated than it might seem because you have to take into account the fact that wages affect overall income, and therefore you have to separate the effect of the income shift and the pure effect of the wage effect while holding income constant — this is called the compensated elasticity. Viewing labour as the negative of leisure, an increase in wages increases income and therefore, viewing leisure as a normal good, more leisure is consumed — therefore you work less. On the other hand, increasing the wage also increases the price of leisure separate from this wealth effect — you have to give up higher wages by working less in order to consume more leisure, so you "buy" less leisure due to its high price and therefore you work more. This effect goes the opposite way, so you have to find a way to separate these two effects when estimating the elasticity.

But there is an additional subtlety: you have to know how long-lasting the wage change will be. If it is only temporary then the effect will be different from the effect if the wage change is permanent. That is, a worker who is offered work at a Christmas fair knows the work will be temporary, but a factory worker who is promoted to a higher wage as a foreman will have a different response to the new wage because it is permanent. This latter effect requires characterising the willingness to intertemporally substitute labour supply, and it is of greater interest to us because the intertemporal elasticity of substitution is the same as the risk aversion parameter γ in our growth model. These additional dynamic effects were examined by MaCurdy (1981).

How does labour supply elasticity allow us to estimate the intertemporal elasticity? This is motivated in the paper by Chetty (2006). The papers in this literature posit that the utility function has two goods, the first is consumption and the second is leisure:

$$u(C) + v(L)$$

An individual who "buys:" more consumption does so by sacrificing leisure — the same as increasing his labour. A change in the wage means that the first order condition for the leisure, $v'(L) = \lambda w$ (L is leisure) interacts with the first order condition for consumption, $u'(C) = \lambda$ (viewing the price of consumption as 1.0): as we have seen before, the ratio of the marginal utilities is the ratio of the prices,

$$\frac{v'(L)}{u'(C)} = w$$

and therefore you can infer behaviours of the utility of consumption — which is where the intertemporal elasticity lives — from the behaviour of labour. There is more about this in the Bonus Material section.

There is yet another aspect of labour supply that is also of greater relevance for us: the behaviour towards risk, which was not incorporated into the early labour supply models.

The estimates of γ from the many studies building on these ideas is that γ is small, somewhere between 0 and 2.0. They are compelling because the samples from which the data is drawn typically consists of thousands or tens of thousands of individuals with a broad range of characteristics and spanning years or decades to capture the dynamic effects. Therefore, when we estimate γ via the estimated Sharpe ratio from the aggregate stock market, and separately from the behaviour of consumption, we not only want those estimates to agree with each other, we want them to be compatible with the findings of this micro literature.

Hansen and Jagannathan's Test

The first of the tests we discuss compares the estimated γ using two separate approaches: the stock market-based estimate and the consumption-based estimate, and then assesses their statistical similarity. This idea was introduced in the paper by Hansen and Jagannathan (1991) (using discrete-time methods).

We employ widely used notation from the literature. The common notation for the risk-free rate in the literature is R_F — that's what we've been calling r, and the expected to return to the market portfolio, which in the literature is often called R_M, is what we have been calling μ_M. And then there's also the volatility of the market portfolio, which we can still call σ_M. These are all empirically observable, although there's statistical error associated with those observations. There is an additional quantity that we can observe, which is consumption C_t, and our models have been concerned with consumption to a large degree. So there are a lot of interrelationships between these variables, as we've seen as we've gone along.

The tests that were done on these models starting in the 1980s or so and continuing especially through the 1990s, uncovered anomalies relative to the predictions of the model, and these anomalies came to be known as puzzles. One of the puzzles was the fact that the equity premium, the difference between the average market portfolio return μ_M and the risk-free rate r, seems to be too large to make sense with the other things about the model that we know; this was famously established by the work of Mehra and Prescott (1985). In particular, to rationalise the equity premium being so large, one needs to posit that γ, which we are now going to refer to as the coefficient of relative risk aversion, needs to be much larger than makes intuitive or empirical sense. It needs to be something like 10, when it would be more reasonable, based on observations of behaviour in other realms by applied microeconomists, as we detailed in the discussion above, to have a value on the order of 1 or 2 — no bigger than that. That bothered people and gave evidence that the models were actually possibly wrong, sparking a hunt for alternative theories.

Why does that conclusion bother anybody? Well, these models have things we like. They have optimisation; they are about individual behaviour, and economists fundamentally think that optimisation is something everybody does. And firms as well. And as we've seen, there are consequences of optimization behaviour.

The other thing that we like is equilibrium. Setting the portfolio weight to α to 1 had a lot of logic behind it, and it led to this assertion that we're talking about the macro economy. If α is equal to 1 has some very strict implications for the behaviours that that we are interested in, for it to not work is bothersome because you have to come up with alternatives and there really aren't any good alternatives. So this has been an ongoing area of research and controversy.

One of the things that we discovered at a theoretical level is that the Sharpe ratio is also equal to the product $\gamma\sigma$:

$$\frac{R_m - R_f}{\sigma} = \gamma\sigma \tag{12.1}$$

That was that was an implication of the equilibrium version of the Merton model. We can observe the ingredients of the left-hand side of this equation: the risk-free rate, the average return to the market, and the volatility σ. We can use these observables to estimate the Sharpe ratio and then divide that by σ, and we have an estimate of γ.

Estimating γ with stock market data

We looked at the returns and volatility for the Nasdaq using data from Table 9.1. We looked at over a much longer period from 1971 all the way to 2020, with a mean annual return of about 0.12; the volatility came in at 0.19, giving us a Sharpe ratio is 0.64. Those numbers are ballpark reasonable looking.

We can also look at alternative versions of these numbers from other sources. First, the volatility can be obtained from the implied volatility from the VIX, which is a deliberately constructed index of the annual volatility of the market return R_M. The VIX takes the implied volatility from all of the options on a representative group of the constituents of the S&P 500 and aggregates those volatilities together to give you an estimated market volatility of the market return. Historically, the VIX numbers are in the same ballpark as the ones we actually estimated ourselves; they mostly range in the 0.1–0.2 range. Our estimate of volatility 0.19 lies in this range.

You can also get Sharpe ratio estimates from external sources. By using the SPX index, the estimated Sharpe ratio ranges below and above 1.0, falling to around 0.6 in some places and going above 1.0 in some places, to around 1.5. The number we got by estimating it on our own is actually ballpark within those estimates.

To estimate these quantities, you have to take averages. And because this is something that's using data that's constantly changing over time, you have to decide: do I average over the last 10 days or the last 10 years when I calculate these volatilities and returns and so on? That's a subject for time-series econometrics. We're not going to fret about it here, but we have been able to get a little bit of intuition for what the numbers are, ballpark at least.

Estimating γ using stock market data. Using the S&P500 from 2012 to 2021, we get an average annual market portfolio estimated return R_M of 0.1–10%. Using the VIX volatility series obtain an estimate of the volatility σ of 0.19. And if we assume the return on Treasuries is about 0.01, then the Sharpe ratio resulting from all of that is about 0.47. Dividing by the volatility again on the right-hand side of (12.1), we obtain an estimated γ of about 2.5. That's a bit high, but it's not horribly high.

Estimating γ with consumption data

We now turn to estimating γ a second way, using consumption data. First, some reminders about our model. From the Merton model, consumption is a linear function of wealth:

$$C_t = B^{-\frac{1}{\gamma}} W_t$$

The linear coefficient of wealth in the consumption function was this parameter $B^{-\frac{1}{\gamma}}$.

We also had a solution for the state price ξ_t in terms of wealth as well:

$$\xi_t = BW_t^{-\gamma} \rightarrow C_t = \xi_t^{-\frac{1}{\gamma}} \tag{12.2}$$

Not linear but it is a direct solution. And if you solve these two equations together, you can note that consumption is a function of the state price, and that's not completely surprising. That's just another way of saying the first-order condition in the optimization of the Lagrangian is the inverse of the marginal utility of the Lagrange multiplier.

Recall that we interpreted the state price as a kind of Lagrange multiplier. And the nice thing is, because of the martingale property using the risk neutral measure, we were able to show that ξ_t has a solution that looks like this:

$$\xi_t = e^{-\frac{1}{2}\gamma^2\sigma^2 t - \gamma\sigma Z_t} \tag{12.3}$$

Taking the logarithm of equation (12.2) and using the solution (12.3) yields

$$\begin{aligned} \ln(C_t) &= -\frac{1}{\gamma}\left(-\frac{1}{2}\gamma^2\sigma^2 t - \gamma\sigma Z_t\right) \\ &= \frac{1}{2}\gamma\sigma^2 t + \sigma Z_t \end{aligned}$$

The change in the log of consumption, which is the percentage change in consumption, looks like the following:

$$d\ln(C_t) = \frac{1}{2}\gamma\sigma^2 dt + \sigma dZ_t \tag{12.4}$$

It has a fixed rate of growth that is driven by γ and σ, and it has a volatility that involves σ as well.

Since we can observe consumption over time, we can estimate the elements of the right-hand side of equation (12.4): the drift or expected return or average percentage growth rate of consumption and the volatility of that consumption. And so by doing the calculation of the average of the rate of change of the log of consumption and then dividing that by the variance of the rate of change of consumption as estimated, of course, then we get γ:

$$2\frac{E\left[d\ln(C_t)\right]}{\mathrm{var}\left(d\ln(C_t)\right)} = \gamma$$

This was the approach used by Hansen and Jagannathan (using a discrete-time approach).

Estimating γ using consumption data. Using consumption data, using the percentage change in consumption from 2002 to 2007, excluding the data for the global financial crisis of 2008, we get an average growth rate of consumption of 0.029; the estimated volatility of consumption growth is 0.04, which gives you an estimated γ of $2 \times \frac{0.029}{0.04^2} = 36$, which is extremely high. This is an example of the equity premium puzzle:, consumption isn't volatile enough to justify a γ that's in a reasonable range.

However, note that the sample interval is from 2002 to 2007; what if we add in later years? Well, we know that consumption went down and as a result of the 2008 global financial crisis and the 2020–2021 pandemic has also caused the downturn in consumption. And that will also lower the average of it but also increase the estimated volatility of consumption. And that changes everything. If we add in the later years which have the higher volatility than the average growth rate remains roughly similar at 0.022, but the volatility changes to 0.15, and the estimated γ falls to just 1.9, which is intuitively and empirically much more reasonable.

Excess Volatility Puzzle

We can conclude that if you only include the pre-2008 numbers, then the γ you get is way too big. But if you use the post-2008 data as well, the γ falls to more reasonable levels. That's quite interesting: in the original literature on this so-called excess volatility problem or puzzle, which came up in the 1980s and 1990s, that was well before the 2008 crisis and this new higher-volatility period. Researchers during that time were well aware of the low volatility and even coined a name for it: "The Great Moderation."

One of the proposed explanations for the perceived anomalous behaviour of the empirical estimates of the model vs. the actual model was that even though we don't observe much volatility in the data, especially volatility of consumption, people in the model, the people in the real world are aware that bad things can happen. And they have happened. World War II is the leading example, but there are other examples of very bad events. And of course, we're experiencing them now. There are the three big bad things: pestilence, war and famine. And we've ticked two of those boxes recently. And of course, the financial crisis is the fourth example of a bad outcome. Two economists, Rietz (1988), and separately and later, Barro (2006), proposed this as an explanation: that people are aware that these bad things can happen, even if they have not yet happened. People's awareness that they are potentially there as outcomes lead them to behave as if the volatility is much higher than what we observe by just estimating volatility during quiescent periods.

And so what we have done in a very crude way here, of course, is to verify that they were right, once those bad events have actually taken place.

The upshot is that the two estimates of γ that are driven by the model, the Sharpe ratio estimate and the consumption volatility estimate, are, in fact roughly similar, once the higher volatility that was realised in the last two decades has been taken into account.

Barone-Adesi *et al.* Test

A second expression of the failure to empirically confirm the model is described in Barone-Adesi *et al.* (2020). In that literature, researchers looked at the state price process, which they call the pricing kernel and which we know is also a kind of Lagrange multiplier. It is a function of wealth. Combining the equations we wrote out in earlier development, for example, in equation (12.3), we can write

$$\xi_t = BW_t^{-\gamma}$$

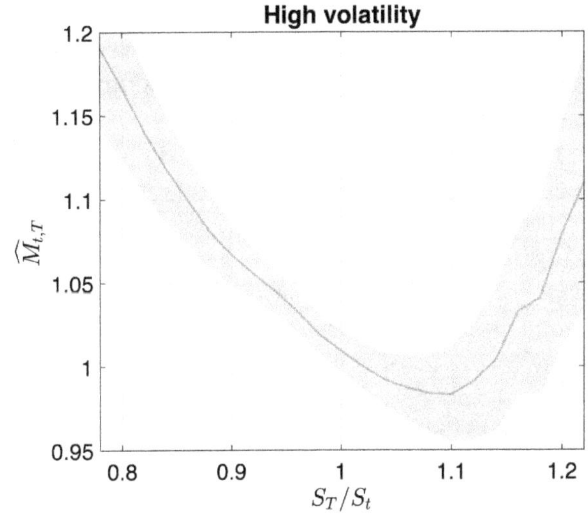

Figure 12.1. Pricing kernel estimated from past volatility is U-shaped.
Source: Barone-Adesi *et al.* (2020, Figure 1). Used by permission.

This has a specific behaviour that we can talk about. If wealth W_t goes up, then because we're taking that to a negative power, ξ_t will go down. Therefore, if we plot ξ_t as a function of W_t, then we should get a downward sloping line. That's a very clear prediction of this version of the model, which we can test if we can estimate wealth W_t and the state price ξ_t from data.

Barone-Adesi *et al.* (2020) carried out this estimation, and the result is illustrated in Figure 12.1. The horizontal axis is the return for the market portfolio, which is used as a proxy for wealth: the higher the return at time T, $\frac{S_T}{S_t}$, relative to some initial value S_t of the portfolio, the higher your wealth.

The state price is measured on the vertical axis. Barone-Adesi *et al.* use the symbol M to denote the state price instead of ξ, but otherwise it's basically the same thing. The prediction is that the estimated curve should be downward sloping. However, as the figure shows, instead of a downward sloping line they obtained a U-shaped line. This violates the prediction of the model, and as such constitute another puzzle.

Barone-Adesi *et al.* had an insight, which was to propose to improve the estimation by recognising that the measurement of σ is not so straightforward. We ourselves have already crudely estimated σ by looking at the volatility of the historical returns to the stock market portfolio. We saw that the estimates are in the ballpark between 0.1 and 0.2.

However, that's looking backwards. If you did that in 2007, if you estimated σ by looking at the volatility of the returns to the stock market portfolio up until late 2007, you would misestimate σ because looking forward, the people in the market were well aware that there was a lot of uncertainty developing, and that means σ would have gone up. Viewing the value of the VIX as the market's forward-looking estimate of volatility, it had started to rise by the end of 2007. By October of 2008, when the crisis was in full swing, the VIX went to over 80. But a retrospective measure of volatility, that is, just looking at the volatility of past SPY returns at that moment, would not generate that number.

But how would we detect that? Barone-Adesi and his co-authors said, OK, the market knows that the current value of σ is determined by current events, and if we're about to have a collapse of the financial system that the participants are anticipating, of course, the true σ is going to be very high.

In developing the model we have assumed that σ is a constant; our model does not allow for the possibility that σ can change over time[1]; this is a weakness of the model. A richer model would be required to properly account for that; it is possible to construct such a model and it is also possible to estimate how σ behaves over time empirically, allowing σ to change gradually over time in a statistically describable way. If you estimate σ that way, you still have the problem that even though σ can change, you might not pick up the a large change in σ that has occurred because of events such as, for example, one country invading another country unexpectedly.

How do you handle that? You look at the implied volatility because the implied volatility picks up the market's sentiments about what's coming. There are thousands and thousands of people attempting to optimise, which means that they're gathering information aggressively so as to not make financial mistakes, and they are expressing their information in their trading behaviour, which in

[1]As a purely statistical matter, one can estimate the statistical process for a changing σ_t using GARCH.

turn translates into the pricing of the options. And then from there, we can back out because those options are presumably priced using the Black–Scholes formula and its extensions.[2]

If that's been done correctly, we can back out the implied volatility and get what the market thinks is coming in the future, rather than estimating it from the past. That was the Barone-Adesi *et al.* strategy.

Now, in addition to that, recall that the $\mathbb{Q}$ measure has this property that it's the product of the so-called physical measure times the state price ξ_t that we have gotten to come out of our models in several different ways now. If we have a way of getting $\mathbb{Q}$ and we have a way of getting $\mathbb{P}$, then we can figure out ξ_t by dividing $\mathbb{Q}$ by $\mathbb{P}$:

$$d\mathbb{Q} = \xi_t d\mathbb{P} \implies \xi_t = \frac{d\mathbb{Q}}{d\mathbb{P}}$$

That is the very nice insight of Barone-Adesi *et al.* So if you can find $\mathbb{Q}$ and find $\mathbb{P}$, you'll have ξ: $\frac{d\mathbb{Q}}{d\mathbb{P}}$. And if you have ξ, then you can explore whether that graph in Figure 12.1 actually slopes down or whether it's U-shaped.

And so how do you get $\mathbb{Q}$? Well, this is where that little factoid we discussed earlier comes in: the second derivative of the option price on SPX shares is actually equal to $\mathbb{Q}$, and we can get at the second derivative either empirically by looking at different Ks — different strike prices — for the option on the SPX, or just use the formulas and substituting the implied volatility from the options on SPX shares into the second derivative directly.

How do you estimate this so-called physical measure? The physical measure is directly influencing and driving the things we can observe and in particular, the market portfolio S_t is being driven by the physical measure. Therefore, if we estimate the expected return on the market and the volatility in the market, then we're indirectly estimating the distribution of Z_t, and so we can actually build it up from those observations in a pretty direct way. Thus, to estimate $\mathbb{P}$, look at the return process for S&P500 series $\ln\left(\frac{S_t}{S_{t-1}}\right)$, then estimate the mean and volatility.

[2]There are a number of nuances that we have not incorporated here that lead to major embellishments of the Black–Scholes model. Actual market participants use these embellished and expanded models.

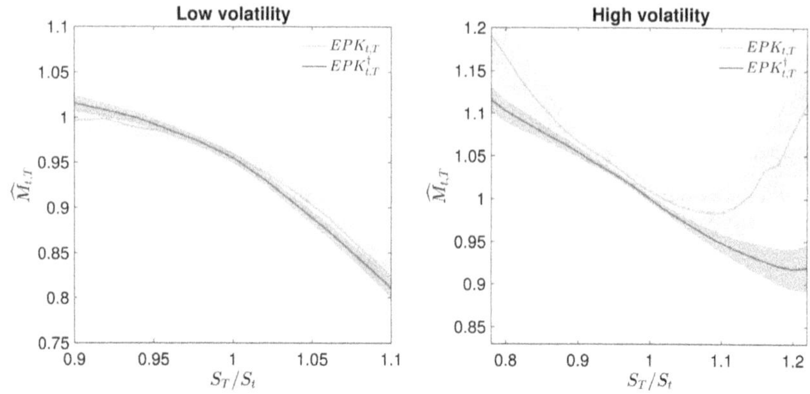

Figure 12.2. Pricing kernel estimated from implied volatility. Dark lines use option estimate of ξ_t.

Source: Barone-Adesi *et al.* (2020, Figure 4). Used by permission.

When you get $\mathbb{Q}$ and $\mathbb{P}$ you can plot the resulting estimate of ξ_t against wealth or a proxy for wealth, which is the change in the value of the S&P 500.

In periods when volatility is low, we get the downward sloping curve in the left panel of Figure 12.2. No problem. If you use the σ estimated from retrospective data, you look at the returns over time during periods of high volatility, you get a U-shaped curve, shown in the right panel of Figure 12.2, and as previously shown in Figure 12.1. But if you allow for the fact that σ can be higher in periods of high volatility, and, importantly, using the implied volatility estimate of σ, you obtain the dark curve in the right panel, which is downward sloping. It works. You continue to get the downward slope. And so by using the forward-looking volatility based on the market's actual anticipation of volatility, you get the right answer.

Thus, this very beautiful little model that we have, which has the things we like, especially optimisation and equilibrium and which incorporates stochastic elements, actually works.

Exercises

Exercise 12.1. Empirical tests of the stochastic equilibrium model using UK data. Download the spreadsheets from FRED, the Federal Reserve data repository, which contain the following information:

- UK stock market returns (https://fred.stlouisfed.org/series/SPASTT01GBM657N).
- returns to low-risk UK bonds (https://fred.stlouisfed.org/series/IRLTLT01GBM156N).
- UK consumption data (https://fred.stlouisfed.org/series/NAEXKP02GBQ659S).
- VIX implied volatility index (https://fred.stlouisfed.org/series/VIXCLS).

Be sure to convert all data to annual rates of return (stock market, bonds, and implied volatility) or annual rates of growth (consumption).

Carry out the following tasks, filling in the results on your spreadsheet:

(i) Calculate the risk aversion coefficient using the consumption growth data.
(ii) Calculate the Sharpe ratio divided by the variance method discussed in slide 3 (estimate the volatility directly using the data in the spreadsheets and the Excel variance calculator).
(iii) Repeat the above exercise but use the *average* implied volatility from the VIX spreadsheet.
(iv) Briefly compare and contrast the results.

Exercise 12.2. Empirical tests of the stochastic equilibrium model using German data. Use summary statistics for the following data:

- German stock market data.
- Returns to low-risk German bonds.
- German consumption data.
- VIX implied volatility index.

(i) Calculate the Sharpe ratio.
(ii) Estimate the CRRA parameter γ using the Sharpe ratio. There are two possible approaches: state and explain each approach.
(iii) Calculate the CRRA parameter γ risk aversion coefficient using the consumption growth data. There are two possible approaches: state and explain each approach.
(iv) Briefly compare and contrast the results.

Exercise 12.3. Empirical tests of the stochastic equilibrium model using Canadian data. Use summary statistics for the following data:

- Canadian stock market data.
- Returns to low-risk Canadian bonds.
- Canadian consumption data.
- VIX implied volatility index.

Carry out the steps in Exercise 12.2.

Bonus Material

Estimating γ: What "micro" studies show in a bit more detail

How does labour supply elasticity allow us to estimate the intertemporal elasticity, γ? This is motivated in the paper by Chetty (2006). The papers in this literature posit that the utility function has two goods, the first is consumption and the second is leisure:

$$u(C) + v(L)$$

λw (L is leisure) interacts with the first order condition for consumption, $u'(C) = \lambda$ (viewing the price of consumption as 1.0): as we have seen before, the ratio of the marginal utilities is the ratio of the prices:

$$\frac{v'(L)}{u'(C)} = w$$

If you posit that both u and v are geometric,

$$u(C) + v(L) = \frac{C^{1-\gamma}}{1-\gamma} + \frac{L^{1-\eta}}{1-\eta}$$

you can express the ratio conditions explicitly, and you can then infer behaviours of the utility of consumption — which is where the intertemporal elasticity lives — from the behaviour of labour:

$$\frac{L^\eta}{C^\gamma} = w \quad \to \quad C = (wL^\eta)^{\frac{1}{\gamma}}$$

$$\frac{u'(C_1)}{\frac{1}{1+\rho}u'(C_2)} = \frac{1}{\frac{1}{1+r}} \quad \to \quad \frac{\frac{v'(L_1)}{u'(C_1)}}{\frac{v'(L_2)}{\frac{1}{1+\rho}u'(C_2)}} = \frac{1}{\frac{1}{1+r}}\frac{w_1}{w_2}$$

Taking the ratio of the marginal utility ratio over time, we can recall the two-period intertemporal model of consumption and use the ratio condition from the geometric utility example. For geometric utility, this becomes

$$\frac{u'(c_1)}{\frac{1}{1+\rho}u'(c_2)} = \frac{1}{\frac{1}{1+r}} \quad \to \quad \frac{C_2^\gamma}{C_1^\gamma} = \frac{1+r}{1+\rho}$$

Note that we have two conditions: the intratemporal relationship between labour and consumption, and the intertemporal relationship between consumption in different periods. Thus, we can write

$$\begin{aligned}
L_1 &= (w_1 C_1^\gamma)^{\frac{1}{\eta}} \\
&= \left(w_1 C_2^\gamma \left(\frac{1+\rho}{1+r}\right)\right)^{\frac{1}{\eta}} \\
&= \left(w_1 \left(\frac{L_2^\eta}{w_2}\right)\left(\frac{1+\rho}{1+r}\right)\right)^{\frac{1}{\eta}} \\
&= w_1^{\frac{1}{\eta}} \left(\frac{L_2}{w_2^{\frac{1}{\eta}}}\right)\left(\frac{1+\rho}{1+r}\right)^{\frac{1}{\eta}} \\
&= \left(\frac{w_1}{w_2}\right)^{\frac{1}{\eta}} L_2 \left(\frac{1+\rho}{1+r}\right)^{\frac{1}{\eta}}
\end{aligned}$$

This captures the intertemporal substitution of labour. If wages fluctuate over time, then we can run a regression of labour (L_t is actually leisure!) on past labour and on the change in wages over time. We can rearrange this equation so that labour (leisure) in period 2 is a function of the wage pattern and also of lagged labour:

$$L_2 = L_1 \left(\frac{w_2}{w_1}\right)^{\frac{1}{\eta}} \left(\frac{1+r}{1+\rho}\right)^{\frac{1}{\eta}}$$

$$\rightarrow \ln(L_2) = \ln(L_1) + \frac{1}{\eta} \ln\left(\frac{w_2}{w_1}\right) + \frac{1}{\eta} \ln\left(\frac{1+r}{1+\rho}\right)$$

This happens because the individual intertemporally substitutes labour by "saving" it through the consumption decision. When formulating it on the final line, we see that a relative increase in the period-2 wage induces an increase in period-2 labour, L_2. Similarly, we see that if the interest rate rises, period 2 labour rises relative to period 1; this is because the individual "invests" his period-1 labour and receives a payoff in period 2. This is the idea behind labour elasticity estimates such as those of MacCurdy (1981).

This allows us to estimate η, and then in turn we can use this estimate in the equation expressing the marginal rate of substitution between labour and consumption:

$$\frac{L^\eta}{C^\gamma} = w.$$

We can formulate a regression model by taking the logarithm of this equation, allowing us to recover an estimate of the risk aversion parameter γ.

These ideas generalise to the infinite-horizon settings in which we analyzed pure consumption models. We can also incorporate labour into the growth model; labour becomes a factor of production, so the production function becomes $(1-L)^{1-\alpha}K^\alpha$.

A model of survival

In Chapter 1, we noted that there isn't really a utility function in your brain, but that we can get utility-like behaviour by assuming that people maximise their probability of survival. The Majumdar and Radner (1991) survival model attacks the problem as maximising the overall probability of survival in the long run. We can get the flavour of the model with a simpler approach using stochastic control.

An individual must consume a fixed fraction ϕ of his wealth:

$$C_t = \phi W_t$$

He gets only a fixed amount of utility from this consumption however: his utility is $\overline{u}$ as long as his wealth is high enough to sustain consumption. More precisely,

$$u(c) = \begin{cases} \overline{u} & W > \underline{\mathrm{W}} \\ 0 & W \leq \underline{\mathrm{W}} \end{cases}$$

Individuals solve the following problem:

$$V(W_0) = \max_{\alpha} E \int_0^{\infty} e^{-\rho t} u(C_t) dt$$

subject to the constraint

$$dW_t = (r(1-\alpha)W_t + \alpha\mu W_t - C_t)dt + \alpha\sigma W_t dZ_t$$

that is, just as in the Merton model.

The HJB equation is then

$$\rho V = \max_{\alpha} \Big\{ u(\phi W) + V'(W)(r(1-\alpha)W + \mu\alpha W - \phi W) \\ + \frac{1}{2}\alpha^2\sigma^2 W^2 V''(W) \Big\}$$

Since consumption is fixed by ϕ, c is not a control. Also, since everything stops when the lower bound is hit, we have the boundary condition

$$V(\underline{\mathrm{W}}) = 0$$

Thus, when wealth dips so low that the interest payments cannot sustain a minimum payment, the continuation value goes to zero.

Strictly speaking this is not equivalent to termination in the sense of Radner and Majumdar; the wealth process can continue evolving and go below the minimum $\underline{\mathrm{W}}$, and then return to a level above the threshold at a later date. However the boundary condition is equivalent to the requirement of termination the first time this boundary is hit.

In order to gain intuition, we assume that the following parametric restriction holds:

$$r = \phi$$

This assumption does not have any economic justification, although note that it is equivalent to requiring that consumption equal the interest payments on the risk-free asset.

We can solve the model in steps as follows:

(i) We first find the optimal α in terms of the value function and its derivatives:

$$\alpha = -\frac{\mu - r}{\sigma^2}\frac{V'}{WV''}$$

If the model behaves as we expect, V'' will be negative, and therefore α will be positive.

The portfolio weight is very similar to the portfolio weight in the basic Merton model: it is driven by the return to risk ratio and the elasticity term $\frac{V'}{WV''}$. In the Merton model, the elasticity term reduced to the inverse of the risk aversion parameter; here it will also reduce to a fundamental parameter, even though technically there is no risk aversion *per se*.

We can then state the HJB equation using the solution from (i) and the parametric assumptions:

$$\rho V = \overline{u} + \frac{1}{2}\frac{(V')^2}{V''}\left(\frac{\mu - r}{\sigma}\right)^2$$

This is a very nonlinear equation, however we can note that

$$\frac{d}{dW}\frac{1}{V'} = -\frac{V''}{(V')^2}$$

This result can be used to solve the HJB equation in two steps.

(ii) We now make an additional assumption: we model maximising survival as maximizing discounted utility without discounting, that is with $\rho = 0$. This, along with the parametric assumptions and the boundary conditions, gives a tractable approach. Thus, solve the Bellman equation and boundary condition assuming $\rho = 0$.

We next define an auxiliary variable, $Y(W) \equiv \frac{1}{V'}$. Combining this variable with the assumption that $\rho = 0$, the HJB equation becomes

$$Y'(W) = \frac{1}{\overline{u}}\frac{1}{2}\left(\frac{\mu - r}{\sigma}\right)^2 \equiv A$$

It is key that A is a constant. This differential equation is much simpler and is easy to solve. It has solution

$$Y(W) = AW + B$$

where B is a constant to be determined.

Using the solution for Y and the definition of Y, we can solve for V:

$$V' = \frac{1}{Y} = \frac{1}{AW + J}$$

Thus,

$$V(W) = \int_{\underline{W}}^{W} \frac{1}{Ax + B} dx$$

which has a logarithmic solution:

$$V(W) = \frac{\ln(AW + B)}{A}$$

We can now impose the boundary condition:

$$V(\underline{W}) = 0 \quad \rightarrow \quad \frac{\ln(A\underline{W} + B)}{A} = 0$$

$$\rightarrow \quad B = 1 - \frac{1}{\overline{u}}\frac{1}{2}\left(\frac{\mu - r}{\sigma}\right)^2 \underline{W}$$

You can verify that the value function V is increasing in wealth, and also that V is concave, that is, $V'' < 0$.

We can now examine the behaviour of the solution. The nonlinear elasticity term can be written as

$$\frac{V'}{WV''} = \frac{(AW+B)}{AW} = 1 + \frac{B}{AW} = 1 + \frac{1 - A\underline{W}}{AW} = 1 - \frac{\underline{W}}{W} + \frac{1}{AW}$$

For large values of wealth, this term becomes approximately 1 because $\frac{\underline{W}}{W}$ and $\frac{1}{AW}$ shrink as W increases. In that case, the optimal action is to diversify the portfolio between the riskless and risky assets, just as in the Merton model.

For smaller values of W (if A is small, which in turn can happen if $\overline{u}$ is large), the nonlinear term exceeds 1, so the investor *increases* his portfolio weight α on the risky asset. This is precisely what Radner and Majumdar found. The reasoning is that the investor is hoping that the high risky return will drive his wealth in a positive direction and thus increase his survival odds.

It is the behaviour of the value for large values of wealth that is of greater interest. In an economy with many individuals, each having different wealth, it is the wealthiest individuals who will drive the market, because they constitute the bulk of the trades simply due to their greater wealth. Those individuals by our reasoning have risk-aversion parameter 1. You can show one additional interesting fact: our geometric utility function $\frac{c^{1-\gamma}}{1-\gamma}$ is equivalent to $\ln(c)$, that is, logarithmic utility, for $\gamma = 1$.[3] Thus, we have an additional theoretical

[3]There is a detail: you have to add a constant to the utility function, expressing it as $\frac{c^{1-\gamma}-1}{1-\gamma}$. This is anodyne in that the derivative of utility is what matters for optimization and the constant term does not affect this. But unfortunately this expression becomes $\frac{0}{0}$ for $\gamma = 1$ — we can't compute the formula for $\gamma - 1$ directly. However, you can use L'Hopital's rule from calculus: the ratio for $\gamma = 1$ is the same as the ratio of the derivatives of the numerator and denominator with respect to γ. But you have to be careful when you take the derivative of the numerator: better to express it as

$$\frac{e^{(1-\gamma)\ln(c)} - 1}{1-\gamma}$$

The ratio of the derivatives (with respect to γ, not c) is then

$$\frac{e^{(1-\gamma)\ln(c)}\ln(c)}{-1}$$

For $\gamma = 1$, this is $\ln(c)$.

prediction driven by the survival model: that the risk aversion parameter is approximately 1.0, reinforcing the finding of the micro literature that γ is small.

If we apply this additional theoretical prediction to our main result, Hub's equation, we have that the return to risky assets is simply the sum of the risk-free rate and the variance of the market return process:

$$\gamma = 1 \quad \rightarrow \quad \mu = r + \sigma^2$$

We can put numbers to this. Supposing that the real return to risk-free bonds is the US Treasury rate (using TIPS, inflation-adjusted bonds) is about 0.02, and using the square of the VIX, which in normal times has a value of about 0.15, we obtain $\mu \sim 0.0425$ — somewhat lower than the actual historical return of about 0.075 (adjusted for inflation).

Chapter 13

Unfinished Business

There are several directions that we could go in if we had the technical stomach for it. The first direction is stochastic growth. It is certainly possible to write down and partially solve stochastic growth models, and there is a large literature on this. To obtain closed form solutions for continuous-time stochastic growth models is far more difficult however. A rudimentary stochastic growth model with closed form solutions is set out in Appendix C.

The second direction to go is to add labour and wages to the model. This is somewhat straightforward but adds clutter that would distract from the main messages of the book.

The third direction concerns boundary conditions, especially the so-called transversality condition. This would take us to a much higher technical level, one that would also be a distraction from the economic focus.

We have focused entirely on representative-agent models of the economy. But in the real world there is heterogeneity, especially of wealth. Can we model this heterogeneity, and does heterogeneity undo our main results?

We have also stayed away from discussing how individuals and firms make use of information in their optimizations, and there is a large literature focusing on the consequences of including information in behaviour and its impact on equilibria.

Finally, we made a seemingly innocuous assumption that individuals commit to repaying their debts in our discussion of the work of He and Pages (1993) model of consumption. This is actually not innocuous at all.

Appendix A

Integration by Parts: An Essential Tool

Take the derivative of the product of two functions using the product rule:

$$\frac{d}{dx}FG = F'G + FG' \tag{A.1}$$

That's pretty easy to remember because it has a kind of symmetry to it.

Reminder: The integral of a derivative of a function is the function evaluated at the limits of integration:

$$\int_a^b f'(x)ds = f(b) - f(a)$$

Use this idea to integrate the derivative of the product — the left-hand side of (A.1):

$$\int_a^b \frac{d}{dx}F \times G\,dx = F(b)G(b) - F(a)G(a) = F(x)G(x)\Big|_a^b$$

Applying the rule, put in the upper limit of integration and subtract the function of the lower limit of integration.

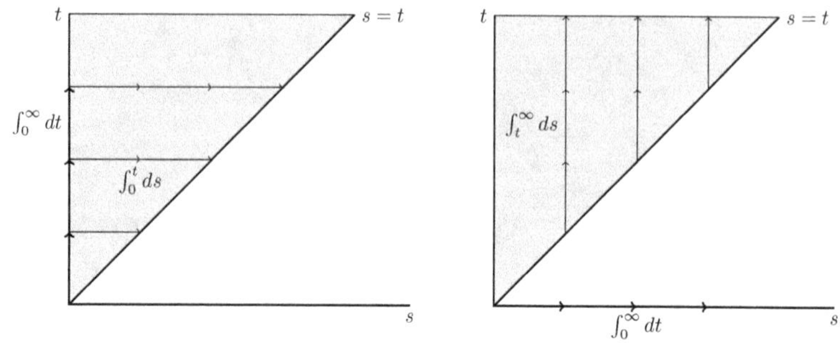

(a) (b)

Figure A.1. Switching the order of integration. (a) Initial order of integration. (b) Reversed order of integration.

We are also integrating the right-hand side of the derivative of the product:

$$F(x)G(x)\Big|_a^b = \int_a^b F(x)G'(x)dx + \int_a^b G(x)F'(x)dx$$

Now we just rearrange the order. This is the standard formula for integration by parts:

$$\int_a^b F(x)G'(x)dx = F(x)G(x)\Big|_a^b - \int_a^b G(x)F'(x)dx$$

Figure A.1 shows the intuition. It expresses integration by parts as the change in the direction of integration.

Stochastic Integration by Parts

There is a stochastic version of integration by parts. It looks similar to the deterministic version, but there is an extra term in the formula, driven by the stochastic terms. A reference is the work of Rezaeyan and Baloui (2013).

The intuition follows the same path as the derivation of the deterministic result: take the differential (not the derivative, since we are in the stochastic setting), using the rule for the differential of a product, then integrate and move terms across the equals sign.

To begin, we suppose there are two stochastic processes, F_t and G_t:

$$dF_t = \mu_F dt + \sigma_F dW_t$$
$$dG_t = \mu_G dt + \sigma_G dW_t$$

A key feature of these processes is that they are driven by the same Brownian process, W_t.

The product of these two processes, F_tG_t, can be analysed using Ito's lemma. In the main text, when we discussed Ito's lemma, we assumed that there was only one process entering into the process of interest, that is, we determined how to find the differential $df(F_t)$. To do this, we took the Taylor expansion of f and found that there were terms in the expansion that were coefficients of dt, dW_t, dt^2, $dtdW_t$, and so on. We argued that all terms would be vanishingly small except those involving dt and dW_t, and the product dW_t^2, which is converted (via an argument about the variance of dW_t) into dt.

When we have a function of two processes, $f(F_t, G_t)$, as we have here, the Taylor expansion of f has cross-product terms, f_{FG} and f_{GF}. The coefficients are the corresponding cross terms $\frac{1}{2}\sigma_F dW_t \sigma_G dW_t$ and also $\frac{1}{2}\sigma_G dW_t \sigma_F dW_t$. Applying the rules that we have recalled above yields the sum $\sigma_F\sigma_G dt$:

$$\begin{aligned}\frac{1}{2}\sigma_F dW_t \sigma_G dW_t + \frac{1}{2}\sigma_G dW_t \sigma_F dW_t &= \left(\frac{1}{2}\sigma_F\sigma_G + \frac{1}{2}\sigma_G\sigma_F\right) dW_t^2 \\ &= \sigma_F\sigma_G dt\end{aligned}$$

It is useful to note that we can represent this cross-product term as the following product:

$$dFdG = \left(\left(\mu_F + \frac{1}{2}\sigma_F^2\right) dt + \sigma_F dW_t\right)\left(\left(\mu_G + \frac{1}{2}\sigma_G^2\right) dt + \sigma_G dW_t\right)$$

When we expand this product we obtain nine terms. These can be grouped as coefficients of dt^2, $dtdW_t$, and dW_t^2. The dt^2 and $dtdW_t$ terms vanish; what is left is the dW_t^2 terms; recalling the product rule from stochastic calculus,

$$dW_t dW_t = dt$$

the product becomes

$$dFdG = \sigma_F \sigma_G dt$$

which was our previous result.

Applying these ideas to the full differential of the product, we have

$$\begin{aligned} d(FG) &= \left(\mu_F G + \frac{1}{2}\sigma_F^2\right) dt + \sigma_F G dW_t \\ &\quad + \left(\mu_G F + \frac{1}{2}\sigma_G^2\right) dt + \sigma_F \sigma_G dt \\ &= GdF + FdG + \sigma_F \sigma_G dt \\ &= GdF + FdG + dFdG \end{aligned}$$

where the final term comes from taking the cross-partial for Ito's lemma when there are multiple processes entering into a function. These terms matter because both F_t and G_t are driven by the same Brownian motion, W_t.

The stochastic integration by parts formula begins, as with the deterministic integration by parts rule, by integrating this formula:

$$\int d(FG) = \int GdF + \int FdG + \int dFdG + F_0 G_0$$

where $F_0 G_0$ is the initial value. The left-hand side is easy:

$$\int d(FG) = FG$$

We can then rearrange the terms to arrive at the stochastic integration by parts formula:

$$\int FdG = FG - \int GdF - \int dFdG - F_0 G_0$$

which is the same as the deterministic formula except for the term $\int dFdG$ — but in practice this term will be tractable because in cases of practical interest it takes the form $\int \sigma_F \sigma_G dt$.

Appendix B

Proof of No Arbitrage (Self-Financing Portfolio)

We asserted in Chapter 9 that all stocks must have the same Sharpe ratio in equilibrium, otherwise there would be arbitrage. Let's think more about the meaning of this.

Doubling in Continuous-Time

Let's approach this with continuous-time ideas: specifically, use the general idea of *boundaries.*

The continuous-time approach would be as follows. First, make an initial purchase of one share of the stock with price X_0 at time 0, where the stock price rate of return evolves according to

$$\frac{dX_t}{X_t} = \mu dt + \sigma dZ_t$$

To make it easy, borrow the money for this; because the debt will then compound at the riskless rate, you will owe $e^{rt}X_0$ when you cash in your winnings at time t.

Next, set a target level for the stock price $\overline{X} > X_0$ so that $e^{rt}\overline{X} > e^{rt}X_0$: when the stock price hits it, sell it and repay the loan. Let's also suppose that the drift μ is greater than r *under the risk-neutral measure* $\mathbb{Q}$ *for the market portfolio.*

If we can set the target arbitrarily, and if the stock will eventually hit it *in finite time* with probability 1, then we would have an arbitrage opportunity; the present value of the profit would be

$$e^{-rT}\left(e^{rT}\overline{X} - e^{rT}X_0\right) = \overline{X} - X_0 > 0$$

regardless of the future hitting time T. Thus, like the net profit in the Monte Carlo doubling story, the profit is a constant, so it is analogous to the €1.

It is crucial that the probability density for T — call it $\phi(T)$ — is positive over *finite* hitting times: then the *expected* payoff is just the integral of the density over those times, times the fixed profit:

$$\int_{T=0}^{\infty}(\overline{X} - X_0)\phi(T)dT > 0$$

This is what we have to prevent, otherwise there is an arbitrage. (Now you see that in the Monte Carlo doubling story there is no discounting; we would have to adjust it a bit if there were discounting).

Mechanics of Doubling

If there is an arbitrage opportunity then we don't have an equilibrium: the continuous-time version of the doubling strategy would be a money pump which all market participants would attempt to exploit, which is infeasible. We see that the way to shut off the money pump is to impose the Sharpe ratio condition.

Let us rephrase the problem slightly: to obtain an arbitrage, we need to show that

$$e^{\mu t + \sigma Z_t - rt} = \frac{\overline{X}}{X_0}$$

at some finite time with certainty — the equivalent of finally getting red at the roulette wheel after doubling the bets. If we take the logarithm of this expression, the problem is equivalent to showing that

$$\mu t + \sigma Z_t = rt + \ln\left(\frac{\overline{X}}{X_0}\right)$$

at some finite time, with certainty. Therefore, if the probability of hitting in finite time is less than 1, we *don't* have a guaranteed arbitrage.

To initiate this line of argument, it is useful to isolate the Brownian motion term:

$$Z_t = \frac{\ln\left(\frac{\overline{X}}{X_0}\right)}{\sigma} - \frac{(\mu - r)t}{\sigma}$$

(For notational brevity, we write this as $Z_t = a + bt$ while we develop the argument.) This problem has a solution that we can examine; an aspect of its interest for us is that it involves a Girsanov transformation.

The density of the hitting time

The next step of the solution process is to characterise the probability density of the *timing* of a Brownian process hitting barrier $a > 0$, starting from time 0. Denoting the *first passage time* to the barrier a by T_a, the density is as follows (from Karatzas and Shreve, 2012, p. 96):

$$P^{\mathbb{Q}}[T_a \in dt] = \frac{a}{\sqrt{2\pi t^3}} e^{\left[-\frac{a^2}{2t}\right]}$$

You get this by noting that the probability that $Z_t < a$, $P[Z_t \leq a] = 2P\left[z \leq \frac{a}{\sqrt{t}}\right]$, where z is a standard normal; the fact that we multiply by 2 has to do with the fact that this is a *first* passage — there might be others subsequently![1]

Briefly, the argument comes from the *reflection principle*: suppose we start a Brownian motion from zero and are interested in $P[T_a \leq t]$. We look at the Brownian path at some time t *after* it has already crossed a at time T_a. Once it has crossed a, *any* path that evolves above a has a symmetric (reflected) path from there, below a. Thus, the *joint* probability of the upper paths and $T_a < t$ is $P[T_a < t, Z_t > a]$, and $P[T_a < t, Z_t < a]$ is equal to it because of the symmetry. But these two possibilities exhaust all of the possible paths emanating from the crossing point a; thus the total probability is just twice the probability that Z_t is above the crossing point, $P[Z_t > a]$. Thus,

[1] A reference is the work of Karatzas and Shreve (2012, pp. 79–80).

$P[T_a < t] = 2P[Z_t > a]$. Now you standardise Z_t — remember it has variance t — and you get

$$P[T_a < t] = P[Z_t < a] = P\left[z < \frac{a}{\sqrt{t}}\right] = \frac{1}{2\pi}\int_{\frac{a}{\sqrt{t}}}^{\infty} e^{-\frac{z^2}{2}}\,dz$$

Now you can differentiate this to obtain the density above.

Hitting time density for an increasing barrier

Now let's expand to the more general situation: the probability of the Brownian process Z_t hitting the line $a + bt$. First of all define the stopping time notation as follows: $T_{a,b}$ is the stopping time to hit the line $a + bt$, so $T_{a,0}$ is the previously defined simpler passage time T_a.

Now consider the problem of calculating the expectation $E\left[e^{-\theta T_{a,b}}\right]$.[2] The first step is the Girsanov transformation: we can define a new Brownian measure $\mathbb{R}$ such that $\bar{Z}_t \equiv Z_t - bt$ is Brownian under $\mathbb{R}$, with measure coefficient $e^{-ab-b^2\frac{T_{a,0}}{2}}$, that is, the expectation can be expressed as

$$E^{\mathbb{Q}}\left[e^{-\theta T_{a,b}}\right] = E^{\mathbb{R}}\left[e^{-\theta T_{a,0}}e^{-ab-b^2\frac{T_{a,0}}{2}}\right] = e^{-ab}E^{\mathbb{R}}\left[e^{\left(-\theta-\frac{b^2}{2}\right)T_{a,0}}\right]$$

that is, we have the previous expectation for crossing the "flat" barrier a with $\alpha \equiv (-\theta - \frac{b^2}{2})$. By consolidating this, the expectation can be calculated using the result for the previous simpler problem for crossing the boundary a.

By carrying out the Girsanov transformation, we can now use the probability density for the "flat" crossing time $T_{a,0}$

$$P[T_{a,b} < t] = \int_0^t \frac{a}{\sqrt{2\pi\tau^3}} e^{-\frac{a^2}{2\tau}-ab-\frac{b^2\tau}{2}}$$

where we used the Girsanov adjustment factor to adjust the density. You can compute this integral by doing a variation on completing the square and also noting that the original density for $T_{a,0}$ remains a valid density and integrates to 1.

---

[2]The derivations can be found at Stack Exchange: https://math.stackexchange.com/questions/133628/distribution-of-hitting-time-of-line-by-brownian-motion.

We are not interested in this integral directly, however, but rather the density, which we can obtain by differentiating with respect to t. By differentiating and completing the square we obtain the density:

$$P[T_{a,b} \in dt] = \frac{a}{\sqrt{2\pi t^3}} e^{-\frac{(a-bt)^2}{2t}}$$

Exercise B.1. (i) Take this derivative. (ii) Complete the square in the numerator.

Using the Density to Calculate the Expected Passage Time

We are now ready to use the density to calculate the appropriate expectation. We can use the fact that if we take the expectation of $e^{-\alpha T_{a,b}}$ we can then differentiate the result, set α to zero, and obtain the (negative of the) expected hitting time. (To see this, do a Taylor expansion of $e^{-\alpha T_{a,b}}$ and set α to zero; this is basically a moment generating function argument.)

If this expected time is finite, we have an arbitrage. Calculating $E^{\mathbb{R}}\left[e^{-\alpha T_{a,0}}\right]$ is straightforward because you can just complete the square inside the normal density:

$$E^{\mathbb{R}}\left[e^{-\alpha T_{a,0}}\right] = e^{-ba+a\sqrt{b^2+2\alpha}}$$

Now we find the derivative of this expectation and set α to zero:

$$E^{\mathbb{R}}[T_{a,0}] = \frac{d}{d\alpha} E^{\mathbb{R}}\left[e^{-\alpha T_{a,0}}\right]\Big|_{\alpha=0}$$

$$= \frac{a}{\sqrt{b^2+2\alpha}} e^{-ba+a\sqrt{b^2+2\alpha}}\Bigg|_{\alpha=0} = \frac{a}{\sqrt{b^2}} e^{-ba+a\sqrt{b^2}} = \frac{a}{b}$$

Now remember our definitions:

$$a = \frac{\ln\left(\frac{\overline{X}}{X_0}\right)}{\sigma} \qquad b = -\frac{(\mu - r)}{\sigma}$$

Substituting these definitions of a and b; by varying μ we obtain the expected time to cross the boundary:

$$\frac{\ln\left(\frac{\overline{X}}{X_0}\right)}{(\mu - r)}$$

(Note that the negative sign for b is lost by squaring and taking the square root.)

It is evident that we obtain a finite expectation if $\mu > r$; to prevent arbitrage we must have $\mu = r$; this yields an infinite first passage time T, so the density over finite passage times is zero, which is what we need. (We can't have $\mu < r$ either because then you could set up a short and a shrinking boundary rather than a growing one; the argument would then be the same.)

Conclusion

Our conclusion is that under the risk-neutral measure for the market, to prevent arbitrage (and therefore to have an equilibrium) *all* stocks must obey the market Sharpe ratio:

$$\frac{\mu_X - r^f}{\sigma_X} = \frac{\mu_M - r^f}{\sigma_M}$$

and under $\mathbb{Q}$ we must have $\mu_X = r^f$. As we saw in Chapter 9 and in the work of Ewald and Taub (2022), this is equivalent to the basic CAPM equation necessarily holding for all stocks:

$$\mu_X = r^f + \beta_X(\mu_M - r^f)$$

Thus, the risk-neutral measure and the CAPM are equivalent.

Appendix C

Stochastic Growth

In this appendix, we unify the equilibrium Merton portfolio model with the basic growth model. In the Merton model, we assumed that the risky portfolio model had a fixed return process that was not related to optimisation, but we know from deterministic growth model that rates of return ultimately stem from the solution of an investment problem.

Basic Setup

Our agenda has been to develop and analyse closed form examples wherever possible. There are a number of directions we could go with this for stochastic growth. The first is to impose logarithmic utility and a geometric production function; this is the approach of the work of Brock and Mirman (1972) using discrete-time methods.

Another approach to stochastic growth is to analyze the behaviour at the steady state; however, because productivity shocks are constantly perturbing the economy away from the steady state, the analysis concerns the "stochastic steady state," with the emphasis on characterising the probability distribution of capital and consumption around the stochastic steady state. Merton (1975) uses this approach, but it is quite technical as it concerns deriving probability distributions.

A third approach is to again use geometric utility, but to impose equality between the CRRA risk aversion coefficient, γ, and α, the elasticity parameter of the production function, k^{α}, in order to facilitate achieving a closed form solution in a continuous time setting; this is the approach used in the work of Menoncin and Nembrini (2018). This approach has the disadvantage of entangling the effects of risk aversion with the productivity of capital. This is the approach we will use, nevertheless, as we will still be able to isolate and highlight the impact of the stochastic elements in the production function by benchmarking them against the models we already have in hand.

Our main agenda is to explore the impact of production risk on capital accumulation: does it hasten it or impede it? Additionally, we would like to spell out the impact of risk on firm value.

Menoncin and Nembrini's Model

Menoncin and Nembrini posit is a fundamental stochastic process that expresses technological progress and also stochastic shocks:

$$dZ_t = \mu dt + \Omega dW_t$$

where W_t is a Brownian motion process. The drift μ and volatility Ω are potential functions of Z_t, however we assume that they are constants. Importantly, the notation here is different from the notation in previous chapters: Z_t is not a pure Brownian motion but rather is a diffusion process with drift.

Output is a function of capital:

$$Y_t = A(Z_t)K_t + B(Z_t)K_t^\gamma$$

where Z_t is a stochastic process separate from W_t, The functions $A(Z_t)$ and $B(Z_t)$ can thus be viewed as technology shocks; the technical term is total factor productivity (TFP) shocks. The second part of the production function, $B(Z_t)K_t^\gamma$, is familiar from the deterministic growth model we analyzed in Chapter 4, except that we have imposed equality between α and γ. We did not encounter the linear part of the production function in the deterministic growth model, but it is allowable because the increasing and concave character of the production function is maintained.

The presence of the linear shock A_t means that capital can grow on average, that is, there is no steady state even if we eliminate the stochastic features entirely. To be more specific, if we eliminate the stochastic elements of the model, then the marginal product of capital becomes $A + B\gamma K^{\gamma-1}$. If A is greater than the subjective rate of time preference ρ, then the representative agent will attempt to accumulate capital until the steady state is attained, but this is unachievable because the marginal product of capital can never fall to that level. As a result, growth continues indefinitely. On the other hand, if A is less than the rate of time preference, the geometric part of the production function adjusts to achieve balance as we saw in the chapter on deterministic growth.

Returning to the richer model in which the coefficients A and B are non-zero and possibly stochastic, we can note that the output function resembles the asset process in the Merton portfolio model: a non-zero shock term A_t corresponds to the positive drift in the return to the risky asset.

Capital grows in a familiar way:

$$dK_t = (Y_t - c_t)dt + \sigma_K K_t dW_t^K$$

The Brownian shock W_t^K is distinct from the Z_t process that affects the productivity of capital.

Combining with the expression for output Y_t, the K_t process becomes

$$dK_t = (A(Z_t)K_t + B(Z_t)K_t^\gamma - c_t)dt + \sigma_K K_t dW_t$$

We can immediately see that if $B(Z_t) = 0$ and $A(Z_t)$ is deterministic, then we essentially have the Merton portfolio model. On the other hand, if we set A to zero and also eliminate the risk from capital growth, then we have $Y_t = BK_t^\gamma$, that is, the deterministic growth model.

The utility function has familiar CRRA form[1]:

$$U(c) = \frac{c^{1-\gamma} - 1}{1 - \gamma}$$

[1]Note that we have the form

$$\frac{c^{1-\gamma} - 1}{1 - \gamma}$$

rather than

$$\frac{c^{1-\gamma}}{1 - \gamma}$$

as in earlier chapters; as we noted in the survival model of Section 12, this slightly more general form allows us to consider the case in which $\gamma = 1$.

taking note that the risk aversion parameter γ is also the production function elasticity. The agent wants to optimise discounted expected utility:

$$\max_{\{c_s\}_t^\infty} E\left[\int_t^\infty e^{-\rho(s-t)}\frac{c_s^{1-\gamma}-1}{1-\gamma}ds\right]$$

where we have been a little bit more fussy to emphasise that is is the entire path of consumption that is being chosen, $\{c_s\}_t^\infty$.

The HJB equation recognises two state variables, Z_t, the underlying TFP shock process, and capital K_t. For our purposes, we want to isolate the effects of the productivity and return shocks from each other, so the cross-correlation between W_t^K and Z_t can be taken to be zero. The resulting HJB equation is

$$\rho J = J_t + \max_c\left[\frac{c_t^{1-\gamma}}{1-\gamma} + \left(A_tK_t + B_tK_t^\gamma - c_t\right)J_K\right] + \frac{1}{2}\sigma_K^2K_t^2J_{KK} + \mu J_Z + \frac{1}{2}\Omega^2J_{ZZ} \tag{C.1}$$

The optimal consumption solution is

$$c_t^* = J_K^{-\frac{1}{\gamma}}$$

that is, the inverse marginal utility function of the equivalent of the Lagrange multiplier that would apply here, as we noted in our development of the Merton model.

Menoncin and Nembrini examine two subcases of this model. In the first, the B coefficient is zero, leading to an extension of the Merton model in which the expected return to risky investment, (μ in the notation of the Merton model), is itself stochastic, that is, A_t is stochastic.

In the second subcase, Menoncin and Nembrini make the opposite simplification, assuming that A_t is zero and B_t is a positive constant.

The stochastic productivity case: $B = 0$, $A \neq 0$

Menoncin and Nembrini first analyse the case in which B is zero, that is, the production function is linear in capital. The additional shocks stemming from the stochastic fluctuations in productivity then alter the resulting behaviour of the model. The model is then like the Merton model but in which the drift of the risky asset, μ, is stochastic. This adds an element of risk.

One aspect of setting B to zero is that, as the production function is then linear, profit is zero and there is no interesting theory of the firm arising from the model.

Menoncin and Nembrini demonstrate that optimal consumption is a linear function of capital, as in our previous portfolio models:

$$c_t^* = \left(E^\gamma\left[\left(\int_t^\infty e^{-\int_t^s \phi(Z_u)du} ds\right)^\gamma\right]\right)^{-\frac{1}{\gamma}} K_t$$

but where, importantly, a measure change has been undertaken, with the expectation E^γ being taken under the new measure; the measure change occurs for reasons unrelated to our earlier applications; it is a transformation needed to apply the Feynman-Kac solution method to the equation. Details of the derivation of this result are set out in the Bonus Material at the end of this appendix.

Note the similarity of the coefficient term $(\cdot)^{-\frac{1}{\gamma}}$ with the coefficient term $B^{-\frac{1}{\gamma}}$ that arises in the Merton model.

The function ϕ is defined as

$$\phi(Z_t) \equiv \frac{\rho + \frac{1}{2}(1-\gamma)\gamma\sigma_K^2 - (1-\gamma)A(Z_t)}{\gamma}$$

The only stochastic element here is the A_t function, which is the stochastic TFP shock on the linear part of the production function. Thus, we can simplify the solution as follows:

$$c_t^* = E^\gamma\left[\left(\int_t^\infty e^{-\frac{\rho+\frac{1}{2}(1-\gamma)\gamma\sigma^2}{\gamma}(s-t)+\frac{1-\gamma}{\gamma}\int_t^s A_t du} ds\right)^\gamma\right]^{-\frac{1}{\gamma}} K_t$$

If A_t is stochastic, although we can bring out the exponential of the constant terms, the nonlinearity stemming from the γ exponent surrounding the integral means that we cannot pass the expectation operator through the integral, although some abstract conclusions are possible concerning the magnitude of the expected value term.

Menoncin and Nembrini examine the behaviour of this term when A_t is stochastic by imagining that A_t follows a mean-reverting process:

$$dA_t = \alpha(\overline{A} - A_t)dt + \sigma_A\sqrt{A_t}dW_t^A$$

The drift term is positive if A_t is less than $\overline{A}$, causing A_t to drift towards $\overline{A}$; conversely, the drift term is negative if A_t is greater than $\overline{A}$, causing A_t to drift towards $\overline{A}$.

In that case, the integral can be approximated by using the mean value $\bar{A}$, and then we can solve the integral by using our rules for the integral of an exponential function. It is important to note, however, that by restricting attention to this approximation, we are eliminating the influence of the risk attached to the stochastic productivity shock.

Under the mean-reversion technology assumption, and imposing the approximation $A_t \approx \bar{A}$, we can approximate the integral as follows:

$$\begin{aligned}
&\int_t^{\infty} e^{-\frac{\rho-\frac{1}{2}(\gamma-1)\gamma\sigma^2}{\gamma}(s-t)+\frac{(1-\gamma)}{\gamma}\int_t^s A_t du} ds \\
&\approx \int_t^{\infty} e^{-\frac{\rho-\frac{1}{2}(\gamma-1)\gamma\sigma^2}{\gamma}(s-t)+\frac{(1-\gamma)}{\gamma}\bar{A}(s-t)} ds \\
&= \int_t^{\infty} e^{\left(-\frac{\rho-\frac{1}{2}(\gamma-1)\gamma\sigma^2}{\gamma}+\frac{(1-\gamma)}{\gamma}\bar{A}\right)(s-t)} ds \\
&= e^{-\left(-\frac{\rho-\frac{1}{2}(\gamma-1)\gamma\sigma^2}{\gamma}+\frac{(1-\gamma)}{\gamma}\bar{A}\right)t} \int_t^{\infty} e^{\left(-\frac{\rho-\frac{1}{2}(\gamma-1)\gamma\sigma^2}{\gamma}+\frac{(1-\gamma)}{\gamma}\bar{A}\right)s} ds \\
&= e^{-\left(-\frac{\rho-\frac{1}{2}(\gamma-1)\gamma\sigma^2}{\gamma}+\frac{(1-\gamma)}{\gamma}\bar{A}\right)t} \frac{1}{\left(-\frac{\rho-\frac{1}{2}(\gamma-1)\gamma\sigma^2}{\gamma}+\frac{(1-\gamma)}{\gamma}\bar{A}\right)} \\
&\quad \times e^{\left(-\frac{\rho-\frac{1}{2}(\gamma-1)\gamma\sigma^2}{\gamma}+\frac{(1-\gamma)}{\gamma}\bar{A}\right)s}\Bigg|_t^{\infty} \\
&= -\frac{1}{\left(-\frac{\rho-\frac{1}{2}(\gamma-1)\gamma\sigma^2}{\gamma}+\frac{(1-\gamma)}{\gamma}\bar{A}\right)}
\end{aligned}$$

Substituting into the formula for consumption, we obtain

$$\left[\left(\frac{1}{\left(\frac{\rho-\frac{1}{2}(\gamma-1)\gamma\sigma^2}{\gamma}-\frac{(1-\gamma)}{\gamma}\bar{A}\right)}\right)^{\gamma}\right]^{-\frac{1}{\gamma}}=\frac{\rho}{\gamma}+\frac{1}{2}(1-\gamma)\sigma^2-\frac{(1-\gamma)}{\gamma}\bar{A}$$

Consumption is therefore

$$c^{*}=\left(\frac{\rho}{\gamma}+\frac{1}{2}(1-\gamma)\sigma_K^2-\frac{1-\gamma}{\gamma}\overline{A}\right)K_t$$

We can compare this solution with the solution for the Merton portfolio model with CRRA preferences:

$$C=B^{-\frac{1}{\gamma}}W$$

That is, consumption is a linear function of wealth, and from equation (7.5),

$$B^{-\frac{1}{\gamma}}=\frac{\rho}{\gamma}-\frac{1-\gamma}{\gamma}\left(r+\frac{1}{2}\frac{(\mu-r)^2}{\gamma\sigma^2}\right)$$

We explored the details of this constant when bonds are zero, which is the same situation the capital growth model presumes from the start. The conditions for zero bonds were that

$$\mu=r+\gamma\sigma^2 \quad r=\rho-(1+\gamma)\gamma\sigma^2 \quad \rightarrow \quad B^{-\frac{1}{\gamma}}=\rho+\frac{1}{2}(1-\gamma)\gamma\sigma^2$$

Thus, the stochastic growth model with linear productivity shocks duplicates the Merton model but with the additional term $\frac{1-\gamma}{\gamma}\overline{A}$ arising from the productivity shocks. However, if we set $\bar{A}=\rho+\frac{1}{2}(1-\gamma)\gamma\sigma^2$, then the Menoncin and Nembrini's ϕ expression reduces to

$$\rho+\frac{1}{2}(1-\gamma)\gamma\sigma^2$$

which exactly duplicates the Merton model formula; thus, by choosing to ignore the risk from the productivity process and setting A_t equal to its mean reverting value, and choosing that value appropriately, we don't get any added mileage out of the stochastic productivity model.

The capital growth process

Of greater interest is the stochastic process for optimal capital. This has the following structure:

$$\frac{dK_t^*}{K_t^*} = \left(A_t - E^{\gamma}\left[\left(\int_t^{\infty} e^{-\frac{\rho-\frac{1}{2}(\gamma-1)\gamma\sigma^2}{\gamma}(s-t)+\frac{(\gamma-1)}{\gamma}\int_t^s A_t du} ds\right)^{\gamma}\right]^{-\frac{1}{\gamma}}\right) dt$$

$$+\sigma_K dW_t$$

Interestingly, only the A_t productivity shocks, not the B_t shocks on the geometric part, matter for the capital process. The A_t shocks cause the drift of the return to capital process to itself be stochastic, and we can calculate the expected value of the return.

If A_t follows a mean reverting process as above, we have

$$\frac{dK_t^*}{K_t^*} = \left(A_t - \left(\frac{\rho}{\gamma} + \frac{1}{2}(1-\gamma)\sigma_K^2 - \frac{1-\gamma}{\gamma}\overline{A}\right)\right) dt + \sigma_K dW_t$$

and thus the A_t term drives the capital growth process; we can look for parameterizations such that this is an ergodic steady state, that is, zero drift. This occurs using the mean-reverting process and the natural mean that we already established, that is, $\bar{A} = \rho + \frac{1}{2}(1-\gamma)\gamma\sigma^2$. Assuming approximate zero drift, we can then solve for the capital process:

$$K_t \approx e^{-\frac{1}{2}\sigma^2 t+\sigma W_t}$$

Nonlinear production function: $A = 0$, $B \neq 0$

Menoncin and Nembrini then consider the more general case in which $B \neq 0$, that is, output comes from a geometric production function.

The $B \neq 0$ case adds substantial complication to the analysis. There are two directions to go with this case. In the first, we would allow $B(Z_t)$ to be stochastic, that is, there would be stochastic productivity shocks on the nonlinear production function. To isolate the effect of this formulation, we could suppress the other stochastic elements of the model by setting the linear productivity shocks A_t to zero, and also the capital accumulation process would be deterministic, that is, σ_K would be zero. Using our orchard analogy, any new trees would grow without risk, but the fruit the orchard bears would be stochastic and nonlinearly affected by the size of the orchard, K_t.

The second direction is to retain these other stochastic elements but to make $B(Z_t)$ a constant, that is, the production function would be like that of the deterministic growth model. However, the interaction of the other stochastic elements with the nonlinear production function still lead to substantial complications.

Menoncin and Nembrini begin their treatment of the $B \neq 0$ case by embellishing the type of preferences of the agent in the model to HARA, hyperbolic absolute risk aversion, which is a generalisation of CRRA preferences:

$$u(c) = \frac{c^{1-\gamma} - \bar{c}}{1-\gamma}$$

where $\bar{c}$ is a "subsistence" level of consumption. There is an additional parameter, δ, that when integrated into the model in the form of the ratio $\frac{\bar{c}}{\delta}$, permits a solution.

Their production function has the form

$$Y_t = A_t\left(K_t + \frac{\bar{c}}{\delta}\right)dt + B_t\left(K_t + \frac{\bar{c}}{\delta}\right)^{\gamma}$$

where $\bar{c}$ and δ are extra parameters that we discuss later, and remembering that the exponent in the nonlinear part of the production function was α in our deterministic growth model, but here the assumption $\alpha = \gamma$ has been used. Similarly, the capital growth process is

$$d\left(K_t + \frac{\bar{c}}{\delta}\right) = ((Y_t - C_t)dt + \sigma dW_t)\left(K_t + \frac{\bar{c}}{\delta}\right)$$

that is, a geometric process.

Menoncin and Nembrini then develop the solution for consumption, similar to our previous derivations:

$$C_t = \bar{c} + \left(K_t + \frac{\bar{c}}{\delta}\right)E^{\gamma}\left[\left(\int_t^{\infty} e^{-\int_t^s \phi(Z_u)du}ds\right)^{\gamma}\right]^{-\frac{1}{\gamma}}$$

where the expectation is taken under the changed measure discussed in the development of the solution above. Thus, the solution is very close to the solution we developed above with $B = 0$, except for the extra terms $\bar{c}$ and $\frac{\bar{c}}{\delta}$. Thus, consumption is still linear (strictly speaking, affine) in the modified capital process $(K_t + \frac{\bar{c}}{\delta})$.

Directly solving for the K process with integrating factor

Menoncin and Nembrini conduct a calibrated numerical simulation with a simplified version of the model. They assume that there are no linear productivity shocks ($A_t = 0$) and the volatility of the investment shocks is constant. They also assume that the nonlinear production function does not have stochastic productivity shocks, that is, B_t is a constant. After solving for consumption and defining the auxiliary variable

$$\hat{K}_t \equiv \left(K_t + \frac{\bar{c}}{\delta}\right)^{1-\gamma} \tilde{K}_t \equiv \left(K_t + \frac{\bar{c}}{\delta}\right)^{1-\gamma}$$

which is the inverse of the marginal product of capital. They can state the capital state process as

$$d\tilde{K}_t = \left(-(\delta+\phi)\tilde{K}_t + B\hat{K}^{\gamma}\right) dt + \sigma \tilde{K}_t dW_t$$

This equation can readily be solved using an integrating factor (see Section 6 in Chapter 6). We can then set $\bar{c} = 0$, derive the marginal product of capital and use it to discount firm profits, which are also a function of the solution. The result will be one that can be benchmarked against the deterministic growth model to illustrate the impact of stochastic shocks to investment returns on profits. Alternatively, we can derive the Radon–Nikodym derivative for the $\hat{K}$ process and use the risk-free rate to discount profits.

After substituting the consumption solution into the capital growth process, they obtain an explicit solution for $(K_t + \frac{\bar{c}}{\delta})$:

$$\tilde{K}_t = \left(\frac{(K_0 + \frac{\bar{c}}{\delta})^{1-\gamma}}{\Gamma_t} e^{(1-\gamma)\int_0^t g_s ds} + (1-\gamma)Be^{(1-\gamma)\int_0^t g_s ds} \int_0^t \frac{\Gamma_s}{\Gamma_t} ds\right)^{\frac{1}{1-\gamma}}$$

where

$$g_t \equiv A_t - \frac{1}{2}\gamma\sigma^2 - E^{\gamma}\left[\left(\int_t^{\infty} e^{-\int_t^s \phi(Z_u)du} ds\right)^{\gamma}\right]^{-\frac{1}{\gamma}}$$

and

$$\Gamma_t = e^{\frac{1}{2}(1-\gamma)^2\sigma^2 t - (1-\gamma)\sigma W_t}$$

and where assumptions have been made so that A_t, g_t, and other elements of the model have been assumed non-stochastic. We can also set $\bar{c} = 0$ to obtain the CRRA solution.

Profit and value of the firm

If we set A to zero and B positive, profit is then positive. The risk in the model does not complicate the decisions of the firms: they still invest as dictated by the equality of the marginal product of capital with the interest rate. What does change, however, is the interest rate: it is now driven by risk, and thus both the marginal product of capital and the discounting that determines the value of the equity in a firm.

Profit is output net of factor payments, which is, as before, the rental cost of capital:

$$\pi_t = f(K_t) - r_t K_t = Y_t - f'(K_t)K_t$$

There are now several complications. First, the production function includes risky shocks. Second, the marginal product of capital, and hence the interest rate, are now stochastic.

The marginal product of capital is straightforward:

$$f'(K_t) = A(Z_t) + \gamma B(Z_t)K_t^{\gamma-1}$$

Substituting into the profit formula,

$$\begin{aligned}\pi_t &= A(Z_t)K_t + B(Z_t)K_t^{\gamma} - A(Z_t)K_t - \gamma B(Z_t)K_t^{\gamma} \\ &= (1-\gamma)B(Z_t)K_t^{\gamma}\end{aligned}$$

It is evident that if $B = 0$, profit is zero. Conversely, if $B \neq 0$, the profit is positive but the $A(Z_t)$ element of the model has no effect on profit. To analyze profit and firm value, therefore, we can focus on the model with the restriction with only the nonlinear production function term, that is, $A(Z_t) = 0$.

The value of a share is the discounted expected value of the profits:

$$E\left[\int_t^{\infty} e^{-\int_t^s dr_s}\pi_s ds\right] = E\left[\int_t^{\infty} e^{-r_s(s-t)}\pi_s ds\right]$$

Since the interest rate, and hence the discount rate, are stochastic, this must be accounted for in the discounting. By choosing the appropriate measure change, we can then discount by the risk-free rate, which might itself be stochastic in this setting.

Valuing the firm

In order to value the firm, we take the discounted expected value of the firm's profits, which we derived above. The challenging aspect of the valuation is to determine the discount rate, but we know that in equilibrium the discount rate must equal the marginal product of capital. So, roughly speaking, the discounted expected value is

$$E\left[\int_0^\infty e^{-\int_0^t K_s^{\gamma-1}ds}(1-\gamma)K_t^\gamma dt\right]$$

where we have again used the assumption that $\alpha = \gamma$.

The problem with this calculation is that the marginal product of capital involves terms like $e^{(1-\gamma)\sigma W_t}$, but these terms appear in the exponent of the discount factor, so we have the exponential of an exponential of a stochastic process, which does not lend itself to closed form solutions.

In addition to simulating the discounted share value of a firm, we would be interested in characterising the stochastic process of the return to holding the asset; this would correspond to the return to holding the market portfolio — the S&P500 in the real world — something that we were very focused on in earlier chapters. Since $\tilde{K}$ is the inverse of the marginal product of capital, we can obtain this from the solution for $\tilde{K}_t$ using Ito's lemma:

$$d\tilde{K}^{-1} = \left(-\tilde{K}^{-2}\mu_{\tilde{K}} + \frac{1}{2}\sigma_{\tilde{K}}^2\tilde{K}^{-3}\right)dt - \sigma_{\tilde{K}}\tilde{K}^{-2}dW_t$$

and this can also be simulated numerically.

As we previously noted, we can undertake the same no-arbitrage measure change as in the equilibrium Merton model framework. In that case, all of the complication entailed by the nonlinear production function can be swept under the rug, that is, it is absorbed in the Radon–Nikodym derivative ξ_t, and which is also the state price, which we have encountered before. Thus, if we want to fully solve the model we would need to solve for ξ_t, and this would require numerical approximations that are a bit more intricate than those we have encountered in this book.

Bonus Material

Solution of the HJB equation

Due to the geometric structure of the Menoncin–Nembrini model, we can conjecture that the value function is also geometric in form but with an additional additive term:

$$J(K_t, Z_t) = F(Z_t)\frac{K_t^{1-\gamma}}{1-\gamma} + G(Z_t)$$

(see the work of Menoncin and Nembrini, 2018, p. 234). This is where the assumption that $\alpha = \gamma$ is being used: the geometric term $K^{1-\gamma}$ has to mesh with the marginal product of the production function $K^{\alpha\ 1}$.

It is key that the B coefficient, which weights the nonlinear part of the production function, appears only in the G subequation. It will turn out that consumption is determined only by the F subequation; therefore, we can conclude that the nonlinear part of the production function does not directly affect the consumption solution.

Substituting into the HJB equation (C.1) yields two separate equations in F and G:

$$0 = F_t + \mu F_Z + \frac{1}{2}\Omega^2 F_{ZZ} - \gamma F\phi(z_t) + \gamma F^{1-\frac{1}{\gamma}}$$

$$0 = G_t + \mu G_Z + \frac{1}{2}\Omega^2 G_{ZZ} - \rho G + F B_t$$

These are both PDEs and therefore require additional analysis. Menoncin and Nembrini use the Feynman–Kac approach, in which the solution is expressed as an expectation at the boundary.

It is worth understanding a bit more clearly the steps leading to the cleavage into the two separate equations for F and G. If we first substitute $F(z_t)\frac{K^{1-\gamma}}{1-\gamma}$ into the HJB equation, then we will have derivatives with respect to K and at the end of the process we will have a collection of terms multiplying $K^{1-\gamma}$ and other terms:

$$\rho F\frac{K^{1-\gamma}}{1-\gamma} = \left[\frac{((FK^{-\gamma})^{-\frac{1}{\gamma}})^{1-\gamma}}{1-\gamma} + (A_t K_t + BK_t^{\gamma} - (FK^{-\gamma})^{-\frac{1}{\gamma}})FK^{-\gamma}\right]$$
$$+ F_t\frac{K^{1-\gamma}}{1-\gamma} - \frac{1}{2}\sigma^2\gamma F K^{1-\gamma} + \mu F_Z\frac{K^{1-\gamma}}{1-\gamma} + \frac{1}{2}\Omega^2 F_{ZZ}\frac{K^{1-\gamma}}{1-\gamma}$$

where the square-bracketed terms are associated with the optimisation. After carrying out some cancellations, consolidation and multiplying by $(1-\gamma)$, we are left with

$$\begin{aligned}\rho F K^{1-\gamma} = &\Big[(F^{-\frac{1-\gamma}{\gamma}})K^{1-\gamma} + (1-\gamma) \\ &\times (A_t F K^{1-\gamma} + BF - (F)^{-\frac{1}{\gamma}+1}K^{1-\gamma})\Big] \\ &+ F_t K^{1-\gamma} - \frac{1}{2}\sigma^2\gamma(1-\gamma)FK^{1-\gamma} + \mu F_Z K^{1-\gamma} \\ &+ \frac{1}{2}\Omega^2 F_{ZZ} K^{1-\gamma}\end{aligned}$$

Gathering $K^{1-\gamma}$ terms and dividing by $K^{1-\gamma}$, and further gathering terms on the left-hand side to begin constructing the ϕ coefficient, and also assigning the BF term to the G equation only, yields

$$\begin{aligned}&\left(\rho - (1-\gamma)A_t + \frac{1}{2}\sigma^2\gamma(1-\gamma)\right)F \\ &= F_t + \left[\left(F^{-\frac{1-\gamma}{\gamma}}\right) + (1-\gamma)\left(-F^{-\frac{1}{\gamma}+1}\right)\right] \\ &\quad + \mu F_Z + \frac{1}{2}\Omega^2 F_{ZZ} \\ \rightarrow \quad &\gamma\left(F\phi - F^{1-\frac{1}{\gamma}}\right) = F_t + \mu F_Z + \frac{1}{2}\Omega^2 F_{ZZ}\end{aligned} \tag{C.2}$$

which is the equation for F_t. For the G equation, all terms involving a derivative J_K disappear.

Feynman–Kac solution

The Feynman–Kac solution process has three steps. In the first step, we state an ordinary differential equation in a new variable X_t, where X_t is defined by the differential equation

$$\dot{X} = \gamma\left(X\phi(z_t) - X^{1-\frac{1}{\gamma}}\right)$$

To understand where this formalism comes from, note that in the PDE for F (C.2), there is an HJB part and a "utility" part, $-\gamma(F\phi(z_t) + F^{1-\frac{1}{\gamma}})$; that part of the equation determines X_t. The Feynman–Kac solution method ultimately takes an expected value of this element at its boundary. Since the boundary condition for the value function is $J_t = 0$ at $t = \infty$, the boundary for F_t is also $F_t = 0$ at infinity.

The equation for X_t is an ordinary differential equation and therefore a standard solution formula can be used. This standard solution for X_t is then

$$X_t = \left(\int_t^{\infty} e^{-\int_t^s \phi(Z_u)du} ds \right)^{\gamma} \tag{C.3}$$

where the upper limit of infinity reflects the boundary condition $X_t = 0$ at infinity.

The reason for computing X_t is that it can now be treated as the "exogenous" part of the partial differential equation in (C.2) and the expectation that is the main idea of Feynman–Kac can then be applied.

In the second step, Menoncin and Nembrini undertake a measure change, defining

$$dW_t = (1 - \gamma)\sigma dt + dW_t^{\gamma}$$

so that the Z_t process becomes

$$dZ_t = \mu dt + \Omega dW_t^{\gamma}$$

under that measure.[2] As a result of the measure change, the drift of Z_t under the measure $\mathbb{Q}^{\gamma}$ is the same as the drift coefficient in the PDE for F_Z in equation (C.2); this is what is needed to make use of the Feynman–Kac solution method.

In the third step, we take the expected value of the boundary function X_t — this is the main aspect of the Feynman–Kac solution method. Beginning with the F function, the solution is the expectation

$$F(z_t) = E^{\gamma}[X_t]$$

where the expectation is taken under the modified measure, and where X_t satisfies the boundary condition for F_t, namely X_t tends

[2]Since we have eliminated the W–Z covariance in our discussion, the term driven by that covariance, which appears in Menoncin and Nembrini's full model, has been dropped.

to zero as t tends to infinity — this is satisfied because as the lower limit of the integral in (C.3) tends to infinity, the integral necessarily becomes zero.[3]

The general Feynman–Kac solution is the sum of two parts. The first part is the expected value of the function you are solving for at the boundary, discounted in a particular way, and the second part is the expected value of an integral of the "utility function" or driving process part of the PDE, that is, the part not involving F. For the purpose of discussion, call this the "exogenous" element of the PDE.

The solution for the function X_t consists of noting that the form $d\gamma(F\phi - F^{1-\frac{1}{\gamma}})$ is a derivative of a function of F. Integrating this function yields the solution for F itself. The integrated form involves only "exogenous" functions, namely ϕ, and so we discount this function before taking the expectation. The discount factor is the coefficient of the F term in the PDE for F_t, however there is no longer such a term, and therefore the discount factor is zero, and we simply take the straight expectation of X_t to obtain the solution for F.

The solution for F_t is then

$$F_t = E^\gamma\left[\left(\int_t^\infty e^{-\int_t^s \phi(Z_u)du} ds\right)^\gamma\right]$$

The solution for the additive term G_t uses the solution for F_t, also using Feynman–Kac. Since the additive term $-\rho G$ appears in the PDE for G_t, we discount the "exogenous" or driving process part of the PDE, FB (because F appears exogenous to the G_t process), when taking the expectation:

$$G(Z_t) = E\left[\int_t^\infty e^{-\rho(s-t)} F(Z_s)B(Z_s)ds\right]$$

where the expectation is taken with respect to the original probability measure.

The surprising thing about this solution is that the coefficient of the nonlinear production function element, B, does not directly affect

[3] As a mathematical nuance, we need to reassure ourselves that the integrand does not get too wild as t goes to infinity; this in turn means ϕ must not get wild. For the cases we are considering, this is clearly the case.

consumption, whereas the coefficient of the linear part of the production function, A does affect it via the ϕ term. The nonlinear term does indirectly affect consumption however because it influences capital accumulation, and the the total capital from which consumption is taken is affected.

Intuition for Feynman–Kac solution

One can prove the basic Feynman–Kac idea using stochastic calculus. However, we can also note that the HJB is a PDE and the PDE is just another way to express a stochastic differential equation for V_t. If we can further assert that the SDE obeys a terminal condition, $V(T) = g(T)$, and also that it is a martingale, then the current solution $V(t)$ is just $E[V(T)] = E[g(T)]$ by the martingale property. The Feynman–Kac solution is then just be an extension of this idea.

Answers to Selected Exercises

Chapter 4

Exercise 4.2.

(i) **Answer.**

$$H = \frac{1 - e^{-\gamma c}}{\gamma} + \xi\left(\frac{1 - e^{-\alpha k}}{\alpha} - c\right)$$

(ii) **Answer.**

$$e^{-\gamma c} = \xi_t \to c = -\frac{\ln(\xi_t)}{\gamma}$$

(iii) **Answer.**

$$\dot{\xi}_t = \xi_t(\rho - f'(k_t)) = \xi_t(\rho - e^{-\alpha k})$$

(iv) **Answer.** At the steady state,

$$f'(\overline{k}) = \rho \to e^{-\alpha \overline{k}} = \rho \to \overline{k} = -\frac{\ln(\rho)}{\alpha}$$

(v) **Answer.**

$$\overline{r} = f'(\overline{k}) = \rho$$

(vi) **Answer.**

$$\frac{1-e^{-\alpha\bar{k}}}{\alpha} - \rho e^{-\alpha\bar{k}} = \frac{1}{\alpha} - \left(\frac{1}{\alpha}+\rho\right) e^{-\alpha\bar{k}}$$

(vii) **Answer.**

$$\frac{1}{\rho}\left(\frac{1-e^{-\alpha\bar{k}}}{\alpha} - \rho e^{-\alpha\bar{k}}\right)$$

(viii) **Answer.** The interest rate satisfies

$$\frac{d}{dt}f'(k_t) = \alpha k_t^{\alpha-1}\dot{k}_t$$

Now substitute from the state equation and integrate:

$$r_t = \int_0^t \alpha k_s^{\alpha-1}\dot{k}_s ds$$

Exercise 4.3.

(i) **Answer.**

$$H = \gamma\ln(c) + \xi\left(\alpha\ln(k-1) - c\right)' \qquad k > 1$$

(ii) **Answer.**

$$\frac{\gamma}{c} = \xi_t \rightarrow c = \frac{\gamma}{\xi_t}$$

(iii) **Answer.**

$$\dot{\xi}_t = \xi_t(\rho - f'(k_t)) = \xi_t\left(\rho - \alpha\frac{1}{k_t - 1}\right)$$

(iv) **Answer.** At the steady state,

$$f'(\bar{k}) = \rho \rightarrow \alpha\frac{1}{k_t - 1} = \rho \rightarrow \bar{k} = 1 + \frac{\alpha}{\rho}$$

(v) **Answer.**

$$\bar{r} = f'(\bar{k}) = \rho$$

(vi) **Answer.**

$$\alpha \ln(\bar{k} - 1) - \rho\left(1 + \frac{\alpha}{\rho}\right)$$

(vii) **Answer.**

$$\frac{1}{\rho}\left(\alpha \ln(\bar{k} - 1) - \rho\left(1 + \frac{\alpha}{\rho}\right)\right)$$

Exercise 4.4.

(i) **Answer.**

$$q_t = q_H e^{\rho t}$$

(ii) **Answer.**

$$c_t = q_H^{-\frac{1}{\gamma}} e^{-\frac{\rho}{\gamma}t}$$

(iii) **Answer.**

$$\dot{S}_t = -q_H^{-\frac{1}{\gamma}}(e^{-\frac{\rho}{\gamma}t})$$

This can be integrated directly, with initial condition $S_0 = S_H$.

(iv) **Answer.** This can be integrated directly, with initial condition $S_0 = S_{T_P} - P$, that is, we take the end state from the previous step and subtract the fixed amount needed for planting as the initial condition.

(v) **Answer.**

$$\begin{aligned}\int_0^{T_P} e^{-\rho t} u(c(t))dt &= \int_0^{T_P} e^{-\rho t}\frac{c^{1-\gamma}}{1-\gamma}dt \\ &= \int_0^{T_P} e^{-\rho t}\frac{q_H^{-\frac{1}{\gamma}}\left(e^{-\frac{\rho}{\gamma}t}\right)^{1-\gamma}}{1-\gamma}dt\end{aligned}$$

$$= \frac{q_H^{-\frac{1-\gamma}{\gamma}}}{1-\gamma} \int_0^{T_P} e^{-\rho t} e^{-\frac{\rho(1-\gamma)}{\gamma} t} dt$$

$$= \frac{q_H^{-\frac{1-\gamma}{\gamma}}}{1-\gamma} \int_0^{T_P} e^{\left(-\rho - \frac{\rho(1-\gamma)}{\gamma}\right) t} dt$$

This integral can be solved explicitly.

(vi) **Answer.** The approach is the same, however the initial value of q_t is the terminal value from the previous step.

(vii) **Answer.** We substitute for the integrals we solved in the previous steps into the two-value equations (4.5) and (4.6) and solve for the two values.

(viii) **Answer.** The solution must result in the grain reaching a value of zero after exactly one year. If the initial costate is too low, the grain will be consumed too fast and will hit zero before the next harvest; conversely, if the initial value is set too high, there will be excess grain after a year, and that grain could have been consumed.

One can find the q_H that solves this condition via trial and error, however, as is pointed out in the paper, there is a marginal condition that provides an additional condition: $q_{T_P} = V'(s_{T_P})$, the transversality condition. Note the similarity of this condition with our previous development of Lagrange multipliers: the costate is a multiplier, and the multiplier is the marginal value of "income" — which is the quantity of grain, S_t.

Chapter 5

Exercise 5.1. Answer. At the optimal size, the growth rate equals the interest rate:

$$CX_T^{-\alpha} = r \quad \rightarrow \quad X_T = \left(\frac{r}{C}\right)^{-\frac{1}{\alpha}}$$

Chapter 6

Exercise 6.3. Answer. If z is normal $N(0,t)$, the mean of $e^{sz(t)}$ is $e^{\frac{1}{2}s^2 t}$. That is,

$$E[e^{sz}] = \frac{1}{(2\pi t)^{1/2}}\int e^{sz}e^{-\frac{z^2}{2t}}\,dz = \frac{1}{(2\pi t)^{1/2}}\int e^{-\frac{1}{2}(\frac{z^2}{t}-2zs+s^2t)+\frac{1}{2}s^2t}dz.$$

Chapter 7

Exercise 7.2.

(i) **Answer.**

$$dW_t = W_t((\alpha_t\mu + (1-\alpha_t)r)dt + \alpha_t\sigma dZ_t)$$

(ii) **Answer.**

$$\rho V = \max_{\{\alpha\}} \frac{w^{1-\gamma}}{1-\gamma} + (\alpha\mu + (1-\alpha)r)wV_w + \frac{1}{2}(\alpha\sigma)^2 w^2 V_{ww}$$

(iii) **Answer.**

$$(\mu - r)wV_w + \alpha\sigma^2 w^2 V_{ww} = 0$$

(iv) **Answer.**

$$V(w) = B\frac{w^{1-\gamma}}{1-\gamma}$$

$$V_w = Bw^{-\gamma}$$

$$V_{ww} = -B\gamma w^{-\gamma-1}$$

(v) **Answer.**

$$(\mu - r)wV_w + \alpha\sigma^2 w^2 V_{ww} = 0 \rightarrow \alpha = -\frac{\mu - r}{\sigma^2}\frac{wV_w}{w^2V_{ww}} = \frac{\mu - r}{\sigma^2}\frac{1}{\gamma}$$

Exercise 7.3.

(i) **Answer.**

$$dW_t = (\alpha_t \mu + (1 - \alpha_t) r) dt + \alpha_t \sigma dZ_t$$

(ii) **Answer.**

$$\rho V = \max_{\{\alpha\}} u(w) + (\alpha\mu + (1-\alpha)r)V_w + \frac{1}{2}(\alpha\sigma)^2 V_{ww}$$

(iii) **Answer.** w does not appear:

$$(\mu - r)V_w + \alpha\sigma^2 V_{ww} = 0$$

(iv) **Answer.** Conjecture that the value function has a form similar to the form of the utility function, that is, it is an exponential function of w

$$V(w) = C - Be^{-Aw}$$

It is tempting to set $A = \gamma$ from the beginning but leave that for later.

$$V_w = ABe^{-Aw}$$

$$V_{ww} = -A^2 Be^{-Aw}$$

(v) **Answer.**

$$(\mu - r)V_w + \alpha\sigma^2 V_{ww} = 0 \to \alpha = -\frac{\mu - r}{\sigma^2}\frac{V_w}{V_{ww}} = \frac{\mu - r}{\sigma^2}\frac{1}{A}$$

Thus, we again obtain the result that the Sharpe ratio appears, and as we see, the unknown coefficient A will involve the risk-aversion factor γ.

(vi) **Answer.**

$$\begin{aligned}\rho\left(C - Be^{-Aw}\right) &= \frac{1 - e^{-\gamma w}}{\gamma} \\ &+ (\alpha\mu + (1-\alpha)r)\, ABe^{-Aw} \\ &- \frac{1}{2}(\alpha\sigma)^2 A^2 Be^{-Aw}\end{aligned}$$

Thus, we preserve the structure of the conjectured solution if we set $A = \gamma$.

(vii) **Answer.**

$$
\begin{aligned}
C &= \frac{1}{\rho}\left(\frac{1}{\gamma}\right) \\
-\rho B &= -\Bigg(-\frac{1}{\gamma} + (\alpha\mu + (1-\alpha)r)\,AB - \frac{1}{2}(\alpha\sigma)^2 A^2 B \\
&= \Bigg(-\frac{1}{\gamma} + (\alpha\mu + (1-\alpha)r)\,\gamma B - \frac{1}{2}(\alpha\sigma)^2\gamma^2 B\Bigg) \\
&= \Bigg(-\frac{1}{\gamma} + \left(\frac{(\mu - r)^2}{\sigma^2\gamma}) + r\right)\gamma B - \frac{1}{2}\left(\frac{\mu - r}{\sigma}\right)^2 B\Bigg) \\
&= \Bigg(-\frac{1}{\gamma} + \left(\frac{1}{2}\left(\frac{\mu - r}{\sigma}\right)^2 + r\gamma\right) B\Bigg)
\end{aligned}
$$

(viii) **Answer.**

$$
\begin{aligned}
C &= \frac{1}{\rho\gamma} \\
B &= \frac{\frac{1}{\gamma}}{\rho + \left(\frac{1}{2}\left(\frac{\mu - r}{\sigma}\right)^2 + r\gamma\right)} \\
&= \frac{1}{\rho\gamma + r\gamma^2 + \frac{1}{2}\left(\frac{\mu - r}{\sigma}\right)^2\gamma}
\end{aligned}
$$

Exercise 7.4.

(i) **Answer.**

$$dW_t = W_t((\alpha_t\mu + (1-\alpha_t)r)dt + \alpha_t\sigma dZ_t)$$

(ii) **Answer.**

$$\rho V = \max_{\{\alpha\}}\left\{\ln(\gamma w) + (\alpha\mu + (1-\alpha)r)wV_w + \frac{1}{2}(\alpha\sigma)^2 w^2 V_{ww}\right\}$$

(iii) **Answer.**

$$(\mu - r)wV_w + \alpha\sigma^2 w^2 V_{ww} = 0$$

(iv) **Answer.**

$$V(w) = A + B\ln(\gamma w)$$
$$V_w = B\frac{1}{w}$$
$$V_{ww} = -B\frac{1}{w^2}$$

(v) **Answer.**

$$(\mu - r)wV_w + \alpha\sigma^2 w^2 V_{ww} = 0 \to \alpha = -\frac{\mu - r}{\sigma^2}\frac{wB\frac{1}{w}}{w^2\left(-B\frac{1}{w^2}\right)}$$
$$= \frac{\mu - r}{\sigma^2}$$

(vii) **Answer.**

$$\rho\left(A + B\ln(\gamma w)\right) = \ln(\gamma w)$$
$$+ \left(\alpha\mu + (1-\alpha)r\right)wB\frac{1}{w}$$
$$-\frac{1}{2}(\alpha\sigma)^2 w^2 B\frac{1}{w^2}$$

Cancelling w terms yields

$$\rho\left(A + B\ln(\gamma w)\right) = \ln(\gamma w)$$
$$+ \left(\alpha\mu + (1-\alpha)r\right)B$$
$$-\frac{1}{2}(\alpha\sigma)^2 B$$

We need to get the $\ln(\gamma w)$ terms to cancel; set $B = \frac{1}{\rho}$, yielding

$$\rho A = +\left(\alpha\mu + (1-\alpha)r\right)\frac{1}{\rho}$$
$$-\frac{1}{2}(\alpha\sigma)^2\frac{1}{\rho}$$

which can be solved for A.

Exercise 7.5.

(i) **Answer.**

$$dW_t = W_t((\alpha_t\mu + (1-\alpha_t)r)dt + \alpha_t\sigma dZ_t)$$

(ii) **Answer.**

$$\rho V = \max_{\{\alpha\}}\left\{-\frac{1}{2}(-w)^2 + (\alpha\mu + (1-\alpha)r)wV_w + \frac{1}{2}(\alpha\sigma)^2 w^2 V_{ww}\right\}$$

(iii) **Answer.**

$$(\mu - r)wV_w + \alpha\sigma^2 w^2 V_{ww} = 0$$

(iv) **Answer.**

$$\begin{aligned} V(w) &= -\frac{1}{2}B(-w)^2 \\ V_w &= B(-w) \\ V_{ww} &= -B \end{aligned}$$

(v) **Answer.**

$$(\mu - r)wV_w + \alpha\sigma^2 w^2 V_{ww} = 0 \to \alpha = -\frac{\mu - r}{\sigma^2}\frac{wB\frac{1}{w}}{w^2\left(-B\frac{1}{w^2}\right)} = \frac{\mu - r}{\sigma^2}$$

$$\begin{aligned} &(\mu - r)wV_w + \alpha\sigma^2 w^2 V_{ww} = 0 \\ &\to (\mu - r)w(B(-w)) + \alpha\sigma^2 w^2(-B) = 0 \\ &\qquad \to \alpha = \frac{(\mu - r)w(B(-w))}{\sigma^2 w^2(-B)} = \frac{(\mu - r)}{\sigma^2} \end{aligned}$$

(vi) **Answer.**

$$\begin{aligned} \rho\left(-\frac{1}{2}B(-w)^2\right) = &-\frac{1}{2}(-w)^2 \\ &+ (\alpha\mu + (1-\alpha)r)\, w(B(-w)) \\ &- \frac{1}{2}(\alpha\sigma)^2 w^2(-B) \end{aligned}$$

Cancelling w terms yields

$$\frac{1}{2}\rho B = \frac{1}{2} + (\alpha\mu + (1-\alpha)r)\,B - \frac{1}{2}(\alpha\sigma)^2 B$$

Substituting the solution for α yields

$$\frac{1}{2}\rho B = \frac{1}{2} + \left(r + \frac{(\mu - r)^2}{\sigma^2}\right) B - \frac{1}{2}\left(\frac{(\mu - r)^2}{\sigma^2}\right) B$$

$$\left(\frac{1}{2}\rho - r\right) B = \frac{1}{2} + \frac{1}{2}\left(\frac{(\mu - r)^2}{\sigma^2}\right) B$$

This is a linear equation in B, which can be solved for B.

Chapter 9

Exercise 9.1.

(i) **Answer.**

$$V_X = ABx^{A-1} \qquad V_{XX} = (A-1)ABx^{A-2}$$

(ii) **Answer.**

$$\begin{aligned} dV &= \left(\mu_X X_t V_X + \frac{1}{2}\sigma_X X_t^2 V_{XX}\right) dt + \sigma_X X_t V_X dZ_t \\ &= \left(\mu_X ABX_t^A + \frac{1}{2}\sigma_X (A-1)ABX_t^A\right) dt \\ &\quad + \sigma_X X_t ABX_t^{A-1} dZ_t \\ &= AV\left((\mu_X + \frac{1}{2}\sigma_X(A-1))dt + \sigma_X dZ_t\right) \end{aligned}$$

(iii) **Answer.** X_t must have drift as follows when we change the measure as stated. In that case,

$$dX_t = X_t\left((\mu_X - \theta\sigma_X)\,dt + \sigma_X dZ_t^*\right)$$

Using Ito's lemma then yields

$$dV_t = AV_t\left((\mu_X + \frac{1}{2}\sigma(A-1) - \sigma_X\theta)dt + \sigma_X dZ_t^*\right)$$

(iv) **Answer.**
$e^{-rt}V$ does not obey the property even though X_t does obey it; V_t cannot stand as an asset in equilibrium unless A satisfies a specific property.

(v) **Answer.**

$$\beta = \frac{V_X x \sigma_X}{V \sigma_M} = \frac{ABx^{A-1} x \sigma_X}{Bx^A \sigma_M} = \frac{A\sigma_X}{\sigma_M}$$

Exercise 9.2.

(i) **Answer.**

$$V_X = -x \qquad V_{XX} = -1$$

(ii) **Answer.**

$$\begin{aligned} dV &= \left(\mu_X X_t V_X + \frac{1}{2}\sigma_X^2 X_t^2 V_{XX}\right) dt + \sigma_X X_t V_X dZ_t \\ &= \left(\mu_X X_t(-X_t) - \frac{1}{2}\sigma_X^2 X_t^2\right) dt + \sigma_X X_t(-X_t) dZ_t \\ &= \left(-\mu_X X_t^2 - \frac{1}{2}\sigma_X^2 X_t^2\right) dt - \sigma_X X_t^2 dZ_t \\ &= -2\left(\mu_X + \frac{1}{2}\sigma_X^2\right) V_t dt - 2\sigma_X V_t dZ_t \end{aligned}$$

(iii) **Answer.** The Sharpe ratio is $\theta \equiv \frac{\mu_M - r}{\sigma_M}$. Define

$$Z^* = Z_t + \theta t \rightarrow dZ^* = dZ_t + \theta dt$$

$$dS = \mu_S S_t dt + \sigma_S S_t (dZ_t^* - \theta dt)$$

$$dS = (\mu_S - \theta) S_t dt + \sigma_S S_t dZ_t^* = r S_t dt + \sigma_S S_t dZ_t^*$$

Thus,

$$\begin{aligned} de^{-rt} V_t &= -re^{-rt} V_t dt + e^{-rt} dV_t \\ &= -re^{-rt} V_t dt + e^{-rt}(r S_t dt + \sigma_S S_t dZ_t^*) \\ &= e^{-rt} \sigma_S S_t dZ_t^* \end{aligned}$$

which is a martingale.

(iv) **Answer.** The Sharpe ratio must be the same:

$$\frac{dV_t}{V_t} = -2\left(\mu_X + \frac{1}{2}\sigma_X^2\right)dt - 2\sigma_X dZ_t \to \frac{\mu_X + \frac{1}{2}\sigma_X^2 - r}{\sigma_X}$$
$$= \frac{\mu_M - r}{\sigma_M}$$

(v) **Answer.**

$$\beta = \frac{xV_X\sigma_X}{V\sigma_M} = \frac{x * (-x)\sigma_X}{-\frac{1}{2}(-x)^2\sigma_M} = 2\frac{\sigma_X}{\sigma_M}$$

Bibliography

G. Barone-Adesi, N. Fusari, A. Mira, and C. Sala. Option market trading activity and the estimation of the pricing kernel: A bayesian approach. *Journal of Econometrics*, 216(2): 430–449, 2020.

R. J. Barro. Rare disasters and asset markets in the twentieth century. *The Quarterly Journal of Economics*, 121(3): 823–866, 2006.

D. T. Breeden and R. H. Litzenberger. Prices of state-contingent claims implicit in option prices. *Journal of Business*, 51(4): 621–651, 1978.

W. A. Brock and L. J. Mirman. Optimal economic growth and uncertainty: The discounted case. *Journal of Economic Theory*, 4(3): 479–513, 1972.

R. Chetty. A new method of estimating risk aversion. *American Economic Review*, 96(5): 1821–1834, 2006.

G. Clark. The cost of capital and medieval agricultural technique. *Explorations in Economic History*, 25(3): 265–294, 1988.

C. O. Ewald and B. Taub. Real options, risk aversion and markets: A corporate finance perspective. *Journal of Corporate Finance*, 72: 102164, 2022.

G. Gamow. *One, Two, Three–Infinity: Facts and Speculations of Science.* Viking Press, New York, 1961.

L. P. Hansen and R. Jagannathan. Implications of security market data for models of dynamic economies. *Journal of Political Economy*, 99(2): 225–262, 1991.

H. He and H. F. Pages. Labor income, borrowing constraints, and equilibrium asset prices. *Economic Theory*, 3: 663–696, 1993.

H. Hotelling. The economics of exhaustible resources. *Journal of Political Economy*, 39(2): 137–175, 1931.

H. G. Johnson. *Lectures in Economics: The Theory of Income Distribution*, Vol. 3. London: Gray-Mills, 1975.

M. I. Kamien and N. L. Schwartz. *Dynamic Optimization: The Calculus of Variations and Optimal Control in Economics and Management.* Dover Publications, Mineola, 2012.

I. Karatzas and S. Shreve. *Brownian Motion and Stochastic Calculus,* Vol. 113. Springer Science & Business Media, New York, 2012.

R. E. Lucas Jr. Asset prices in an exchange economy. *Econometrica: Journal of the Econometric Society,* 46(6): 1429–1445, 1978.

T. E. MaCurdy. An empirical model of labor supply in a life-cycle setting. *Journal of Political Economy,* 89(6): 1059–1085, 1981.

M. Majumdar and R. Radner. Linear models of economic survival under production uncertainty. *Economic Theory,* 1(1): 13–30, 1991.

A. M. Malz. A simple and reliable way to compute option-based risk-neutral distributions. FRB of New York Staff Report, 677, 2014.

D. N. McCloskey and J. Nash. Corn at interest: The extent and cost of grain storage in medieval england. *The American Economic Review,* 74(1): 174–187, 1984.

R. Mehra and E. C. Prescott. The equity premium: A puzzle. *Journal of Monetary Economics,* 15(2): 145–161, 1985.

F. Menoncin and S. Nembrini. Stochastic continuous time growth models that allow for closed form solutions. *Journal of Economics,* 124(3): 213–241, 2018.

R. C. Merton. Optimum consumption and portfolio rules in a continuous-time model. *Journal of Economic Theory,* 3(4): 373–413, 1971.

R. C. Merton. Optimum consumption and portfolio rules in a continuous-time model. In *Stochastic Optimization Models in Finance.* Academic Press, New York, 1975, pp. 621–661.

J. Norstad. Black-Scholes the Easy Way. 1999.

F. P. Ramsey. A contribution to the theory of taxation. *The Economic Journal,* 37(145): 47–61, 1927.

R. Rezaeyan and E. Baloui. Stochastic differential equations and integrating factor. *International Journal of Nonlinear Analysis and Applications,* 4(2): 62–67, 2013.

T. A. Rietz. The equity risk premium a solution. *Journal of Monetary Economics,* 22(1): 117–131, 1988.

N. L. Stokey, R. E. Lucas, and E. Prescott. *Recursive Methods in Economic Dynamics.* Harvard University Press, Cambridge, 1989.

B. Taub. A model of medieval grain prices: Comment. *The American Economic Review,* 1048–1053, 1987.

K. Wicksell. *Interest and Prices.* Ludwig von Mises Institute, Auburn, 2007 (original 1936).

Index

O

P

R

S

T

www.ingramcontent.com/pod-product-compliance
Lightning Source LLC
LaVergne TN
LVHW011808200926
848484LV00005B/1112